# The Egyptian Pyramid Mystery Is Solved!

## Volume 1: The Mysteries

# The Egyptian Pyramid Mystery Is Solved!

## Volume 1: The Mysteries

Margaret Morris

Edited by William E. Morris, Jr.

Frontispiece: Amenhotep-son-of-Hapu of Athribis as an elderly scribe, with Pharaoh Amenhotep III in the background. Amenhotep-son-of-Hapu was a high priest of Amun, he was considered an intermediary between humankind and the god Amun. Although his statues were made with granite, inscriptions on a papyrus roll he holds are almost completely worn down from worshippers touching them in the temples of Karnak, where at least some of his statues stood. A great many touches are required to obliterate deeply incised hieroglyphics in such hard material. This statue is one of about ten found at Karnak, four of which were found in the temples. Photograph by Jon Bodsworth.

Amenhotep-son-of-Hapu was the architect responsible for the construction of the 60-foot-high Colossi of Memnon, which stood in front of the now-vanished Mortuary Temple of Pharaoh Amenhotep III. There is every reason to think that Amenhotep-son-of-Hapu was an expert in the long-lost (but now fully recovered), once-sacred technology that is the subject of the volumes of this book. The background image of Pharaoh Amenhotep III (under whom Amenhotep-son-of-Hapu served) is based upon a photograph of a limestone sculpture in the Luxor Museum taken by Professor B.V. Bothmer.


ISBN 0-9720434-0-3

Library of Congress Control Number: 2003109450

ancient mysteries, architecture, building, Egypt, history, history of science and technology, pyramids, stone

Edited by William E. Morris, Jr.

Contact Margaret Morris at her Web site: http://www.margaretmorrisbooks.com

First Edition



Scribal Arts
16863 Lenore St.
Detroit, MI 48219
U.S.A.

Printed in the United States of America on acid-free paper

# Contents

# DEDICATION

This book is dedicated to the memory of geophysicist and geochemist Dr. Edward J. Zeller (1925–1996), who was a Director of the Radiation Physics Laboratory at the University of Kansas at Lawrence. This book is also dedicated to his research partner and widow physicist Dr. Gisela A. Dreschhoff, who succeeded Dr. Zeller as Director of the Radiation Physics Laboratory after his passing in 1996.

# ACKNOWLEDGEMENTS

To write this book, I needed scientific, technical, and other forms of support. I was fortunate to obtain such support from the people listed below. Most of the scientific and technical expertise and assistance applies to the scientific solution presented in Volume 2 of this book:

First, I thank Robert G. Magnuson for performing computer maintenance, formatting, and a myriad of other tasks involved in the creation of this book. This book would not exist without his long, steady support, assistance, and encouragement.

I am enormously grateful to geologists Robert G. McKinney and Dr. Edward J. Zeller. I am greatly privileged to have consulted with them over the years to resolve difficult geological problems. I doubt that I would have started this book without their encouragement, in-depth knowledge, and great willingness to volunteer their help in the interest of science.

The extent of Robert G. McKinney's contributions over the past 13 years are hard to put into words. I owe him a tremendous amount of thanks.

The same is true for geophysicist Dr. Edward J. Zeller, who was always very generous with his time although in the midst of his own remarkable contributions to science. As a scientist and individual, Ed was rare and will always be sorely missed by his friends, family, and colleagues in the scientific community. I am proudly dedicating this book to him and to his widow physicist Dr. Gisela A. Dreschhoff of the University of Kansas.

Geologist Dr. Luciano Ronca was a professor at Wayne State University, in Detroit, Michigan, when I made his acquaintance in 1990. He kindly introduced me to his former professor Ed Zeller that year because of Ed's exceptional qualifications, and for this I will always be grateful.

Geologist James Shelton, of SIP Technologies, in Mandeville, Louisiana, has made a fine contribution to this book by providing an analytical statement for Appendix 2 of Volume 2.

I thank astronomer Dr. Edwin C. Krupp, Director of the Griffith Observatory in Los Angeles, California, for preparing a statement for Volume 2 of this book.

Above all, I owe thanks to the internationally recognized French scientist Dr. Joseph Davidovits. This book is based on the scientific and archaeological research of the award-winning materials scientist Dr. Joseph Davidovits. I began working as his historical assistant in 1984, when he founded the Institute for Applied Archaeological Science (IAPAS) at Barry University, in Miami Shores, Florida. The IAPAS was established to revive worthwhile ancient technology and to advance the clarity of ancient history.

I would like to put on record my thanks to William E. Morris, Jr., for introducing me to the work of Dr. Joseph Davidovits in 1983. The occasion occurred after a presentation at Brookhaven National Laboratory by Joseph Davidovits and Liliane Courtois, the latter of the Center for Archaeological Research, in Paris. I thank William E. Morris, Jr. also for applying his professional editing skills to this book.

My Mother wrote letters on behalf of this work, and I extend my appreciation for these efforts.

I extend my thanks to materials scientist Dr. Rustum Roy, former Head of the Materials Research Institute, at Pennsylvania State University, for his actions on behalf of this research, and to Dr. Mike Silsbee, Head of the Pennsylvania State University Materials Research Laboratory, for his efforts.

I wish to thank zeolite expert Dr. Robert Colpitts, who has held a number of industrial and university positions, for advising me.

I offer a great many thanks to materials scientist Dr. Michel Barsoum, of the Materials Engineering Department of Drexel University, in Philadelphia, Pennsylvania, for his efforts on behalf of this body of research. I sincerely appreciate his enthusiasm and commitment to expanded research.

I wholeheartedly thank Dr. Linn W. Hobbs, Professor of Materials and Professor of Nuclear Engineering in the Department of Materials and Engineering at MIT. Dr. Hobbs kindly read a prepublication draft of this book and suggested a number of advanced tests to perform on samples of pyramid stone at MIT. I thank Dr. Hobbs, too, for interesting graduate student Katherine Kershen in designing and conducting a test project with him at MIT.

My thanks are also extended to Katherine Kershen for the aforementioned efforts and for reviewing a prepublication draft of this book. I appreciate her suggestions and her calculation, which appears in Volume 2, with regard to building Khufu's pyramid.

I extend my gratitude to Senior Engineer George Gardiner, of the International Chimney Corporation, in Williamsville, New York. George Gardiner kindly provided input concerning the serious problems involving transporting enormous monolithic structures.

I am grateful to Jon Bodsworth for his wonderful photographs of Egyptian antiquities. Jon has visited Egypt many times and also several museums to collect thousands of excellent photos. Jon generously supplied me with copies of several of his photos for publication here. Everyone can enjoy the charm of his on-line collection by visiting his Web site: http://home.freeuk.net/egyptarchive/html/home.html

Acoustics engineer and CymaScope inventor John Reid, who conducted acoustical testing in the King's Chamber of the Great Pyramid, also kindly provided photographs for publication here. I wholeheartedly extend my appreciation to him for his contribution.

My thanks are extended to precision mold maker Gary Mellinger. Gary has 28 years of precision-casting experience with Spokane Industries, in Spokane, Washington. His contribution appears in Volume 2.

I offer my gratitude to Systems Engineer Mike Carrell, who is now retired after 38 years with the former RCA Corporation, where he held the position of principal member of the technical staff. Mike made a number of contributions to this book.

George Havach, a technical editor for the U.S. Geological Survey, has benefited this work. My many thanks are in order for his consulting geological reference material and his great encouragement and enthusiasm.

The ancient names Imhotep, Amenhotep-son-of-Hapu and Kha-em-waset must be included here. We all owe these priestly natural scientists a debt of gratitude for their remarkable contributions to the world's unprecedented architecture.

I thank all of my readers. Anticipating reaching you has inspired me to continue on through the years despite the opposition and difficulties involved in completing this work. I sincerely hope you enjoy this book and benefit from it.

# List Of Illustrations

# TABLES

# Chapter 1

# A Secret Of The Ages Revealed

Some ancient Egyptian artifacts made with very hard stone, like diorite and quartzite, defy reproduction when modern steel hand tools are used. Nonetheless, many thousands of such artifacts were fashioned during the Late Stone Age. Many people are surprised to learn that the Egyptians built the most admired and mysterious monuments of all time—Egypt's Great Pyramids—when tools were at the Late Stone Age level. At that time, the strongest metal available was copper, a relatively soft metal. The hardest limestone blocks in the pyramid complexes (consisting of pyramids, temples and other sacred architecture) are too hard and intricately fit to have been cut on such a massive scale with copper tools, or with these instruments along with abrasive sand. Indeed, assuming the Great Pyramid was completed or nearly completed during the 24-year reign of Pharaoh Khufu, as Egyptologists assert, its scale is too large for the myriad of form-fitted pyramid blocks and the overall near-perfect giant pyramid shape to have been cut with these primitive stone-cutting devices. Experts estimate that the Great Pyramid contains over two million blocks.

In the 5$^{th}$ century B.C., the Greek historian Herodotus visited the Great Pyramid when its blocks were pristine and unblemished. Herodotus reported seeing a myriad of casing blocks 30 feet long covering the outside of the Great Pyramid! We must exercise caution when accepting measurements in ancient texts (the Greek world used different measurement systems, and scribes made errors). But Herodotus' report matches that of Abd el-Latif, who visited Giza around A.D. 1200. Abd el-Latif also reported seeing a myriad of 30-foot-long blocks casing the Great Pyramid as far as the eye could determine. Egyptologists have been astonished to find that the backs of the casing blocks remaining on all of the monuments at Giza, site of the Great Pyramid, conform exactly to the intricate irregularities of the front faces of the blocks behind them! How can we believe that these huge form-fitting blocks were so precisely cut with stone and copper tools and abrasive sand on such a gigantic scale? The Great Pyramid was originally covered by 20 acres of smooth casing blocks that angled to produce the overall pyramid shape. It stands to reason that something is wrong with the accepted theory of pyramid construction.

Many theories about how the Great Pyramid was built have been offered, but

1. THE ENTRANCES TO THE GREAT PYRAMID ARE SHOWN: THE GREAT PYRAMID INCORPORATES AN ESTIMATED 2½ MILLION BLOCKS. PHOTOGRAPH BY JON BODSWORTH

there are several basic requirements a theory must meet. Theories other than the one presented in these pages do not take all of these requirements into consideration. Most theories actually ignore most of them. We will explore the requirements in these pages. Once they are clearly set out, it becomes obvious that only one theory meets all of them.

Many pyramid blocks are of a hardness that can be roughly cut with a hard form of bronze. But Egyptology has determined that hard bronze was not available to Egyptians of the Pyramid Age, when the Great Pyramids arose. Since the inception of Egyptology, more than 100 years ago, most Egyptologists have assumed that copper tools were adequate for quarrying and carving limestone into pyramid blocks. Egyptologists are only now beginning to recognize, because of hands-on stone-cutting experiments by masons and tool experts, that copper chisels are too soft to be useful for producing the hardest limestone pyramid blocks. Granite, used to make almost five percent of the blocks found in pyramid complexes, is much harder than limestone. If we propose that copper tools could be sufficiently hardened to cut the limestone, then the amount of copper required to cut all the limestone pyramid blocks with copper tools would be staggering. The enormous supplies needed are not accounted for by archaeological findings at the copper mines, and the tools found in sealed tombs are typical, soft copper.

Some Egyptologists, therefore, propose that the ancient workers must have made the millions of pyramid blocks with stone tools, the only other kind available.[1] A critical dilemma results, because stone tools are not suitable for producing the blocks of the Great Pyramid, either. The vast amount of masonry had to be carefully prepared to prevent any distortions that would adversely affect the overall giant pyramid shape, a feat that would be challenging with today's methods. For instance, on the outer surface of the Great Pyramid, casing blocks have been measured to fit as close as 1/500 inch or in perfect contact along their entire joints.

The Great Pyramid also incorporates large blocks and beams made with granite. There was no steel in ancient Egypt for cutting granite, and so this kind of strong metal cannot explain the tight-fitting blocks in the Great Pyramids that conform to one another on all touching surfaces and exhibit flat front surfaces. Similarly, no iron smelting sites are known dating from the Pyramid Age, and no iron has ever been found within a sealed tomb of that period. Granite is so hard that today this rock is cut with diamond, which was also unknown in ancient Egypt according to all of Egyptology.

With a great deal of effort, freshly quarried granite can be gradually cut with copper and sand. But modern experiments using these means have not replicated the remarkable features of granite objects from ancient Egypt. Some granite artifacts studied by W.M.F. Petrie, the father of modern archaeology, show signs of rapid cutting.

According to experts, crisp hieroglyphics cut in some ancient Egyptian objects

2. THE TIP OF THE GREAT PYRAMID OF KHAFRA, AT GIZA, IS STILL POINTED AND COVERED WITH CASING BLOCKS THAT REFLECT MOONLIGHT. PHOTOGRAPH BY JON BODSWORTH

made with granite are of better quality than can be achieved with modern diamond drills. Furthermore, some ancient Egyptian sarcophagi made with granite or other types of hard stone exhibit surface areas, covering many square feet, that are extremely flat. In contrast, it is very difficult to achieve extreme flatness over surfaces larger than a few inches by grinding with abrasives. Clearly, something is fundamentally wrong with the accepted theories of ancient Egyptian masonry. The special means used to create the remarkable masonry work has eluded Egyptology.

The first Egyptologists were baffled by hard-stone artifacts they excavated from the ruins of ancient Egypt.[2] More than a hundred years of subsequent Egyptological research has failed to explain how these same artifacts were made with the means

3. W.M.F. PETRIE MEASURED THE FIT OF THE CASING BLOCKS ON THE GREAT PYRAMID TO BE AS CLOSE AS 1/500 INCH OR IN PERFECT CONTACT. BELOW THE LOWEST TIER IS THE 13-SQUARE-ACRE FOUNDATION, LEVEL TO 7/8 INCH FROM CORNER TO CORNER. PHOTOGRAPH BY JON BODSWORTH

available to the ancient Egyptians. Over the past thirty years or so, several best-selling books have proposed technologically advanced means that do not directly explain the remarkable features of these artifacts or the pyramids.[3] Caught between their contempt for these books and their own embarrassing inability to provide a proper explanation of the enigmas, Egyptologists now mostly trivialize the very same problems that they, just like the first Egyptologists, still cannot explain.

Consequently, the masonry and engineering enigmas I present in these pages are mostly overlooked by contemporary authorities, who simply try to explain away the problems of pyramid construction. As I show below, unresolved masonry and construction problems are often seriously misrepresented in up-to-date, authoritative literature on pyramid building.

Once these enigmas are exposed, it becomes obvious that a fundamentally new theory of pyramid construction is imperative. In the two volumes of this book, I present more than just a solution to the seemingly insurmountable engineering and masonry riddles. We will explore convincing proof that the special ancient technology presented is, indeed, the long-lost secret that explains pyramid construction and other masonry enigmas.

We will explore some severe logistical problems that have been unrecognized until now. We will also consider accepted experiments that have attempted to quarry, carve, hoist, and set limestone blocks with replicated ancient Egyptian cutting implements and lifting devices. When evaluated logically and correctly, these accepted Egyptological studies prove that the prevailing theory of pyramid construction is entirely unworkable. The new light thrown onto the numerous unresolved engineering and masonry puzzles spotlights the gloss with which experts have obscured the facts.

Some of the experiments we will explore used metal and stone tools, sometimes combined with abrasives like quartz sand, to shape rocks of the types used in creating ancient artifacts. These rocks are much harder than the pyramid blocks made with limestone. Some intricately detailed ancient Egyptian artifacts, made of varieties of hard rock like diorite and quartzite, defy replication when using either ancient or modern tools. We will explore the characteristics of some of these artifacts in these pages.

Indeed, hammering diorite will ruin the striking surface of a high-quality modern hammer made of tough tool steel, which is stronger than regular steel. It is difficult to drill into a bed of quartzite using a tungsten carbide (next in hardness to diamond) bit, although thousands of pounds of pressure are applied to the tool bit. Nevertheless, large monolithic objects were made with quartzite, including 60-foot-high statues and beautifully formed sarcophagi. Their features stunned the Egyptologists who discovered them.

Without the advantage of any hard metals or good tools, ancient Egyptian sculptors routinely rendered diorite, quartzite and other types of hard rocks into extraordinary works of art that are unparalleled even today. Some are great artistic masterpieces. A myriad of hard-stone artifacts that defy duplication using power tools (and, according to some highly skilled machinists, even ultramodern tooling systems) emphasize that something is fundamentally wrong with the accepted understanding of ancient masonry techniques.

The solution to the long-standing riddles emerges as self-evident in the volumes of this book, because I show that the collective masonry and engineering mysteries can be explained only by the special ancient technology presented here. The pertinent facts of the masonry and engineering mysteries are simple and straightforward. These facts clearly show the impossibility of the standard construction theory. The Great Pyramid is the most conspicuous testament to a novel and once-sacred technology that subsequently was lost. The existence of this special technology is not speculative or theoretical; it is fully recovered in Volume 2 of this book. The present volume sets out the mysteries that collectively cannot otherwise be explained. Let us begin our journey back to the time when this technology thrived, by exploring the remarkable features that prompted the ancient Greeks to proclaim the Great Pyramid as the First Wonder of the World.

# Chapter 2

# The Great Masonry Wonder

Situated in a desert necropolis in an area that is now the outskirts of modern Cairo, the Great Pyramid is historically unprecedented because of its enormous scale and magnificent design complexities. Experts have calculated that the illustrious monument incorporates about 2.3 million massive blocks, totaling an estimated 93.5 million cubic feet of limestone. It is remarkable that the maximum error between the lengths of its sides is less than 1 percent, although each of the four sides measures 756 feet long at the base of the Pyramid.

Egyptologists are strongly convinced that workers assembled the Great Pyramid without the use of the wheel, hard metal tools, or even the block and tackle. Egyptologists have determined that workers built this famous monument almost a millennium before the wheel was introduced in Egypt for transportation. Bronze, needed for metal tools strong enough to cut fossil-shell limestone, was not introduced until 800 hundred years after this construction so famous for its amazing architectural features was built. Iron, a much stronger metal, came into use even later. Egyptologists are convinced that the Great Pyramid was built centuries before any evidence of the block and tackle in Egypt.

Nevertheless, reckoning that workers labored ten hours per day when building the Great Pyramid, Egyptologists calculate that an average of one block was raised and set in place every two or three minutes! To complete (or nearly complete) the Great Pyramid within the reign of the pharaoh, this astounding construction pace had to continue for about 23 or 24 years. The reign of its builder Pharaoh Khufu lasted that long, from about 2551 to 2528 B.C. Even for a short duration, modern experiments (placing monoliths that do not even approach the upper end of the range of weights of those of the Great Pyramid) have not been able to duplicate this rapid pace.

A fundamental problem exists in studies that calculate lifting pyramid blocks, as follows: Egyptology has averaged the weight of the blocks of the Great Pyramid at 2.5 tons each. The pioneering founder of Egyptology Sir William Matthew Flinders Petrie (1853–1942) calculated this average by estimating the number of blocks in the structure to be about 2.3 million (he arrived at this figure while taking into consideration the 27-foot high mound of rock incorporated into the base of the Great Pyramid). Petrie averaged the main pyramid blocks at 50 x 50 x 26 inches, about 2.5

tons apiece.[1] While there is nothing wrong with averaging block weights in and of itself, most theorists improperly employ weight averaging. They use it as a masking device that allows them to avoid the more difficult calculations involving elevating thousands of much heavier blocks to great heights.

The misleading use of this average makes building the Great Pyramid seem relatively easy. Read almost any authoritative book on pyramid building and you will find that either it raises no serious problems, or you will read a description of how relatively easy the construction process was. In either case, these books have presented highly distorted facts.

Supposedly authoritative literature obscures another truth. Presumably, block sizes diminish at a fairly constant rate as the Great Pyramid ascends. The premise is held, because from the base to the 17$^{th}$ tier block heights progressively diminish from about six down to two tons. But above the 17$^{th}$ tier, some tiers are made of very large blocks. Most calculations ignore these massive blocks high in the Great Pyramid. Let us consider the information on this issue provided by the most authoritative Egyptological source.

Until recently, the standard work on Egyptian building methods was *Ancient Egyptian Masonry: The Building Craft* (1930), by Somers Clarke and Reginald Engelbach. Much new information has come forth since its publication over seventy years ago. The newest and most complete and authoritative replacement is *Building in Egypt* (1991). This new Egyptological standard was written by one of the foremost experts on Egyptian stone masonry Dieter Arnold of the Metropolitan Museum of Art in New York. Arnold based his new standard on prominent studies of recent decades. In *Building in Egypt*, Arnold stated the following about the diminishing block sizes in the Great Pyramid of Khufu (Greek: Cheops):

> At the pyramid of Cheops, the height of steps (which corresponds to that of the casing) starts with 1.49 meters from the ground and ends with 0.58, 0.56, 0.57 and 0.54 meters near the top.[2]

His statement is technically correct. But it gives the impression that block sizes gradually diminish at a fairly constant rate in the entire Great Pyramid. Arnold did briefly acknowledge that some of the tiers (courses) in the core masonry (the main building blocks) of the Great Pyramid comprise larger blocks:

> For the casing blocks of the Cheops Pyramid, Petrie noticed that the height decreases in general but that some courses in between are considerably higher. Such courses appear in a completely irregular pattern in distances of 6, 7, 8, 9, 10, 12, 14, and 16 courses.[3]

Above, Arnold referred to outer casing blocks. In pyramid tiers where casing

4. GREAT PYRAMID TIERS: G. GOYON AND OTHERS MEASURED THE TIERS OF THE GREAT PYRAMID. THEIR MEASUREMENTS SHOW THAT THE TIERS CONFORM TO ABOUT 75 HEIGHTS, WITH A MARGIN OF ERROR OF LESS THAN ½ CM. PHOTOGRAPH BY JON BODSWORTH

blocks remain, the casing blocks generally correspond to the heights of the tiers. Arnold's reference to casing blocks, therefore, generally relates to the height of the tiers of the Great Pyramid. While we see that Arnold briefly mentioned the existence of the tiers made of taller blocks, he did not discuss the considerable added engineering problems posed by elevating these larger blocks to great heights.

Arnold's book does not mention the majority of unresolved difficulties of constructing the Great Pyramid, because he opted to write his authoritative book on ancient Egyptian construction from a Middle Kingdom perspective—when no Great Pyramids were built. Most of Arnold's readers will not recognize the magnitude of unresolved engineering and masonry difficulties associated with the information he presents in his new Egyptological standard.

Measurements establish the exact heights of the tiers of the Great Pyramid (see Appendix). Tier measurements are critically important because the sudden increase in block size at the 19$^{th}$ tier is not apparent from ground level, given the distortion created by perspective when one looks up from the base of the Great Pyramid.

The first measurements of the tier heights were taken when Napoleon and his army were stranded in Egypt during the French Revolution. In 1798 Napoleon and his army invaded Egypt. With them were members of the Commission of Arts and Sciences. During the stay in Egypt savants of the Napoleonic Egyptian Expedition accurately measured the heights of the tiers of the Great Pyramid. Later, various early pioneers of Egyptian archaeology verified the measurements, including Colonel Howard Vyse and J.S. Perring. In the 1970s, French Egyptologist Georges Goyon confirmed the tier measurements.[4]

At the 35$^{th}$ tier of the Great Pyramid, block sizes dramatically increase again. Course 35 is made of blocks just over four feet tall and of varying lengths. Because they are situated so high above ground, their placement presents a greater challenge than blocks at the base of the Great Pyramid that are about five feet high and more than seven feet long.

Though not as sharp, sudden increases in block sizes occur in a number of other tiers. Included are the 67$^{th}$, the 98$^{th}$, the 118$^{th}$, the 144$^{th}$, the 180$^{th}$, and other tiers high in the Great Pyramid. Blocks in tier 201 are taller than those in course four. Some tiers exhibit blocks that occupy the space of the next higher tier, so that these blocks take up the height of two tiers.

Very heavy beams appear in the interior masonry. Several weighing up to 73 tons are situated 160 feet above ground level and higher. To form the tip of the Great Pyramid, a missing capstone of unknown weight rested at a height of nearly 500 feet.

To summarize, theorists usually exclude tiers made of truly heavy blocks high in the Great Pyramid from the block-raising equation. Theorists simply avoid them by generalizing the statistics. They calculate with averaged weights, and therefore exclude specifics about the tall tiers situated at great heights in the Great Pyramid. Keeping in mind that the Great Pyramid was built during the 4th Dynasty, here is an example of this generalization. These are Arnold's remarks about the diminishing block sizes:

> In the period from the Fourth to the Twelfth Dynasty, the shape and size of the casing blocks did not vary significantly. The lowest course usually has the highest steps, starting with 2 to 3 cubits and slowly decreasing with every step upward until it measures about 1 cubit at the top. This was clearly due to the problems of lifting.[5]

Arnold's statement should not be misconstrued as applicable to the core masonry of the Great Pyramid, where course 35 is taller than course two, and tier 201 was measured as taller than course four (as shown in Appendix). Owing to the severe problems posed by raising blocks on inclined ramps, tall tiers made of massive blocks situated high in the Great Pyramid present unresolved engineering problems.

The fairly high degree of uniformity in the heights of the tiers of the Great Pyramid presents a dramatic statistic that accentuates the design complexities of the monument. The remaining tiers were measured to conform to 73 heights, with the very precise measurements showing that tier heights are off less than half a centimeter. The aforementioned tier measurements taken by le Pere and Coutelle of the Napoleonic Expedition illustrate the degree of uniformity. But logistical studies overlook this critically important issue. Clearly, pyramid construction theorists have not fully appreciated the existing logistical difficulties, including the complexities of producing blocks that conform to this design specification.

When Egyptologist Georges Goyon climbed the northeast corner of the Great Pyramid in the 1970s and measured its tiers, he produced charts that exhibit the exact same peaks and plateaus recorded by Napoleon's scholars. Like them, Goyon found that the tier heights suddenly increase and diminish in 19 sharp fluctuations. Goyon was unable to explain this difficult-to-achieve design pattern. He proposed that it is the result of quarrying technique.[6] He assumed the quarrymen cut along the softer strata* in the bedrock to more easily obtain rough building stones. If so, then the stones could

*STRATA ARE SHEETLIKE LAYERS THAT FORM IN THE LIMESTONE DUE TO SLIGHT INTERRUPTIONS IN THE SEDIMENTATION PROCESS.

be relatively uniform, their heights corresponding to the distance between strata.

However, Goyon's idea does not hold water. In 1984 Joseph Davidovits and Hisham Gaber measured the strata in the quarry walls associated with the construction of the Great Pyramid. Their measurements show that the heights of the pyramid blocks are less than the distance between strata. The same is true for the blocks of Giza's Second Great Pyramid, built for Pharaoh Khafra (c. 2520–2494 B.C.).[7]

In short, if the Egyptians cut along the strata to obtain blocks, then they would also have had to pare the blocks down, because the blocks are smaller than the length between the strata. It makes no sense to cut rock that way if one must gain advantage by cutting along strata. Egyptology, therefore, has not explained how the pyramid builders overcame the difficulties of creating the design pattern shown by the measurements of Goyon and others. The strata heights of the Giza bedrock do not correlate with the specific tier heights, the measurements of which are off less than a half

5. SOME CASING BLOCKS REMAIN AROUND THE LOWER PART OF THE GREAT PYRAMID. ABOUT TWENTY ACRES OF CASING BLOCKS ORIGINALLY COVERED THE ENTIRE GREAT PYRAMID AND CREATED ITS SMOOTH, SLOPING FACES. PHOTOGRAPH BY JON BODSWORTH

centimeter for all 73 different heights used to form the 201 steps (tier 201 has been removed since the measurements taken by Napoleon's scholars).

In that case, it follows that gargantuan problems emerge. We encounter the enormous tasks of quarrying, shaping, hauling, sorting, and storing so very many correctly sized blocks. Builders had to make blocks to fit with the various heights of the tiers. Limestone has a strong tendency to crack, most especially if quarried by primitive means (like hitting it with stone pounding balls), so that salvaging smaller units establishes block sorting and storing efforts on an enormous scale. Given the complexities of such an enormous operation (involving millions of blocks to be incorporated into the Great Pyramid in less than 25 years), achieving the 19 sharp height fluctuations and other features described would be challenging with the best modern means.

The inadequacy of Pyramid Age (Late Stone Age) tools for cutting medium-hard to hard fossil-shell limestone blocks to specifications vastly complicates the problem. I dedicate chapters below to experiments with primitive tools, to carefully illustrate a variety of stone-cutting problems. As mentioned, a main problem with the idea that pyramid blocks were cut with copper tools and abrasive sand is the tremendous amount of copper that would be needed compared with actual findings concerning the copper yield from the Sinai mines and other sources. Another consideration is that the overwhelming majority of pyramid blocks exhibit no tool marks (some tool marks on blocks date from the Middle Ages and perhaps the much earlier Hyksos period, when blocks are believed to have been pried at in search of hidden entrances). The absence of tool marks on most blocks makes it more difficult for Egyptologists to determine the overall methods used.

Another masonry pattern further complicates matters. No one has measured the lengths of the blocks of the Great Pyramid, so I cannot present a pattern involving its block lengths. But in 1984 the south and west faces of the Great Pyramid of Khafra, the Second Great Pyramid at Giza, were clearly photographed at the upper level. Joseph Davidovits photographed the blocks below the casing blocks that still cover the tip.[8] He photographed almost 2,000 blocks in tiers with undamaged masonry. His resulting chart reveals that the workers put long blocks next to and above and below shorter blocks. The arrangement staggers the location of joints, creating a stable, interlocking superstructure. The pattern Joseph Davidovits demonstrated vastly complicates the logistical and technical problems that theorists think were involved in cutting, storing, sorting, and selecting the blocks. The pattern in Khafra's pyramid involves millions of massive, appropriately sized blocks. In other words, in addition to the masonry problems of cutting, storing, and sorting explained above, within the context of the accepted construction paradigm workers also had to contend with preparing blocks so that their lengths would correctly form the interlocking masonry pattern.

The Great Pyramid exhibits another design pattern that would be very difficult to execute with either primitive or modern tools. The vast, rough faces of the Great Pyramid (which are now devoid of the smooth casing blocks that converted them from stepped structures into flat-faced pyramids) are constructed so that they are slightly and evenly bowed in. The curvatures are very subtle and difficult to detect when standing at the base. From that vantage point, all four faces appear to be flat. An extraordinary degree of precision was required to achieve this design pattern because the concave curves are regular and subtle. The feature represents another design complexity that greatly compounds the problems of building the Great Pyramid using the means proposed by Egyptology.[9]

Petrie discovered another remarkable design complexity. He surveyed the faces of the Great Pyramid and found that the mean optical plane that touches the most prominent points of the blocks shows an average variation of only 1.0 inch.[10] The near-perfect plane shows how closely blocks conform to the angle of the vast sides of the Pyramid. Although today's Egyptologists advocate that there are few, if any, remaining pyramid construction enigmas, just the features we have considered so far show that too much has been taken for granted.

Another consideration is the high rate of breakage that occurs with all limestone quarrying operations. Even if cracked and broken blocks can be pared down for incorporation into smaller tiers, then this constant reshaping and shuffling of multiton blocks further complicates the sorting and storing quagmire. To form the overall giant pyramid shape, blocks would have had to be prepared and situated so that their top surfaces would conform to the tier immediately above. One of the amazing features of the Great Pyramid is the way large tiers, covering acres, correspond to one another other in such a way as to prevent distortion of the overall pyramid structure.

The Great Pyramid is famous for its tight-fitting joints. While there are now gaps between many of the Great Pyramid's visible building blocks (where mortar between them, used to cushion them against earthquake stress, has disappeared), there are a myriad of tight-fitting blocks. There is no room for the durable, thick pink mortar (such as is found on many Old Kingdom monuments) between these blocks, which fit together very snugly on all touching surfaces. These blocks actually conform to the shape of all neighboring blocks.

Casing blocks, used to produce the outer surface, also fit very closely on all sides with neighboring blocks. Many pyramid and temple blocks exhibit joints, the area where two tight-fitting stones adjoin, that deviate from the vertical plane. That is, some joints are long and wavy or oblique. Some are even L-shaped. Yet, their fit is very snug along the entire lengths of their joints. In some Old and Middle Kingdom (c. 2575–1640 B.C.) structures, 30 percent of the blocks exhibit such formfitting oblique joints.[11] The long, formfitting oblique joints in the Great Pyramid have confounded researchers who have tried to duplicate the feature on a small scale.

The main building blocks of the pyramids are made with local limestone.

Most of the limestone at Giza is formed by the consolidation of round, flat seashells about the size and shape of coins. The fine-grained casing blocks (most of which were removed centuries ago) on the outer surface of the pyramids contrast to this rough grade of limestone. The casing blocks once covered the coarse limestone tiers, converting these stepped structures into pyramids with smooth, flat faces. The casing blocks were made with corners squared at 90-degree angles to a high degree of accuracy. The surfaces of the casing blocks on the pyramids are so smooth and reflective of sunlight that early travelers often mistook them for polished marble.[12]

Remaining casing blocks on the Great Pyramid weigh six to 16 tons each. Egyptologists estimate that there were originally an estimated 115,000 casing blocks forming the smooth outer faces of the Great Pyramid. To create these vast faces, workers used about 2,379,842 cubic feet of fine limestone. One of the mysteries of Egyptology is how each casing block was so closely custom-fitted on all sides with neighboring blocks on such a massive scale. Egyptologists have measured the remaining casing blocks on the Great Pyramid to fit to a mean opening of 1/50 inch. The joints fit as closely as 1/500 inch or in perfect contact.[13]

As mentioned, the backs of casing blocks on the three Great Pyramids of Giza conform exactly to the irregular front faces of the backing blocks behind them. This snug, interlocking fit is amazing by modern standards. The scale on which workers applied the casing blocks to the Great Pyramids renders their joints historically unprecedented. Remaining casing blocks on Khafra's pyramid are even larger on average than those on the Great Pyramid. Some fit together by interlocking tongue-and-groove joints.

In *The Pyramids and Temples of Gizeh* (1883), W.M.F. Petrie discussed casing blocks remaining at the lower north side of the Great Pyramid. He described cement between them that is paper-thin and found between tight-fitting joints that did not need to be filled. Petrie described what he called an "almost impossible" task of controlled handling on a gargantuan scale:

> Several measures were taken of the thickness of the joints of the casing stones . . . the mean thickness of the joint there is .020; and, therefore, the mean variation in the cutting of the stone from a straight line and from a true square, is but .01 on length of 75 inches up the face, an amount of accuracy equal to the most modern opticians' straightedges of such a length. These joints, with an area of some 35 sq. ft. each, were not only worked as finely as this, but cemented throughout. Though the stones were brought as close as 1/500$^{th}$ inch, or, in fact, into contact and the mean opening of the joint was 1/50$^{th}$ inch, yet the builders managed to fill the joint with cement, despite the great area of it, and the weight of the stone to be moved—some 16 tons. To merely place such stones in exact contact

6. THE SPHINX AT GIZA IS SHOWN WITH THE GREAT PYRAMIDS OF KHUFU (GREEK: CHEOPS) AND KHAFRA (GREEK: CHEPHREN) IN THE BACKGROUND. THE PHOTOGRAPH DATES TO BEFORE 1875, WHEN THE SPHINX WAS PARTIALLY BURIED IN SAND. HERODOTUS DID NOT MENTION THE SPHINX IN HIS 5TH CENTURY B.C. DOCUMENTATION OF GIZA, AND SO SOME HISTORIANS SUGGEST THAT IT WAS COMPLETELY BURIED AT THAT TIME. THE SPHINX DOES NOT SIT AT GROUND LEVEL AND IS INSTEAD SITUATED IN A PIT FROM WHICH LIMESTONE WAS REMOVED FOR PYRAMID BUILDING. A COVERING OF SAND PRESERVED THE WEAKLY-BOUND LIMESTONE BODY (THE HEAD IS HARD MATERIAL) OF THE SPHINX OVER THE AGES. IT WAS CLEARED DURING THE 18TH AND 19TH DYNASTIES AND OTHER HISTORICAL PERIODS, ONLY TO BE GRADUALLY BURIED AGAIN BY SANDSTORMS. PHOTOGRAPH BY ELSEVIER, COURTESY OF GRIFFITH INSTITUTE, ASHMOLEAN MUSEUM, OXFORD, U.K.

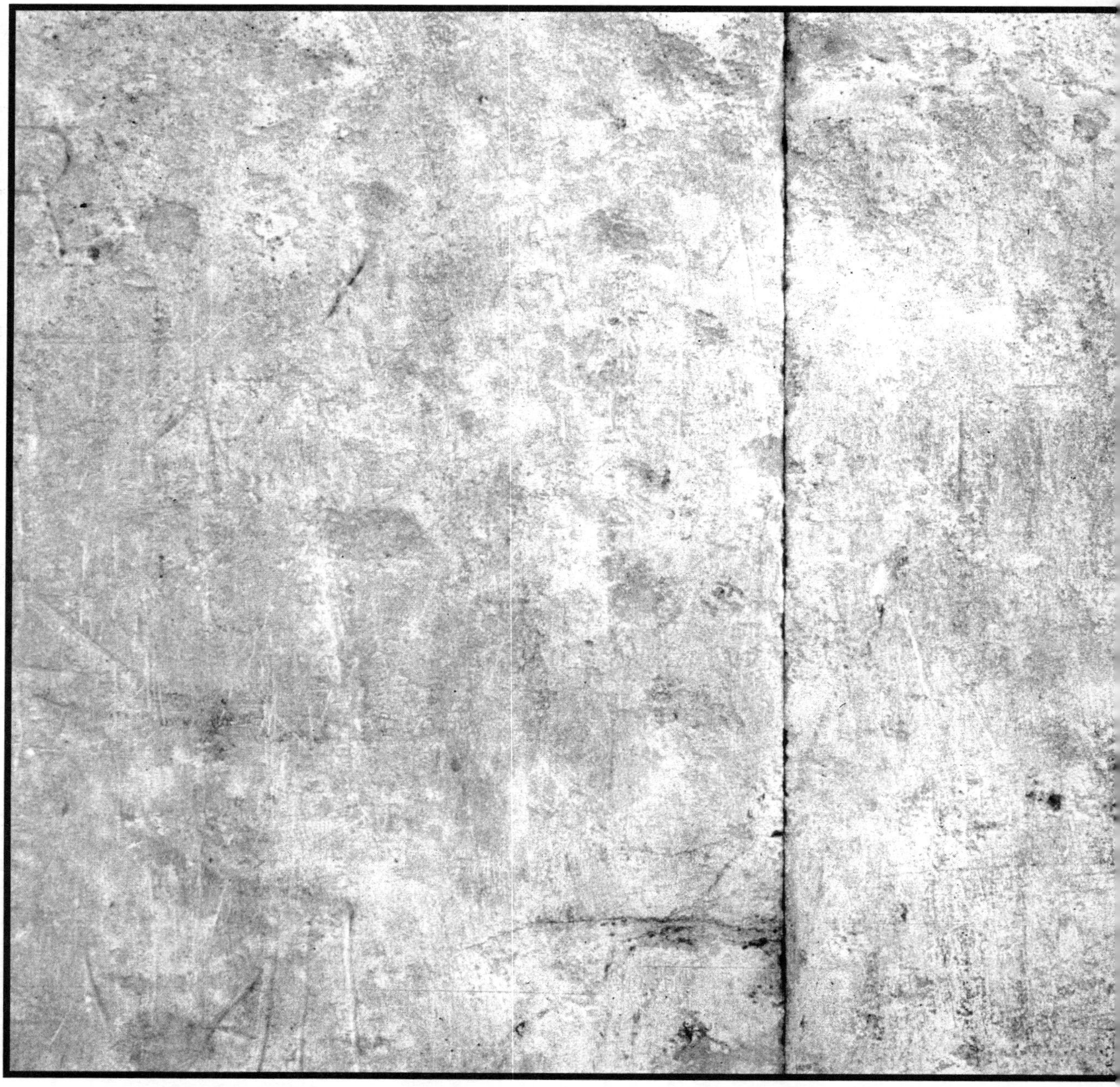

7. GREAT PYRAMID CASING BLOCK JOINT: THE TIGHT-FITTING CASING BLOCKS CONFORM TO EACH OTHER IN SHAPE. SOME JOINTS ARE WAVY, BUT EVEN THESE IRREGULARITIES CONFORM TO ONE ANOTHER.

SOME SURFACES, LIKE THOSE ON THE OUTER CASING BLOCKS SHOWN HERE, ARE SCRATCHED AND CHIPPED AFTER 4,500 YEARS OF SEVERE EXPOSURE. THE PAPER-THIN CEMENT BETWEEN THE CASING BLOCKS IS EXTREMELY DURABLE.

SOME JOINTS ARE SO CLOSE THAT THEY ARE DIFFICULT TO DETECT, LIKE THOSE OF THE BLOCKS THAT CASE THE QUEEN'S CHAMBER. THEY ARE SOMETIMES CALLED HAIRLINE JOINTS.

PHOTOGRAPH BY JON BODSWORTH

> at the sides would be careful work; but to do so with cement in the joint seems almost impossible.[14]

Although the casing blocks on the Great Pyramid are now few in number, a much older account confirms that such tight-fitting joints, filled with paper-thin cement, originally existed on an enormous scale. Although paper thin, this cement is as hard and impervious as the blocks, and proves the existence of a sophisticated cement technology that was lost to Egypt in later times. The older account attesting to 30-foot-long casing blocks separated by the highly durable, paper-thin cement is by Abd el-Latif (A.D. 1162–1231), a physician of Baghdad who visited Giza:

> These pyramids are built of large stones between 10 and 20 cubits long by a breadth and thickness each of 2 to 3 cubits; but most especially worthy of admiration is the extreme nicety with which these stones are fashioned and disposed one above the other. The courses fit so exactly that not even a needle or a single hair can be thrust between the joints. They are cemented together by a mortar which forms a layer the thickness of a leaf of paper. With the composition of this mortar I am totally unacquainted.[15]

As el-Latif's report matches Petrie's accurate account of the close jointing and cementing, it is probably very reliable. The hard and extremely durable cement el-Latif witnessed was no longer made in Egypt in his time. By comparison, modern Portland cement, from which today's buildings are made, lasts no longer than 150 years under ideal environmental conditions. In sharp contrast, the paper-thin cement both Petrie and el-Latif observed has endured for thousands of years.

Like el-Latif, the 5th century B.C. Greek historian Herodotus reported a myriad of casing blocks 30 feet long.[16] Their reports are at odds with the size of blocks seen today at the base of the Great Pyramid. Presumably, in ancient times sand encased the lowest tiers, covering the shorter blocks we see today. Egyptologists speculate that a dense blanket of sand covered areas of Giza so that the 60-foot-high Sphinx was completely buried, explaining why Herodotus did not mention this monument.

Today only a few casing blocks remain on the north and south sides of the Great Pyramid. But el-Latif and Herodotus witnessed the monument when it exhibited formfitting casing blocks, which they reported were up to 30 feet long. We know of one pyramid block that long today. It measures 29½ feet long and about six feet high, and it is incorporated into the entrance of the 5th Dynasty pyramid of Unas, at Saqqara. Given that the average weight density of limestone is 152.5 pounds per cubic foot, the Unas block must weigh between 450 and 500 tons (I do not have its thickness dimension). Consider that blocks at or near that size range were witnessed in great numbers by Herodotus and Abd el-Latif, and then compare their weights with the average of 2.5 tons per block used in almost every pyramid-building calculation found in "authoritative" books on the construction of the Great Pyramid.

There are actually longer blocks in ancient architecture, such as the three blocks in the Temple of Baalbek, in Syria. One of these blocks measures 64 feet long and 14 feet square. However, hauling a great many 30-foot-long pyramid casing blocks on barges from across the Nile presents a truly incredible scenario, as does raising, cementing and fitting such blocks so that they correspond to each other in shape and have flat, correctly angled faces.

The foundation of the Great Pyramid dazzled the first Egyptologists. Slabs of fine-grained limestone are sunk into shallow bedrock. The slabs make up a gigantic square platform that surrounds the Great Pyramid and extends under its edges. The platform has a discrepancy so slight from true square that its accuracy is extraordinary, given its great size. What is more remarkable is that this huge platform, measuring 13 acres, is so accurately level as to be off only 7/8 inch from the northwest to the southwest corner. The slight unevenness might be due to settling.[17] The undersides of the platform slabs conform to irregularities in the bedrock below. That is, each platform slab fits snugly into a particular spot in the irregular bedrock, like a piece in a gigantic puzzle.[18]

The magnificent platform-foundation of the Great Pyramid is only addressed in Egyptological literature in terms of how level surfaces were measured with ancient means.[19] The same literature ignores the germane enigma: How could masons accurately level hard limestone slabs on this vast scale with only abrasives and copper and stone tools? There is no doubt that the limestone is hard, because the platform tolerates the tremendous weight of the Great Pyramid. How could masons cut the undersides of these level platform slabs to conform exactly to irregularities in the bedrock on such an enormous scale?

The overall picture astonished early Egyptologists like W.M.F. Petrie. The Great Pyramid exhibits precise right angles on a supercolossal scale. A gradual incline from casing block to casing block produced huge, beautifully formed triangular pyramid faces that measured about five acres each. The four corners of the Great Pyramid each tapered into triangles that rose almost 500 feet high and met perfectly at a point at the top.[20] The ancient workers made it all to unparalleled precision.

# Chapter 3

# Incredible Construction Speed

The speed at which Egyptology has determined that the Great Pyramid was built remains unduplicated by modern experiments that worked with the range of weights found in the Great Pyramid. Egyptologists use an inscription in the Great Pyramid to help estimate the time it took for the entire monument to be completed. A vault above its King's Chamber exhibits Pharaoh Khufu's reddish-brown painted cartouche, consisting of his royal names enclosed by an oval-shaped frame. Inscriptions date this cartouche to the $17^{th}$ year of his reign. Because the cartouche is located at about half of the height of the Great Pyramid, Egyptologists reckon that the monument soared to that level by year 17 of Khufu's reign.

If these hieroglyphic writings are authentic, as Egyptologists believe them to be, then by Khufu's $17^{th}$ year on the throne, his pyramid was well underway. Its magnificent Grand Gallery and the exquisite granite King's Chamber were already completed, so that the most admired features and about half of the height of the pyramid were finished by the time Khufu had reigned for 17 years. Given that two-thirds of the height of the Great Pyramid contains 96 percent of its total bulk, we see that most of the monument was finished by that time. The most complex features, like the Grand Gallery and King's Chamber, were finished. The construction speed is staggering, especially given the overall perfection and design complexities and the amount of material employed. Experts have estimated that the Great Pyramid contains a total volume of 93.5 million cubic feet of limestone masonry, a figure that some contemporary Egyptologists propose should be modified downward some.

Sometimes experts propose manipulating figures as a mechanism for easing construction problems that are not reconciled. For instance, Khufu's dated cartouche works against theorists who propose doubling or tripling the Great Pyramid's construction time to ease inexplicable construction problems. To reconcile the number of blocks that had to be set per day to build the Great Pyramid in Khufu's 23-year reign, Dieter Arnold proposed extending the life span of Khufu and other prolific pyramid-building pharaohs:

> There can only be one solution . . . namely to increase the lifetime of the pharaoh. . . .[1]

An Egyptologist requires tangible chronological information to adjust the chronology of the pharaohs that was so carefully researched over many years by other Egyptologists. Arnold's proposal lacks such evidence. It also ignores evidence to the contrary, the dated cartouche suggesting that the Great Pyramid was well on its way to completion by year 17 of Khufu's reign.

Egyptology asserts that each pyramid was finished, almost entirely if not completely, during one pharaonic reign. A completed ritual chamber, such as the King's Chamber in the Great Pyramid (situated at about half of the Pyramid's height), was necessary for a pharaoh's funerary rites. Religious doctrine held that the soul of the heaven-sent pharaoh must ascend to his throne among the stars. The ascension point was a ritual chamber in the Primordial Mountain. The pyramids are re-creations of the Primordial Mountain, the rock that religious tradition held was the foundation of the world.

History offers many examples of this burial custom. For instance, thousands of years after the Pyramid Age, King Herod the Great (73–4 B.C.), the Roman-backed king of Judea, adhered to this cross-cultural tradition. Herod had himself buried in a huge structure resembling a volcanic mountain, a re-creation of the Primordial Mountain. A Chinese example is the massive earthen burial mound of the Chin Dynasty's Emperor Shin Huang Ti, built around 210 B.C. in the northeastern province of Shanxi in China.

Ancient Egyptian religious doctrine held that chaos would quickly rule if their god-king did not safely ascend to his heavenly throne, where he continued to govern the activities of heaven and Egypt. The Egyptians made every effort to build the pyramids in time, since few ancient Egyptians lived more than 35 years.

The one-reign construction period held by Egyptology badly clashes with an attempt to build a scale model of the Great Pyramid. In 1975 Japanese engineers from Waseda University, in Tokyo, built a 34-foot-high pyramid four miles south of the Great Pyramids of Giza. Their simplified model did not include any interior halls or chambers. Based on their engineering experiment, the engineers calculated that it would have required not 23 years, but 1,200 years to build the Great Pyramid![2]

A 1,200-year construction period is far more problematic than Dieter Arnold's mere doubling or tripling of the lengths of the reigns of pharaohs who built Great Pyramids. Ancient Egyptian history could not have accommodated more than a 100-year construction period for the Great Pyramid. A brief historical reconstruction shows why.

Pharaohs of the 5th and 6th Dynasties stripped blocks from the earlier Great Pyramids to build their much smaller pyramids. Within about 100 years of the completion of the Great Pyramid, anarchy and social collapse ensued in Egypt. The end of the 6th Dynasty (c. 2152 B.C.) marked the end of the classical civilization of Old Kingdom Egypt. The next centuries of relative impoverishment were not conducive to pyramid construction. The pyramid necropolis underwent serious decline.

By the end of the Middle Kingdom (c. 1640 B.C.), Egypt was occupied by a foreign power: a Semitic group ruled called the Hyksos, probably invaders from Western Palestine. During the Hyksos occupation, the pyramid complexes were gradually despoiled of masonry and probably plundered of treasure. Later, the Hyksos invaders were driven from Egypt (after 1550 B.C.), and this ushered in the period Egyptologists call the New Kingdom. During the early New Kingdom, the state treasury neglected the maintenance of northern Egypt, where the pyramids are located. The neglect was by pharaohs who came into power far to the south. New Kingdom pharaohs

8. THE GIZA PYRAMIDS, WITH KHUFU'S PYRAMID IN FRONT: ALMOST 318 MILLION CUBIC FEET OF LIMESTONE WERE CONSUMED TO BUILD THE GREAT PYRAMIDS OF EGYPT'S 4TH DYNASTY. PHOTOGRAPH BY JON BODSWORTH

from Thebes, deep in the south, proclaimed this city Egypt's new capital. Thebes was the focus of many lavish new construction projects. Theban pharaohs promoting the status of Thebes had little incentive to glorify the area of the old northern Memphite capital that fell to the Hyksos. The pyramids were built in the necropolis that served Memphis and other northern cities like Annu (the city called On in the Bible and Heliopolis by the Greeks). It was not until a millennium after the construction of the Great Pyramid that more work was finally carried out on the badly dilapidated pyramids. The restoration was conducted by the administration of the famous New Kingdom Pharaoh Ramses II.[3]

Ramses' family ties were in the north, and he adorned Memphis and the north with some of Egypt's most sumptuous constructions. His administration repaired several pyramids and restored pyramid maintenance cults.[4]

We see that history cannot accommodate a 1,200-year construction period for the Great Pyramid. Two different disciplines (engineering and Egyptology) have examined the pyramid-construction problem from entirely different perspectives and come to clashing conclusions. The tremendous difference of opinion is striking. Owing to the serious historical constraints, we cannot assume that the Waseda team's estimate of a 1,200-year construction period is correct. Had the Waseda team factored in associated monuments at Giza, like the ¼-mile-long causeway that once led from Khufu's Valley Temple to his Great Pyramid, they may have estimated an even longer overall construction period. On the other hand, if Egyptology is correct, then a highly efficient method—one that Egyptologists have not considered—was used to build the Great Pyramids very rapidly.

An estimate by the German Egyptologist Rainer Stadelmann emphasizes the rapid construction rate: Stadelmann estimated that, in only 60 years, almost 318 million cubic feet of limestone were consumed to build the 4$^{th}$ Dynasty's Great Pyramids.[5]

Some people have tried to solve the puzzle by suggesting that the Great Pyramid is older than the 4$^{th}$ Dynasty reign of Pharaoh Khufu. Proponents of this idea speculate that Pharaoh Khufu usurped a far older, pre-Egyptian monument. They suggest that survivors from Atlantis, the fabled sunken island, built the Great Pyramid.[6] If proponents could prove that the Great Pyramid dates to an earlier period, then the time it took to build it would become an open question. Although some popular books promote an Atlantean origin, there is no sound evidence favoring a construction date before the 4$^{th}$ Dynasty.

Aside from pure speculation, some information comes from a radiocarbon dating test. Bits of wood and charcoal were tested, since these materials appear in the thick pink mortar found here and there on pyramids and associated monuments. The mortar samples came from a number of Old Kingdom monuments, including the Great Pyramid.

A team including Mark Lehner, now on the faculty of the University of Chicago's Oriental Institute, undertook the initial project in 1984–5.[7] Lehner collected the samples and suggested the means of testing. The radiocarbon-14 project dated the Great Pyramid up to 400 years older than the 4th Dynasty. But this team did not recognize that pyramid mortar cannot be accurately dated with the radiocarbon-14 method.

A problem is that pyramid mortar was made with carbon-based material, namely sodium carbonate (a salt present in Egyptian natron). Because natron contains a form of carbon, it pollutes radiocarbon dating tests. Carbon pollution can skew test results.[8] To make pyramid mortar, gypsum, clay, chalky limestone debris and natron were mixed with water; therefore, the natron was carried in solution into the organic debris in the mix.[9] Natron permeated the wood and charcoal bits that were tested.

Regardless of the source of pollution, the strange results of Lehner's radiocarbon dating project do suggest pollution. In Lehner's tests, the first pyramid ever built, attributed to the 3rd Dynasty Pharaoh Zoser, dated as more recent than the 4th Dynasty Great Pyramid.[10] These results sharply conflict with chronology developed through many years of careful Egyptological field and textual research.

One of Lehner's test results indicates that mortar near the top of the Great Pyramid dates older than mortar near the bottom.[11] Workers applied the mortar at the bottom of the Great Pyramid first, so this mortar should date as the oldest. The strange results can suggest that the Great Pyramid was built from the top down, which is hardly a likely scenario.

Mark Lehner's book titled *The Egyptian Heritage: Based On the Edgar Cayce Readings* (1974) advocates that the Great Pyramid is a 12,500-year-old remnant of survivors from Atlantis.[12] Lehner promoted an Atlantean origin for the Great Pyramid throughout most of his career as an archaeo-Egyptologist. This notion is fueled by the lack of a sorely needed, responsible, comprehensive explanation for the Great Pyramid's construction enigmas. Until the true explanation is popularized, Atlantean enthusiasts will interpret masonry features that defy orthodox explanations as the product of an advanced Atlantean civilization—one that they contend the Great Pyramid itself proves must have existed.

Lehner's radiocarbon-14 results, which date the Great Pyramid up to 400 years older than the 4th Dynasty, fit neither the Atlantean nor the orthodox historical framework. We cannot properly construe his flawed test results as evidence justifying a need to lengthen the construction period for the Great Pyramid. No rethinking of the puzzle is warranted based on Lehner's tests.

Rather than out of time and place, the Great Pyramid fits perfectly into the evolution of ancient Egyptian architecture. There was a fairly steady increase in the size of blocks from the first pyramid, built for Pharaoh Zoser in the 3rd Dynasty, to the Great Pyramid. In general, workers built pyramids increasingly taller from the time of Zoser's pyramid to that of the Great Pyramid. The fabulous corbelled walls in the

Grand Gallery of the Great Pyramid have profiles like giant upside-down staircases. They are more grandiose than the corbelled rooms in previous pyramids.[13] The elaboration suggests steady architectural progression.

Large pyramids, including Snofru's Red Pyramid at Dahshur, immediately preceded the Great Pyramid. The Red Pyramid is very similar in construction to the Great Pyramid, also suggesting design progression. The enormous Great Pyramid of Khafra at Giza immediately followed the construction of Khufu's Great Pyramid. Khafra's pyramid is almost as tall and massive as the Great Pyramid. Again, this strongly suggests architectural progression. Khafra's Great Pyramid represents the beginning of an architectural decline that became increasingly dramatic as time went on.

No solid evidence has been put forth to justify an Atlantean origin for the Great Pyramid. The same is true for the Sphinx. To eliminate any doubt, in Volume 2, I evaluate the evidence for redating the Sphinx and Great Pyramid. Without justification for moving the date of construction of the Great Pyramid backward in time, theorists cannot legitimately explain its rapid construction rate.

When reckoning the problems of constructing the Great Pyramid, experimenters rarely raise heavy stones to appreciable heights. To build their 34-foot-high pyramid near Giza, Waseda University engineers resorted to modern means, including a forklift. They did not attempt to build interior features or a limestone foundation. To achieve a level foundation, they poured Portland-cement-based concrete.

The Waseda University experiment employed numerous Egyptian workers to tackle the quarries. The crew increasingly fell behind its deadline. To save time, the team resorted to the use of dynamite to quarry blocks, trucks to haul them, and a forklift to hoist them into place. With modern means, including steel tools for shaping blocks, the crew was unable to meet its deadline. Workers had to complete the pyramid by casting concrete blocks. Of the 700 blocks, with a total weight of 25,353 tons, 300 were poured concrete.[14]

The Public Broadcasting System (PBS) science series Nova later attempted and filmed the construction of a much smaller pyramid. The televised Nova program is titled *This Old Pyramid*, and it first aired as a 90-minute special over PBS stations on November 4, 1992. Nova's goal was to address unresolved problems of constructing the Great Pyramid. Nova incorporated fewer than 200 one- and two-ton blocks into an unfinished 18-foot high miniature pyramid.

The Nova film repeatedly states that their workers used only ancient means to build the miniature pyramid, and the film implies this throughout. But only three or four one-ton stones, needed for the on-camera demonstration, were raised up the miniature ramp manually.[15] The rest were hauled and placed with a front-end loader, a construction vehicle with a hydraulically operated scoop in front! Compare the over two million blocks in the Great Pyramid, placed hundreds of years before evidence of the use of a simple block and tackle in ancient Egypt.

9. The Great Sphinx at Giza with Khafra's Great Pyramid in the background. Orthodox Egyptology includes the Sphinx with Khafra's pyramid complex. Photograph by Jon Bodsworth

Nova used modern steel hand tools to cut and quarry the softest limestone the quarries at Tura have to offer.[16] Nova's pyramid blocks had crude tool marks all over their faces, and their corners were chipped. Gaps between the blocks measured up to 0.2 inch wide. Compare joints as close as 1/500 inch in the Great Pyramid. Compare the 13-acre foundation of the Great Pyramid, measured to be 7/8 inch off level. Nova did not attempt to cut a limestone foundation. Compare the exactness of the Great Pyramids, built when only primitive tools were available for quarrying and shaping rock.

Systems Engineer Mike Carrell contemplated the problem of the level foundation and tiers. For publication here, Mike Carrell prepared this statement stressing the critical importance of a level foundation and accurate tiers:

> Among the remarkable features of the great pyramids are their great weight and the levelness of the tiers. At Giza, the pyramids rest on a hard limestone bedrock, which must have been chosen because it is reasonably level. The first tier of blocks must transmit their weight and the weight of all above them to the bedrock. To do this there must be exact conformity of the lower surfaces of the blocks with the actual surface of the bedrock. Any misfits will concentrate the burden on a smaller area, increasing the stress, and possibly resulting in a fracture.
>
> The same considerations apply to the horizontal interfaces between each successive layer. They must mutually conform to transmit stress, and they must be level, lest errors accumulating from one tier to the next cause distortions in the shape of the pyramid. Producing these necessary features in limestone with the tools available, within the recorded time, presents a seemingly insurmountable task.

Nova's pyramid building experiment did not attempt to meet these requirements.

It is not uncommon for an engineer to introduce a device and claim that it can solve the construction enigmas of the Great Pyramid. Ingenious devices range from simple to highly elaborate, but most have nothing in common with the technological level of the Pyramid Age. Egyptologists have named the 80-year span in which all the Great Pyramids arose (c. 2575–2494 B.C.) the Pyramid Age, which falls into the Late Stone Age's Chalcolithic period (beginning about 4000 B.C.). People of that time had tools made of copper, stone and/or wood, and they had abrasives like sand. Even the simple modern mechanical devices theorists have proposed bear no relationship to ancient Egyptian implements.

Theorists tend to focus on a particular engineering or masonry problem without considering the full range of enigmas. Consequently, proposed solutions are at odds with features of the Great Pyramid and/or with Pyramid Age technology. When responsible new engineering systems are proposed, they come under considerable scrutiny, assuming that they comply with the orthodox paradigm of pyramid construction. Dieter Arnold made this comment:

> But at what point one method or another was used can only—if at all—be determined by detailed technical studies of some of the thirty major pyramids. Before this is accomplished, the most ingenious and scrupulous system developed on the drawing board is nothing but one more example of unproven speculation.[17]

Let us now consider the magnificent interior features of the Great Pyramid and the conundrums they pose.

# Chapter 4

# Enigmatic Interior Features

The grand entrance of the Great Pyramid, on its north face, is a prominent feature. Forming the outside of the entrance is an outstanding double layer of conspicuously large beams that lean against one another at the top to form a triangular arch. Situated about 55 feet above ground level, each of these four beams measures about ten feet in length. In the interior of the Great Pyramid, the flat ceiling of the entrance passage also exhibits heavy beams.

After entering the Great Pyramid, one soon comes to its 129-foot-long Ascending Passageway. In its upper portion, the masonry is finely executed with tight-fitting limestone blocks. Three large blocks made with granite, together 15 feet in length, were placed to plug the remarkable passageway at its lower end.

Most theorists assume that these plugs were stored in the Grand Gallery, above the Ascending Passageway, and then slid down this 129-foot-long expanse into position.[1] But the plug blocks are less than half an inch narrower than the Ascending Passageway itself.[2] They fit very closely to its ceiling. In some places, there is only 1/10 inch clearance.[3] In general, the gap between the tops of the plugs and the ceiling of the corridor is only about 1-1/3 inch.[4] To prevent them from slipping out of position, workers made the granite plugs slightly wedge-shaped. The Ascending Passageway corresponds to their shape.[5]

Sliding these blocks, each about five feet long and weighing about seven tons, down 129 feet so that they will not get hopelessly jammed in the close spaces has been called a staggering feat to comprehend. Large, unbroken portions show their custom, precision fit with one another. Theorists attempt to explain how these plugs were installed, but have not adequately explicated or demonstrated their placement in practice.

Various pyramids and later tombs exhibit dramatic examples of blocks in narrow spaces at the bottom of long, sloping shafts. These extremely tight places allow only a few men to work at a time. Several pyramids are equipped with underground burial chambers containing large stone sarcophagi. The only way into these chambers is through a long, sloping rock-cut shaft. Some of the narrow bedrock shafts are fully paved with tight-fitting blocks made with limestone or granite. In several pyramids, the blocks plugging sloping corridors filled their corridors very exactly.[5] In the 12th

10. ENTRANCE BEAMS: THESE 10-FOOT LONG BEAMS AT THE ENTRANCE OF THE GREAT PYRAMID ARE SITUATED ABOUT 55 FEET ABOVE GROUND LEVEL. PHOTOGRAPH BY JON BODSWORTH

Dynasty pyramid of Pharaoh Senworset I (c. 1971–1926 B.C.), six or seven granite plug blocks weigh up to 20 tons each.[6]

The Descending Passageway is remarkable for its accuracy. Although it is 350 feet long, and runs down into the bedrock at an angle of 26 degrees, it measures only 1/50 inch off square along its entire course! The floor, walls and ceiling of the Descending Passageway were once very smooth surfaces, but now the floor is so damaged that it is very uneven. The Descending Passageway leads to a rough subterranean chamber called the "Pit."

In the Great Pyramid, massive installations made with limestone and called "girdle stones" are remarkable features. Spaced at intervals along the Ascending Passageway, they serve to reinforce it. The Ascending Passageway runs straight

11. THE GRAND GALLERY IN THE GREAT PYRAMID, AS SKETCHED DURING THE NAPOLEONIC EXPEDITION IN EGYPT.

through the girdle stones, which range from 12 to 15 feet long.[7] These giant support structures are just as thick. Altogether, there are four full girdle stones and three half girdle stones. The girdle stones are thought to be a feature unique to the Great Pyramid, and one of those making the Great Pyramid far superior to all others. These masses are never taken into account by engineering studies attempting to explain away construction problems. We can only imagine the difficulties of raising, installing and fitting huge hollow blocks that girdle the width and breadth of the Ascending Passageway.

The Ascending Passageway leads to the most grandiose feature of any pyramid, the Grand Gallery.[8] The Grand Gallery is such an imposing, impressive structure that climbing it leaves an unforgettable impression on the senses. This magnificent construction measures 157 feet long and 28 feet high. Its colossal, finely executed walls, made with white limestone, were elaborately fashioned with great care. The smooth walls are corbelled and made of seven courses of giant blocks. The magnificent corbelled walls look like great upside-down staircases, which start at the ceiling. The design makes the width of the Grand Gallery at its ceiling equal to half of that at its floor.

The Grand Gallery's ceiling, too, is corbelled, made of overhanging block courses that approach one another from opposite sides. The design left a center gap that is bridged by a single block. Engineers recognize the tremendous complexities of constructing this corbelled ceiling, which slopes at a 26-degree angle.

The Grand Gallery leads up to the famous King's Chamber, an extraordinary room made entirely (walls, ceiling and floor) of blocks that were finely executed with red granite.[9] Its walls incorporate 100 huge blocks made in five

12. THE KING'S CHAMBER IN THE GREAT PYRAMID AS PORTRAYED BY LUIGI MAYER IN ABOUT 1800.

courses of nearly equal height. These wall blocks weigh up to 50 tons apiece and are very smooth, flat, and exact. There are almost 300 joints between the blocks, most of which fit so closely that they can be called hairline separations—many are barely detectable to the naked eye.

The King's Chamber measures about 34 feet from east to west, 17 feet from north to south, and it is 19 feet high. The bottom course of wall blocks terminates below floor level. The disconnected construction isolates the floor so that shifting and settling do not cause deformation. The blocks making up the floor are so large that only 21 of them cover the whole floor. The construction of the finely crafted masonry of the King's Chamber has long been a glaring mystery of Egyptology.[10]

Pyramid Age copper chisels will not cut hard red Aswan granite, and no harder metal was available. Other options are lapping or sanding, but it is hard to imagine lapping 50-ton granite blocks so that they conform to each on all contact surfaces, with hairline joints, and have flat faces that form smooth walls. A project to reproduce such blocks by sanding granite has not been undertaken, and producing the King's Chamber with abrasive sand is vastly easier said than done.

The King's Chamber contains no furnishings other than Khufu's hard sarcophagus, which was made with granite and weighs about three tons. It rings like a bell when struck with a hammer. Similarly, the entire King's Chamber is extremely resonant.[11] The prominent early figures of Egyptology William Petrie and Alfred Lucas hotly debated enigmatic artifacts like the cutting lines on Khufu's sarcophagus. The cutting lines prove that the ancient masons cut through the granite at an extraordinarily rapid rate, prompting more recent and unorthodox theorists to assert that highly advanced power tools must have been used. The debate between Petrie and Lucas, which went on for 35 years, concentrated on how the Egyptians could have accomplished the rapid cutting with primitive means.

Stonemason Denys Stocks performed experiments showing that granite can very gradually be cut with copper tubular drills and abrasive sand.[12] It took his team one week to cut through one inch of granite using a copper tube drill and sand as an abrasive. His crew, consisting of two men per saw, gradually cut a core from granite at Aswan, in southern Egypt. The core was covered with intersecting striation marks, such that further work would be needed to create a smooth surface on the small object. The resulting parallel striations were of various widths and depths, and their edges were rough. The means Stocks used do not produce rapid cutting or crisp features; therefore, the matter of how Khufu's sarcophagus was rapidly cut through is unresolved by his experiments. We will consider this topic more fully in a later chapter.

Below the level of the King's Chamber, the so-called Queen's Chamber was built at the 25$^{th}$ course. This room measures 19 feet long x 17 feet wide x 15 feet high. J.P. Lepre eloquently described the Queen's Chamber this way:

> The jointing of the limestone blocks comprising this chamber is so nearly perfect that many of them are practically invisible to the naked eye. Therefore, one receives the mistaken impression that the chamber is carved out of a solid piece of rock rather than built of many individual blocks fitted together. This absolutely perfect jointing is even more astonishing when one considers that the monument is close to 5,000 years old and has experienced numerous earthquakes throughout the centuries.[13]

The heavy beams and blocks in the interior of the Great Pyramid pose unresolved problems for engineers. Any construction ramp must be able to support the heaviest building units of the Great Pyramid. Engineers recognize that earthen ramps would not be strong enough to support even the transport of several core blocks, units that weigh much less than the construction beams.

Engineers who have seriously studied the problems believe that only solid masonry could provide the necessary strength needed for raising numerous blocks on ramps.[14] The ramp designs, however, proposed for the Great Pyramid would consume far too much material for solid masonry to be practical. A very compact earthen ramp may accommodate a limited number of large blocks, but the structure will quickly disintegrate when bearing numerous heavy weights. Egyptology is left without a viable explanation for how pyramid blocks were elevated, a topic we will explore in more depth in a later chapter.

The problem with ramps becomes particularly conspicuous when we consider the nine mammoth granite beams making up the ceiling of the King's Chamber. The beams measure up to 27 feet long. Most of these enormous beams weigh about 54 tons, some about 70 tons. These are the largest building units of the King's Chamber. Collectively, the weight of the granite slabs that make up the flat ceiling is more than 400 tons.[15]

The ceiling of the entrance passage to the King's Chamber incorporates another large granite beam. Measuring ten feet long by eight feet high, it weighs about 45 tons. These enormous monoliths are situated about 160 feet above ground level.

Several cyclopean beams make up the remarkable system of five stress-relieving chambers above the King's Chamber. The pointed roof of the topmost of these chambers reaches to about half of the height of the Great Pyramid. The pointed roof of these chambers is made of 11 pairs of sloping limestone beams each measuring over 20 feet long. They each weigh about 36 tons.

Debate centers on how workers could have transported huge granite beams up to 27 feet long from the Aswan quarries, about 600 miles south of Giza, and then elevated them to the level above the King's Chamber.[16] The heaviest granite building units known at Giza are the 56 built into this general area of the Great Pyramid.[17] Lower in the monument, the ceiling of the Queen's Chamber is made of six pairs of immense beams.

The shafts in the Great Pyramid are extremely long, complex architectural features that required a great deal of extra building effort. These long shafts also provide strong evidence suggesting undetected chambers within the Great Pyramid near the King's Chamber, as follows: The southern shaft of the Queen's Chamber became famous after a robot, designed by German roboticist Rudolph Gantenbrink, climbed it and found that it is blocked by a slab made with limestone. Subsequently, another robot drilled through this slab (popularly called Gantenbrink's Door) and found yet another slab behind it.

After the 2002 Fox-National Geographic TV special revealed this second slab, one of the technicians involved in the project decided to send the robot up the northern shaft in the Queen's Chamber. He commented in a subsequent news report that the robot found that the northern shaft deviates from its straight course to the exterior masonry so as to accommodate the corbelled walls of the Grand Gallery. When I

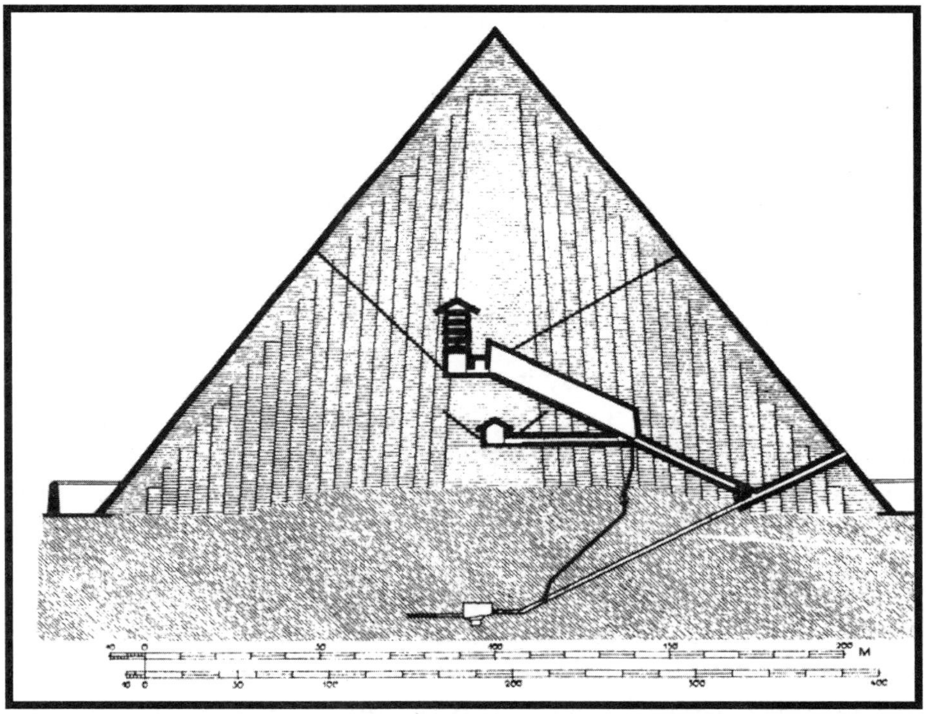

13. GREAT PYRAMID SECTION: IN MOST DIAGRAMS THE SHAFTS ARE SHOWN AS STRAIGHT LINES EXTENDING FROM THE KING'S CHAMBER TO THE EXTERIOR. THIS DIAGRAM SHOWS THE KING'S CHAMBER WITH SHAFTS AND ROOFING STRUCTURES, THE GRAND GALLERY, THE QUEEN'S CHAMBER WITH ITS SHAFTS, THE ASCENDING AND DESCENDING PASSAGES AND THE PIT. THE DIAGRAM IS FROM AHMED FAKHRY, *THE PYRAMIDS* (1969 EDITION), FIGURE 68.

heard his report, I immediately recognized strong evidence of hidden chambers near the King's Chamber. The evidence is so obvious that many other people must have recognized it, too, so that I expect several reports by the time this book is published.

The evidence of hidden areas near the King's Chamber is based on the above-mentioned news report combined with J.P. Lepre's observation of the shafts of the King's Chamber. He found two bends in the southern shaft of the King's Chamber and four in its northern shaft. We can put two and two together and recognize that these bends should accommodate hidden areas, just as the bends in the northern shaft in the Queen's Chamber bends to run around, rather than through, the walls of the Grand Gallery. Here are J.P. Lepre's observations:

> The north channel is rectangular in form, being 5" high by 7" wide, while the south air channel has a stranger configuration. Within the chamber itself is a dome-shaped, representing a quite wide 18" by 24" opening. After a few feet it maintains this basic dome-shape, but is now reduced to a 12"' by 18" aperture which, after a few feet more, narrows to approximately 8" by 12". It maintains these dimensions as it passes through the pyramid's masonry to the 101st outside course, but takes two sharp bends in the process. In the first of these turns it changes its shape from dome to oval, and in the second turn (or its third line of travel), from oval to rectangular or oblong. This is a very strange design, to say the least, one which is classically demonstrative of the architect's propensity to dramatically shift design when it is least expected.
>
> To add to this idiosyncrasy is the fact that, at the first turn or bend, this air channel changes its direction, inclining to the south-southwest from true south; it then alters its direction once more, further south-southwest, at its second turn. The entire direction and configuration is so bizarre that it has thus far defied any logical explanation.
>
> In contrast, the north air channel of the King's Chamber maintains its basic rectangular shape throughout its long journey to the exterior of the edifice. Yet it, too, changes its direction during the course of its travel, and takes, not two, but four distinct bends or turns. For although its basic upward angle is not altered, it deviates, first to the north-northwest, then back to north, then to the north-northeast, finally returning to true north. Thus it curves in a semicircular pattern, and then returns to its original direction.
>
> The reader may wonder how so many turns in such small channels could possibly be sighted by the author or any other viewer; certainly the apertures spoken of are much too tiny to admit a man—or even a very small

child, for that matter. But recall that the beginning 6′ section of the southern air channel measures 18″ by 24″ at its commencement inside the burial chamber and 12″ by 18″ where it reaches its first bend. In the confines of this space it is possible for a small to medium-sized person to crawl forth, and by stretching, to view the two sharp bends which the channel then takes.

In respect to the northern air duct, it is of course not possible to be afforded such a view from the interior of the burial chamber, as the 5″ by 7″ duct cannot admit the body of a viewer, and even if it could, then no one would sight four turns of the duct from a single vantage point.

Fortunately for the interested observer—though sadly for the pyramid—although the first 8′ of this channel has remained perfectly intact, the distance of the next 30′ or so has been excavated by inquisitive explorers who broke through to this section and tunneled northward, following the direction of the channel. They did not begin their excavation where the air channel commences, in the King's Chamber, but broke into the west wall of the short passage leading to that chamber, where an iron grating has now been placed by the Egyptian government to ward off further observation. Within this cavernous tunnel, one can immediately see the first, second and third bends which the air duct takes in this confined area. By stretching one's self at the northern, more narrow end of this tunnel, the fourth bend in the channel can also be seen. Were it not for this fortuitous but barbarous quarrying we would never been made aware of the interesting features of this northern air vent.

While the unorthodox curve in the southern air vent is puzzling, in the northern air channel the direction is even more eccentric, with that channel turning once again to its original direction. One's initial reaction to this deviation is that this duct was shifted and then brought back shortly thereafter in order to avoid something in that area of the King's Chamber north wall. Could we then deduce that there may be a cavity or a passage of a sort in that location that the architect wished to keep secret? This is, of course, pure speculation. Only one thing is certain: that the architect had a purpose in diverting and then redirecting this channel.[18]

In short, putting J.P. Lepre's keen observations together with the National Geographic project information revealing that the northern Queen's Chamber shaft definitely deviates its course to avoid the Grand Gallery, we can recognize strong evidence of hidden chambers near the King's Chamber of the Great Pyramid.

Let us now consider very serious challenges to the orthodox theory of pyramid construction that theorists have not previously recognized.

# Chapter 5

# Egyptology Has No Explanation

The size of the limestone quarries associated with the Great Pyramid places an intolerable strain on the prevailing construction theory. Some years ago, the aforementioned Mark Lehner carried out a mapping project at Giza.[1] The project included measurements of the limestone quarry used for building the Great Pyramid. Lehner found that the amount of stone in the Great Pyramid roughly equals the amount removed from the quarry. Lehner's calculation convinced him that workers quarried all blocks for the Great Pyramid at Giza, except for the casing blocks. They are made of fine-grained limestone from the Tura quarries across the Nile. There is a serious problem with Lehner's assessment: If core blocks were extracted from the Giza quarry to build Great Pyramid, then the quarry should be much larger.

Block quarrying is a wasteful process. Typically, four blocks will crack during quarrying for every usable block, according to limestone geologist Robert L. Folk, professor emeritus of the University of Texas, in Austin. If we assume that cracked blocks are salvageable for making smaller blocks, then we may arrive at a rate of only two cracked per every usable block. The Giza quarries would still be about twice as large as measured by Lehner. The problem, however, is not that simple. Given the ancient methods of block extraction, there is no reason to assume such a generously small quantity of waste rock.

In the 1800s, quarrymen extracted roughly shaped blocks by lining up in quarries with eight-foot-long steel bars. They would strike up and down with the bars, and then twist them to break away large chunks of stone. The process can begin only after removing waste rock from the top surface of the quarry.

Today quarrymen use dynamite to perform this initial clearing of waste rock, which is unsuitable for making blocks. Once this initial cleansing is complete and a rock face of suitable limestone is exposed, quarrymen use chain saws to section the rock face into blocks. They then detach the blocks using a variety of means, including wedges combined with either hydraulics or air pressure. A good limestone quarry will yield 30 percent waste with the benefit of this technology. The 30 percent figure is calculated only after up to 30 feet of top waste rock has been removed. The percentage of waste rock can vary dramatically. A poor quarry might have a 50 percent net yield after the removal of waste rock. When we consider this information relative to pyramid construction, it is apparent that the amount of quarry waste at Giza would be very high, because using ancient quarrying methods for making blocks was even more wasteful than today's techniques.

In 1988 Joseph Davidovits and I pointed out that the quarry associated with the Great Pyramid was too small to have furnished enough blocks to build the monument.[2] Mark Lehner, in *The Complete Pyramids* (1997), now agrees:

> The calculated amount of stone removed - c. 2,760,000 cu. m (97.5 million cu. ft) - compares neatly with the total 2,650,000 cu. m (93.5 million cu. ft) in Khufu's pyramid. Too neatly in fact. There should be more missing that this: modern masons and quarrymen estimate that between 30 and 50 percent of stone was wasted in the extraction of stone. However, the quarry extends an unknown distance to the south, beyond the line of Menkaure's causeway. . . . And much stone was taken from the Central Wadi. . . .[3]

In other words, Lehner thinks that these other unmeasured areas can adequately satisfy our concern. However, for reasons I explain below, there is a serious problem with his calculations.

Egyptology also theorizes that the head of the Sphinx is the remains of a layer of hard rock that was all quarried away to build the Great Pyramids. If we accept this premise, then it is likely that this layer was not very expansive. The reason is that when geochemist Dietrich Klemm selectively gathered samples from the Great Pyramids, he found that only 2.5 percent of the blocks are made of stone that is as hard as the head of the Sphinx. While the body of the Sphinx is very fragile, the head is very hard limestone. Almost 98 percent of the pyramid blocks are limestone that is not nearly as hard.[4] The Klemms' findings, therefore, suggest that any rock layer associated with the head of the Sphinx was not extensive.

Returning to the issue of quarry waste, based on the crude tool marks on walls of the Giza quarries, Dieter Arnold deduced that workers extracted pyramid blocks with simple stone hand tools.[5] Hard rocks, including granite, chert, basalt, quartzite, and hard limestone were used to make crude ax heads. Workers affixed the ax heads to wooden handles with leather strips.[6] Stone axes make a different type of impression on the quarry walls from that of metal chisels with flat cutting edges. Based on existing tool marks, Arnold reckoned that stone axes or broken pieces of flint were somehow used to cut trenches in the quarries until blocks were isolated on all four sides. Next, he suggested, the workers undercut the blocks to separate them from the quarry floor. The method would generate enormous amounts of waste rock, because the trenches would have to be wide enough for men to crouch in when separating the blocks from the quarry floor.

The separation ditches must be proportionally large for large blocks and beams,

14. Pounding Ball: Hard stone balls, like this one in the British Museum, were useful for bashing out underground tunnels and rooms. Photograph by Jon Bodsworth

so that there would be enough space for men to work from below when breaking huge building units from the quarry floor. Extracting truly large blocks is so cumbersome and difficult that today strategically located dynamite charges are used.

Another problem is that the above-described stone axes are unsuitable for quarrying even roughly shaped limestone blocks. During the filming of Nova's *This Old Pyramid*, Mark Lehner tried to shape a block made from the softest limestone of Tura. Lehner's ax, replicated to Dieter Arnold's specifications, was made of diorite, a very hard, tough rock. The limestone block Lehner worked on had already been preshaped with a modern steel tool before he even touched it with his diorite ax. But Lehner's repeated behind-the-scenes cutting attempts were futile. He finally discarded the primitive diorite ax and used an appropriately shaped modern steel tool.

Primitive stone ax heads, held to handles with banding, are unsuitable for the much heavier work of making trenches in bedrock to extract blocks. Flint is very hard, but it is brittle and will break when repeatedly struck against a hard surface. The best tool the ancient Egyptians had for making trenches was the pounder, a heavy chunk of hard rock. These tools will not neatly slice rock, but workers can use them to bash out pits and trenches. Pounding on limestone tends to generate cracks in stone that would otherwise be usable, creating additional quarry waste.

Given the enormous amount of rubble generated by pounding balls and other primitive means of quarrying, the Giza quarries should be a great deal larger than measured by Lehner. It is difficult to think that the unmeasured areas he mentions would make the difference, given that ancient techniques generate a far higher percentage of waste than today's 30 to 50 percent. Besides, as I discuss further below, the areas quarried at Giza do not geologically match the pyramid blocks, and this presents a whole different problem for Egyptology. The areas that were extensively quarried at Giza consist of fragile limestone like the body of the Sphinx. Although most are not as hard as the head, the pyramid blocks are considerably more durable than the body of the Sphinx.

Certain that Pyramid Age Egyptians did not have iron tools for detaching blocks from the quarry floor, some Egyptologists suppose that quarrymen used long wooden levers. The use of long levers requires much more room for men to maneuver, resulting in an increase in size of quarry trenches. We see that this method would result in a further increase in the quarry-size requirements.

Moreover, a great deal of stone was consumed to make causeways. Khafra's causeway is about ¼ mile long and about 15 feet wide. Herodotus witnessed Khufu's great causeway, which reached from the Great Pyramid to Khufu's Valley Temple, and reported that it was made of smooth, fine-grained blocks like the casing. However, Herodotus witnessed the outer casing when the causeway was intact. Thus, he was not able to report information about the core of the monument. The number of

15. STEP PYRAMID OF ZOSER: EGYPT'S FIRST PYRAMID, THE STEP PYRAMID AT SAQQARA, WAS SURROUNDED BY 30-FOOT-HIGH RETAINING WALLS THAT ENCLOSED THE SQUARE-MILE PYRAMID COMPLEX. PHOTOGRAPH BY JON BODSWORTH

16. WHEN RICHARD LEPSIUS AND HIS TEAM VISITED GIZA IN 1842-43, A MYRIAD OF BLOCKS FROM KHUFU'S CAUSEWAY REMAINED AT GIZA. IMAGE: R.C. LEPSIUS, *DENKMALER AUS AGYPTEN UND ATHIOPIEN* (1849), PLATE 20

17. A MODEL OF ZOSER'S PYRAMID COMPLEX CREATED BY J.P. LAUER: THE AMOUNT OF MASONRY NEEDED FOR CONSTRUCTING A PYRAMID COMPLEX INCLUDED BLOCKS FOR THE PYRAMID, A CAUSEWAY LEADING TO THE NILE, RETAINING WALLS SURROUNDING THE COMPLEX, TEMPLES, AND SHRINES.

18. QUARRY NEAR KHAFRA'S PYRAMID: W.M.F. PETRIE NOTICED THAT THE GIZA QUARRY SHOWING THE REMOVAL OF WHOLE BLOCKS IS TOO SMALL TO ACCOUNT FOR THE CONSTRUCTION OF THE GREAT PYRAMID. THIS IS THE ONLY QUARRY AT GIZA SHOWING THE MASSIVE REMOVAL OF WHOLE, QUARRIED BLOCKS. SEE FIGURE 19 FOR ITS VOLUME COMPARED TO THAT OF THE GREAT PYRAMID. PHOTOGRAPH BY JON BODSWORTH

**19.** The diagram compares the size of the quarry near Khafra's pyramid to the size of the Great Pyramid. The volume of the quarry is about two percent of the volume of the Great Pyramid or about three percent of the volume of Khafra's pyramid. Diagram by Mike Carrell, based on Alberto Silotti's *Guide to the Pyramids of Egypt*

blocks used was monumental: Herodotus considered the enormous causeway as, ". . . not much inferior, in my judgment, to the pyramid itself."

Aside from long causeways and temples that required stone, the pyramid complexes were surrounded by high walls made of blocks, which required another vast quantity of stone. For instance, Zoser's Step Pyramid complex, located at Saqqara, measured a square mile and was enclosed by limestone walls 30 feet high. At Giza, the amount and type of stone consumed depends on the thickness of Khufu's walls, which were torn down over the ages.

Another consideration vastly increases the size requirements for the Giza quarries. The standard theory of pyramid construction assumes that the Great Pyramids were built using enormous construction ramps. To make a ramp for the Great Pyramid, a tremendous volume of material would have been required. Engineers have determined, as is further discussed below, that a ramp must be made of solid masonry to be strong enough to support the weight of blocks.

A ramp of the size needed, made of solid limestone masonry, would demand much more material from the quarries than the volume of the pyramid itself. The Great Pyramid contains about 93.5 million cubic feet of limestone, and engineers estimate that a construction ramp must contain a minimum of twice that amount for a ramp of an appropriate incline that extends only part way up the Pyramid.

The size of the ramp depends upon its slope. To produce a workable slope, some engineers multiply the ramp's volume to many times that of the Great Pyramid. To give every advantage to the standard theories, I use a very conservative estimate here to minimize the volume of the ramp as much as possible. Given that any ramp would consume at least as much limestone as the Great Pyramid itself, the Giza quarries should be vastly larger than Lehner can account for by factoring in unmeasured areas at Giza. Besides, quarried areas of the appropriate enormous size would be highly conspicuous, rather than involve the nebulous guessing proposed by Lehner.

Ramps made of stone rubble cemented with clay have been found attached to some of the smaller pyramids. These pyramids are made of blocks small enough to be carried by one or two men. Many books assume that a much larger mud-rubble ramp must have been used to build the Great Pyramid, but engineers who have seriously studied the construction problems insist that only a solid stone ramp would be strong enough to raise the massive blocks of the Great Pyramid.

There is another aspect to the problem involving the size of the Giza quarries, and it further emphasizes the construction enigma facing Egyptology. The main building blocks of the Giza Pyramids look different from and are harder than the limestone in the Giza quarries, where there is extensive evidence of rock extraction. The quarry walls expose the layers of limestone that were removed. Therefore, we know what blocks cut from this material should look like. Because of the distinctly different appearance between the pyramid blocks and the quarry walls, some researchers have concluded that the pyramid blocks must have been transported from afar.

Various studies have shown the fundamental geological differences between the Giza quarries and the pyramid blocks.[7] The first study was by M. Edme Francois Jomard (1777–1862), General Commissioner for the Napoleonic Scientific Expedition, with geologist Francoise Michel de Roziere. They reported the difference in appearance between pyramid stone and Giza bedrock in Jomard's *Description de l'Egypte* (1809–1830).[8] The book includes a drawing of pyramid limestone, which is made of scrambled coinlike seashells. In contrast, scrambled shells do not characterize the quarry walls.

Later, W.M.F. Petrie spent many seasons at Giza studying the problems.[9] The Giza quarries were not cleared in his day, but had there been matching limestone at Giza we can expect he may have been satisfied. But he could not find sufficient signs of block quarrying at Giza to account for the Great Pyramid. Now that the quarries are clear, anyone can compare the area where blocks were quarried (the area is next to Khafra's pyramid) with the well-defined size of the large quarries (we can more precisely call these "excavation pits" because they were heavily excavated but show no signs of block quarrying). The comparison shows that the quarried area is very small compared with the huge excavation pit associated with the Great Pyramid, which equals the volume of the pyramid but exhibits no pounding ball marks or trenches or stubs indicating the massive removal of blocks.

Petrie searched carefully for miles around the Giza area for a limestone outcrop where whole blocks were removed. He could find none and assumed that all of the stone must have come from across the Nile, more than 15 miles away in the Mokattam hills. A serious problem presents itself because Dietrich Klemm subsequently analyzed fossil shells and determined a definite match between those in the blocks of the Great Pyramid and those at Giza in the large excavation pit (commonly called a quarry) where a volume of rock roughly equal to the Great Pyramid was extracted. Egyptology has no explanation for this conflict that will stand up to scrutiny. Only the solution presented in this book can reconcile this problematic matter.

Jumbled shells are a striking characteristic of blocks making up the pyramid complexes. The feature is so common that it would be difficult to find a block in the Giza pyramid complexes that do not exhibit scrambled shells, although many thousands of blocks are visible to the naked eye. In sharp contrast, fossil shells normally lie flat in sedimentary limestone, as they do for the most part in the excavated areas of Giza bedrock. The walls of the so-called quarries (excavation pits) show the sedimentary nature of the rock that was removed.

In *The Great Pyramid in Fact and Theory* (1932), William Kingsland, who did not always agree with Petrie, agreed that the pyramid blocks did not look like Giza limestone:

> The Core Masonry is composed of limestone of varying quality; some of it as pure as that of the Casing Stones, but a good deal of it is what is known as nummulitic limestone, as it contains large quantities of fossil shells resembling coins. It all appears, however, to have come from the Mokattam Hills on the opposite side of the Nile, from the quarries of Masara and Tura.[10]

It is widely recognized that the fine-grained casing blocks that originally covered the pyramids, eliminating their stepped appearance, look like the bedrock of the eastern limestone quarries at Tura. It is widely assumed that the rough nummulitic* limestone building blocks, which make up a large percent of the masonry of the Great Pyramid, were quarried at Giza itself. The information above, indeed, poses dilemmas for Egyptology. It poses the mystery of the mismatch between the heavily excavated limestone at Giza and the pyramid blocks. It also greatly complicates the logistical problems of hauling heavy blocks and beams for constructing the Great Pyramid if these building units had to be transported from a distant site. The closest quarry showing the quarrying of a huge number of nummulitic limestone blocks is far from Giza in Middle Egypt, at the quarry called Zawyet Sultan on the east bank of the Nile near el-Minya.

Another study was made in the 1980s by geologists from Japan's Waseda University. They wanted to test W.M.F. Petrie's observations and compared the walls

*IN LIMESTONE, THE NUMMULITE SHELLS ARE FOSSILIZED DISCS, WHICH ARE SHAPED LIKE COINS. THEIR APPEARANCE INSPIRED THEIR NAME, WHICH COMES FROM THE LATIN WORD *NUMMUS*, MEANING COIN. IN BUNCHES, THEY RESEMBLE A HANDFUL OF COINS, AND THOSE AT GIZA ARE UNUSUALLY LARGE, UP TO THE SIZE OF A QUARTER. THESE ORGANISMS ONCE LIVED NEAR THE BOTTOM OF THE SEA THAT COVERED MUCH OF EGYPT AND NORTHEASTERN AFRICA 50 MILLION YEARS AGO. AS NUMMULITES DIED, THEIR SHELLS BUILT UP ON THE OCEAN FLOOR, OFTEN INTO LARGE BANKS. AT GIZA, THEIR PETRIFIED SHELLS ARE SOLIDIFIED INTO THE LIMESTONE LAYERS OF THE BEDROCK.

of the Giza quarries with the pyramid core blocks. The Giza quarries are far more cleared of debris than in W.M.F. Petrie's time; therefore, the quarried surfaces are now well exposed for observation. The Waseda University team concluded that, in general, the blocks of the Great Pyramid are:

> . . . hard and highly viscous [and that] characteristics of the limestone are different from those of the limestone of the site . . .[11]

In other words, the blocks are different from the middle geological layer at Giza where limestone was extensively extracted. The Waseda geologists did not have enough time to try to determine if matching limestone is found across the Nile, where Petrie assumed millions of blocks must have come from.

In 1984 Joseph Davidovits and Egyptian geologist Hisham Gaber compared Giza pyramid and temple core blocks with the Giza quarries.[12] Joseph Davidovits' theory of pyramid construction is the focus of this book, since it solves all of the problems and enigmas I am explaining. Like the other researchers, Joseph Davidovits and Hisham Gaber observed that, in general, the Giza bedrock does not match the pyramid core blocks. The jumbled shells in pyramid core and backing blocks (immediately behind the casing) contrast sharply with the sedimentary layering characterizing the walls of the Giza rock extraction sites.

This is such an important point that in 1990 I arranged for confirmation by Robert

L. Folk, a leading sedimentation expert. He chose to involve petrographer Donald H. Campbell in our study. In addition to arranging for their studies at Giza and Saqqara, I accompanied them. In general, Folk and Campbell were unable to find pyramid or temple blocks at Giza with sedimentary layering (an exception is a 27-foot-high protrusion of natural bedrock that is incorporated into the Great Pyramid). Robert Folk confirmed that the shells in the pyramid and temple core blocks at Giza are jumbled. He observed normal sedimentary layering characterizing the quarries. In other words, normal sedimentary layering characterizes the quarry walls, which show evidence of extensive rock excavation with pointed picks.

These studies indicate that if the Giza quarries had been well cleared in Petrie's day, then he would have still insisted that millions of limestone core blocks had been hauled from a distant quarry. His assertion presents staggering logistical and archaeological problems. First, the task of hauling a myriad of massive core stones for building the Great Pyramids of Giza is greatly multiplied. Large-scale, long-distance transport systems leading from the quarry to the Nile dramatically increase logistical problems. Dragging heavy blocks requires flat, slick tracks to reduce friction. Dragging blocks across the desert sands is not feasible.

Second, archaeological explorations have found wooden tracks still visible at 12th Dynasty pyramid sites where heavy funerary equipment was hauled over short distances. If hundreds of thousands or millions of pyramid blocks were hauled from the distant quarry of Zawyet Sultan (Egypt's only other huge nummulitic limestone quarry) in Middle Egypt to the Nile to be floated to the harbor at Giza, then a great deal of evidence from the hauling operation would remain. But none has been found.

If we imagine that blocks were brought from Zawyet Sultan to Giza on barges floated along the Nile, then Giza should support the existence of a great many thousands of large barges, given the rapid construction pace. However, at Giza, no evidence of barges or even transport sleds has ever been found, and sleds are unknown for the 4th Dynasty. At Giza, excavators have found a tremendous amount of evidence of the activities of the Pyramid Age of 4,500 years ago, from large funerary boats to a myriad of tiny fish bones left over from the meals of workers. But there is no evidence of great barges that could have brought either casing or core blocks to the Giza Plateau, and no evidence of the thousands of sleds that Egyptologists propose were used to haul blocks up ramps at Giza. The situation presents very strange and extremely severe mysteries of Egyptology, such as the issue of the "missing" limestone quarries of Khufu and the issue of the transport of enormous numbers of massive blocks both to and at Giza.

Another anomaly persists. Owing to breakage during quarrying, there should be millions of cracked and broken blocks at Giza. According to geologist Robert L. Folk, one usable block for every four quarried is typical. There are no appropriately large heaps of broken blocks at Giza. There is limestone rubble and the expected

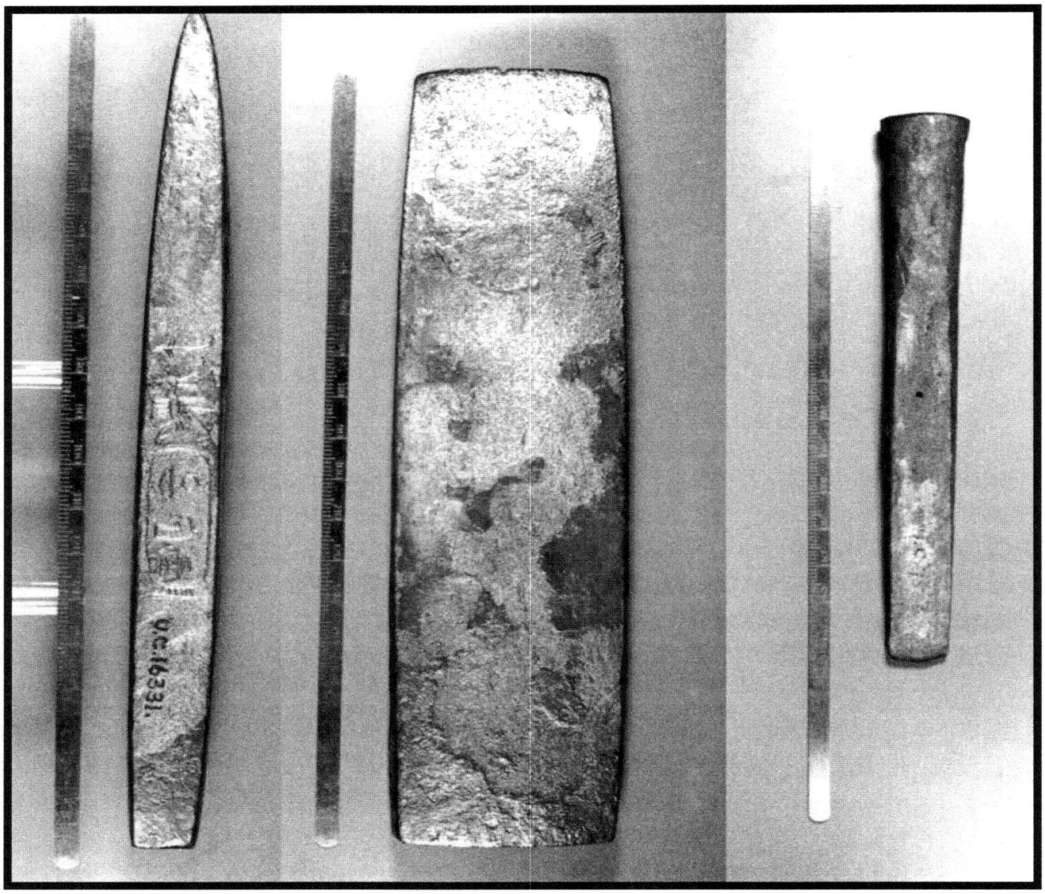


20. Bronze chisels like these in the Petrie Museum, in London, date to about 800 years after the Great Pyramid was built. Pyramid Age chisels were made of copper. Copper chisels and stone pounding balls are inadequate for recycling millions of broken blocks so that they conform to about 75 tier heights, with the margin of error of those tier heights off less than ½ cm. Photographs by John Reid

fallen blocks strewn near the bases of the pyramids.

Historical and early Egyptological reports tell of the dismantling of pyramid tiers in small pyramids at Giza and of how the blocks torn off were dumped nearby. Collectively, the blocks that fell or were torn from the pyramids are relatively few compared with the great number that should exist owing to breakage during quarrying and carving.

A myriad of fragments of 4$^{th}$ Dynasty artifacts have been found at Giza, including bits of vases, sculptures, and faience. Egyptologists have even found mud-brick, which is highly perishable, intact at Giza and dating to the Pyramid Age. Given the presence of these artifacts, how can several million broken blocks vanish without a trace?

Smaller blocks, of the size that might come from recycling or paring down of broken blocks, appear in the small queen's pyramids at Giza. But these structures are small and could not have absorbed the vast amount of stone from broken blocks. No study, based on actual statistics, has addressed the problem of how much stone could be recycled. It is normal for ancient buildings made with cut stone to have large amounts of broken stone blocks somewhere in the area, and usually nearby. This is not the case at Giza.

The Romans and Arabs removed fine limestone blocks from the nearby Old Kingdom capital of Memphis, and the Romans heated such blocks to make lime for cement. But they could not have calcined abandoned blocks at Giza to make lime. Giza limestone is largely bound fossil shells, which is not good for making lime.

It is hard to imagine that so many broken blocks could be recycled to make smaller blocks for later buildings because the amount of limestone is so great and does not show up in known architecture. As is further explained below, the amount of limestone in the Great Pyramids at Giza equals more rock than all of the Theban monuments built with sandstone over a 1,500-year period in later times. The waste from quarrying millions of limestone blocks at Giza should be extremely high, given the tendency of limestone to crack and the primitive tools that existed in the Pyramid Age.

Although every block quarrying operation generates broken blocks, evidence suggests that there never were heaps of broken blocks at Giza. For instance, ancient travelers touring Giza did not report heaps of broken blocks. Herodotus did not report cracked, waste blocks in the 5th century B.C. In the 1st century B.C., the Greek historian Diodorus Siculus commented about the lack of heaps of broken blocks. Diodorus indicated:

> . . . and the most remarkable thing in the account is that, though the constructions were on such a great scale and the country round about them consists of nothing but sand, not a trace remains either of any mound [construction ramp] or of the dressing of the stones, so that they do not have the appearance of being the slow handiwork of men but look like a sudden creation, as though they had been made by some god and set down bodily in the surrounding sand.[13]

Heaps of broken blocks were not reported by the 1st century Roman naturalist Pliny the Elder, either. In 64 B.C., the geographer Strabo reported heaps of fossil-shell rubble, but no heaps of abandoned blocks.[14]

It is unlikely that peasants carried off several million broken blocks to built house foundations (the houses themselves were made of dried mud-brick down to Roman times). Large areas of Giza were covered in sand for most of recorded history, making abandoned stones highly inaccessible. The build-up of sand blowing in from the Libyan Desert is rapid. Without constant maintenance, the 60-foot-high Great Sphinx of Giza will become buried by the encroaching sands in short order.

In summary, Egyptology assumes that workers used primitive stone axes or picks to quarry roughly shaped blocks, since the marks of crude picks appear on quarry walls. Some Egyptologists suppose the use of stone pounding balls, and some suppose the use of long wooden levers. Modern quarry methods produce a great deal of stone rubble, and ancient methods produced far more. Given the demands of the Great Pyramid complex (including a long, wide causeway, retaining walls and temples) and any strong, solid masonry construction ramp, the associated quarries should be much larger. Engineering studies have shown that a solid stone ramp is needed for raising great numbers of massive blocks such as those in the Great Pyramid, and creating such a ramp places tremendous demands on the local limestone quarries in sheer amount of rock consumed.

Furthermore, Egyptology has no explanation for the lack of millions of broken blocks at Giza, and the staggering amount involved is too much to have been absorbed by other known structures. D. Klemm found that the fossil shells in Giza pyramid blocks are of the same type as those in the nearby quarries (huge excavation pits) at Giza. Whereas, Japanese geologists and others who made comparative geological studies showed that the pyramid and temple blocks do not match the limestone quarries (excavation pits) at Giza. Fossil shells are scrambled in the pyramid and temple blocks, but the quarries are characterized by normal sedimentary layering. W.M.F. Petrie and later the Japanese geologists concluded, therefore, that most blocks of the Great Pyramid must have been hauled from a distant site. But all of the Egyptian quarries are known, and the only quarry where enormous numbers of nummulitic limestone blocks were removed is far from Giza, in Middle Egypt, at the quarry of Zawyet Sultan near el-Minya. The site is characterized by post-Pyramid Age block quarrying technique, trench quarrying. No evidence of any hauling system to or at Giza has been found. Accepted theories of pyramid construction are already badly overburdened and cannot tolerate these additional tremendous strains.

# CHAPTER 6

# EGYPTIAN MASONRY MARVELS

While the Great Pyramid is by far the best known example of enigmatic masonry, many other examples attest to the use of a special technology. Experts marvel at but cannot explain how, with only abrasives and primitive hand-tools at their disposal, Predynastic and early dynastic Egyptians fashioned the most perfect and hardest stone dishes of all time.

21. THE TRIAD OF MENKAURE, MADE WITH GREYWACKE AND NOW IN THE CAIRO MUSEUM, IS A MASTERPIECE OF OLD KINGDOM EGYPT. PHOTOGRAPH BY JON BODSWORTH

Artisans made stone dishes and other vessels of a number of rock varieties, including diorite, serpentine, schist, breccia, purple porphyry, red jasper, obsidian, quartz, granite and basalt. Some of the rock types used are too hard to be crafted using iron tools, including basalt, metamorphic schist, diorite and quartzite. The remarkable features of these vessels, such as ultrathin walls that are uniform in thickness, have not been replicated by using abrasive sand and replicas of ancient tools.

Most of the more than 30,000 hard-stone vessels found in Zoser's pyramid, at Saqqara, date before this 3rd Dynasty monument. Many of these stone dishes were made even before writing was invented or copper was smelted.

In 1999 a team from the German Archaeological Institute in Egypt published the discovery of symbol writings more than 5,000 years old (dating between 3300 and 3200 B.C.), found in the tomb of the Pre-Dynastic King Scorpion at Abydos. The finding challenges the long-held consensus that writing was first invented in Mesopotamia, at about the same time. However, some of the hardest vases, made of diorite and basalt, date to the Neolithic Period of the Stone Age (at about 7000 B.C.). Thus, as startling as it may be, based on all available evidence, dwellers along the Nile produced hard-stone vessels that are unparalleled in modern times before they had a rudimentary written language (comprising simple line drawings of natural elements like animals, plants and mountains).

There is no mystery to making simple vessels of soft limestone, Egyptian alabaster or other relatively soft rock types. Alabaster can range from soft to hard and compact. An artisan can shape the soft variety called Egyptian alabaster with primitive tools and abrasives, and a mild acid like vinegar eases the task. But the several thousand hard-stone vessels found remain highly enigmatic. In his *Archaic Egypt* (1987 rev.), W.B. Emery admitted to being baffled:

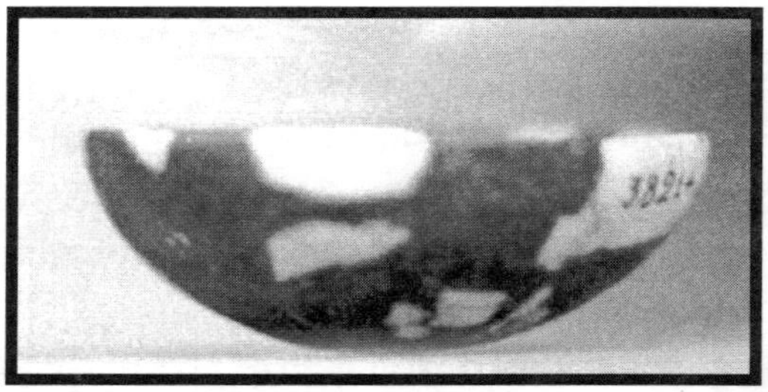

22. BOWL MADE WITH DIORITE IN THE CAIRO MUSEUM. PHOTOGRAPH BY JOHN REID

> Unfortunately, we have no really satisfactory evidence of the method of manufacture of these stone vessels, and, although certain processes of the work are known to us, others remain a complete mystery. How did they achieve such accuracy that when we 'swing' a shallow bowl or dish, no deviation from a perfect circle can be noted? How did they cut rock crystal tubular jars with walls not more than a millimetre [.04 inch] thick?[1]

Relying on Old Kingdom tomb depictions, Emery described methods suitable for drilling varieties of soft stone. For instance, a tomb scene shows boring with a drill weighted with rocks. Emery admitted that the known methods could not explain the difficult-to-achieve crafting of hard-stone vessels with complex features. The jars with narrow necks and wide shoulders greatly impressed him:

> How, for example, was the upward pressure obtained to cut away the interior side of the shoulders? All of these problems as yet remain unanswered and are likely to remain so until perhaps the discovery of a stone vase maker's workshop which will reveal some of his methods.[2]

No one has actually proven the proposed methods by reproducing the problematic features in hard, tough diorite. German scholar Kurt Lange was awestruck by hard-stone vases he examined at Saqqara, not far from Cairo.[3] Some vases have narrow, perfectly undercut flared openings. Like Emery, Lange was perplexed by fully and perfectly hollowed-out vases with long, narrow necks and wide rounded bellies. These vessels are even smooth on the insides, and their walls are of uniform thickness. Tool

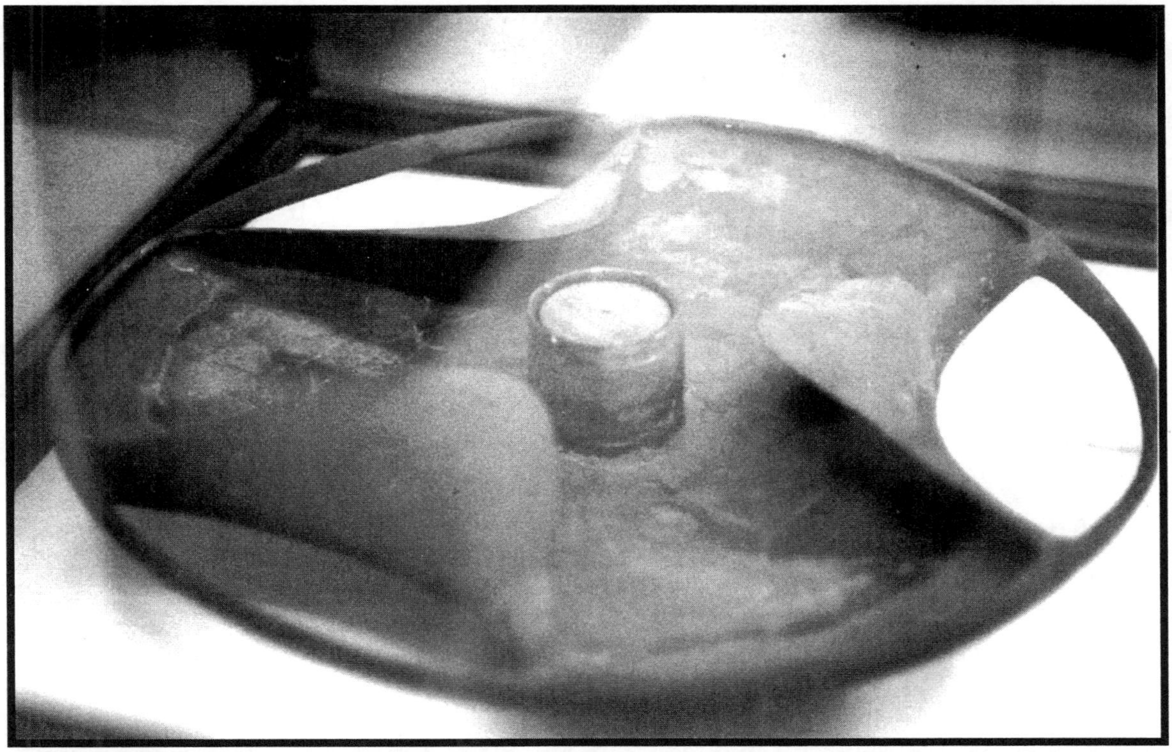

**23. PREVIOUS PAGE: THE UPPER PHOTOGRAPH SHOWS A REMARKABLE ARTIFACT, MADE FROM SCHIST, IN THE CAIRO MUSEUM. THE OBJECT, WHICH MEASURES AT LEAST 24 INCHES IN DIAMETER, EXHIBITS THREE SEGMENTS OR TABS THAT LOOK LIKE THEY WERE FOLDED OR PULLED IN. MACHINISTS ARE AT A LOSS TO ADEQUATELY EXPLAIN THE STUNNING MASONRY WORK.**

**24. THE LOWER PHOTOGRAPH SHOWS A VESSEL, MADE WITH DIORITE, IN THE NUBIAN MUSEUM. THE VESSEL HAS UNIFORM THIN WALLS.**

**PHOTOGRAPHS BY JOHN REID**

experts have not reproduced and demonstrated the tools that can cut these features in hard rock.

Many of the hard-rock vessels are delicately inscribed with the symbols of the Predynastic monarchs, who ruled before the unification of southern and northern Egypt into a nation with its first pharaoh. Some schist vases have flawless, paper-thin edges. Schist is a hard, crystalline rock that easily breaks along its closely set foliations into thin, flaky plates. Its crystalline structure makes this hard rock brittle and greatly compounds the problems of working it to this level of perfection. A vase in the Cairo Museum made of schist has extremely thin, uniform walls. It is difficult to imagine the ancient lathe that could create this vessel in hard schist.

Some vessels rest on small rounded bottom tips. For instance, a granite bowl, nine inches in diameter, balances perfectly on its small, rounded bottom tip. The tiny round base-tip measures less than .15 inch square. When the bowl rests on a level surface, like smooth glass, its top edge is horizontal. Thus, the bowl, in the Cairo Museum, balances perfectly on its round bottom, with its top edge aligned along the horizontal plane.[4]

W.M.F. Petrie pondered long and hard over fragments of hard-stone dishes he found at Giza.[5] He believed that the ancient Egyptians made some 4th Dynasty examples with lathes. Objects made with basalt, diorite and black granite are examples. Narrow, clean cutting lines, which are circular, are conspicuous on the interiors of hard-stone bowls. The primitive lathes known are only capable of shaping wooden objects. No one has explained how a Late Stone Age turning device could cut these unprecedented vessels out of hard stone.

Today's most advanced lathes would not produce such vessels in hard stone. Examples commonly have handles, which interfere with lathe turning, attached at both ends. Gaston Maspero mentioned the early date at which artisans made hard-stone vessels with handles:

> As early as the close of the Predynastic period stone vases were worked in the hardest materials, such as breccia, syenite, quartz, crystal, and diorite, and great alabaster bowls were so finely worked as to be transparent. Stone vases intended for suspension were provided with handles carved at the sides and pierced. Some of the finest of these stone vessels belong to the

> later prehistoric and early dynastic times; they are found also in porphyry, slate, alabaster, diorite, basalt, and other fine stones in the temples of the Fourth and Fifth Dynasties. . . .[6]

Long before the first pyramid was built, Egyptians produced many kinds of masterful works. Artist Nestor l'Hote (c. 1780–1842) worked with one of the great founders of Egyptology Jean Francois Champollion (1790–1832). L'Hote was ecstatic about artwork found in three Old Kingdom *mastabas* by the famous French archaeologist Auguste Mariette (1821–1881) and the distinguished German Egyptologist Karl Richard Lepsius (1810–1884). *Mastabas* are early-style oblong tombs, with sloping sides and flat roofs, that predate the pyramids. Describing the sculptured stones in one of the most ancient such tombs, that of the vizier Menefra of Memphis, l'Hote remarked:

> The sculptures in this tomb are remarkable for their elegance and finesse. The relief is so light that it can be compared with one of our five franc coins. Such perfection in something so ancient confirms the observation that the further one goes back in antiquity towards the origin of Egyptian art, the more perfect are the results of this art, as if the genius of these people, unlike others, was formed in one single stroke.[7]

Moving forward to the 1st Dynasty, we find that heavy stone slabs blocked the entrances of royal tombs at Saqqara. First Dynasty tombs at Helwan, in northern Egypt, are the earliest known burial chambers lined with large limestone slabs. The largest slabs measure more than seven x 13 feet, large enough to cover a whole wall.[8]

The burial chambers located about 90 feet below the later 3rd Dynasty Step Pyramid of Pharaoh Zoser, at Saqqara, are gigantic granite constructions, as are those of Zoser's successors in the Old Kingdom.[9] The ceilings of the crypts beneath Zoser's pyramid are made of huge granite beams with round holes in them. These holes are sealed with round granite plugs that weigh about three tons each. In 3rd Dynasty tombs of Beit Khallaf, in northern Upper Egypt, stone slabs weighing six to seven tons were installed in shafts about 82 feet deep.[10]

By the 4th Dynasty, builders were using blocks weighing more than 200 tons. Among the largest surviving units are limestone blocks incorporated into the Mortuary Temple of the Third Pyramid at Giza, built for Pharaoh Menkaura. These blocks weigh up to 220 tons. Outer limestone wall blocks of the Valley Temple of Giza's neighboring Second Great Pyramid, built for Pharaoh Khafra, are equally as heavy. They each measure about ten x 16 x 26 feet.[11] Some of these large blocks are located more than 40 feet above ground level.

If they had to be lifted with machinery today, then the world's largest crane

25. A SOCKET ABOVE THE DOORWAY OF KHAFRA'S VALLEY TEMPLE AT GIZA. PHOTOGRAPH BY JON BODSWORTH

26. CLOSE-UP OF THE SOCKET ABOVE THE DOORWAY OF KHAFRA'S VALLEY TEMPLE AT GIZA. PHOTOGRAPH BY JON BODSWORTH

would be required. Only two industrial cranes exist with the necessary capacity.[12] They are equipped with onboard counterweights (which prevent them from tipping) weighing more than 150 tons. The booms of the cranes reach to 220 feet.

The early archaeologists Georges Perrot and Charles Chipiez were awestruck by the accomplishments of Khafra's sculptors and others of the Old Kingdom:

> How did the sculptors manage to carve into these rocks which are so hard? . . . Even today it is very difficult when using the best tempered steel chisels. The work is very slow and difficult and one must stop frequently to sharpen the edge of the chisel, which becomes dull on the rock, and then re-temper

> the chisel. But the contemporaries of Khafra, and everyone agrees on this, had no steel chisels.[13]

These archaeologists were marveling at the somewhat larger than life-sized statue of the 4th Dynasty Pharaoh Khafra*, builder of the Second Great Pyramid at Giza, and other marvelous hard-stone statuary. Perrot and Chipiez recognized that tempered steel tools are inadequate for reproducing their crisp detail.

*THE KHAFRA STATUE ROCK TYPE HAS SEVERAL NAMES. IT IS TECHNICALLY CLASSIFIED BY GEOLOGISTS AS AN ANORTHOSITE (SODA-LIME FELDSPAR) GNEISS (MEANING IT HAS A BANDED OR LAMINATED STRUCTURE). THIS DARK GREEN ROCK IS COMMONLY CALLED DIORITE AND, MORE PROPERLY, DIORITE-GNEISS. IT IS ALSO OFTEN CALLED "CHEPHREN (KHAFRA) DIORITE" BY EGYPTOLOGISTS. IN ANCIENT EGYPT, THIS HIGHLY PRIZED ROCK WAS CALLED *MNTT*.

At Giza, archaeologists have excavated innumerable fragments of finely executed bowls made with various types of diorite. Hammering hard diorite with the best modern hardened steel hammer will ruin the striking surface of the tool.

Fully corbelled rooms appear in 4th Dynasty pyramids at Dashur, south of Saqqara. Magnificent examples appear in the Bent Pyramid and the Red Pyramid, both built for Pharaoh Snofru (c. 2575–2551 B.C.).[14] The Bent Pyramid was named for the dramatic inward slope of its upper tiers, and the Red Pyramid was named for the reddish tinge of iron oxide in its limestone. The magnificent three-room burial chamber in the Red Pyramid is considered one of the finest of the Old Kingdom. Built 14 to 16 corbels high and measuring about 14 x 27 feet in width and length and 48 feet high, the chambers are beautifully corbelled on all four sides. Only the corbelled ceiling of the Grand Gallery of the Great Pyramid surpassed the length of these remarkable ceilings.

Egyptologists think that a pivoting stone door opened and closed both the Bent Pyramid and the Pyramid of Meidum. Egyptologists found sockets in sidewalls near entrances that can accommodate door pivots. W.M.F. Petrie believed that the Great Pyramid was similarly equipped with a huge pivoting stone door. He drew evidence from Strabo's *Geographica,* written at about 64 B.C.:

> [The Great Pyramid] a little way up one side, has a stone that may be taken out, which being raised up, there is a sloping passage to the foundations.[15]

Petrie asserted:

> A self-replacing door, which left no external mark, is absolutely required by the fact of the Arabs having forced a passage. Only a flap door, or a

27. The Colossi of Memnon stand about 60 feet high and are made with quartzite, the hardest stone used in Egyptian colossi. The figures were originally monoliths, until Roman restorations under the rule of Septimius Severus. Photograph by Jon Bodsworth

> diagonal-sliding portcullis slab, can satisfy this requirement. A flap door is unequivocally shown to have been used at Dahshur. And Strabo's description of the entrance agrees with such a door, and with no other. Such is the evidence for the closing of the Pyramids by doors; equally proving also the absence of any plugging up of the entrance passages.[16]

Lesser pyramids of the 5th and 6th Dynasties incorporate stunning features, too. A limestone casing block incorporated into the masonry near the entrance of the 5th Dynasty Pyramid of Unas measures about six feet high. Its length is 29½ feet. As mentioned, both Abd el-Latif (A.D. 1162–1231) and Herodotus (5th century B.C.) reported seeing a myriad of similar 30-foot-long blocks incorporated into the outer masonry of the Great Pyramid.

The ceilings of burial chambers in the lesser pyramids are made of giant beams leaning against one another at the top, forming constructions called pointed saddle roofs. An example is the roof over the underground burial crypt of the 5th Dynasty pyramid of Pharaoh Djedkara Isesi at Saqqara.[17] Another is the roof over the crypt of Pharaoh Niuserra's 5th Dynasty pyramid, at Abusir, north of Saqqara. These pointed saddle roofs are exceptional because of the size and number of their beams. The 60 blocks roofing Niuserra's crypt each weigh about 90 tons.[18] A roofing block in Djedkara Isesi's pyramid weighs 24 tons.

As mentioned, there are several examples of heavy blocks underground in narrow caves and shafts, where numerous workers, ramps and long levers will not fit. Burial chambers were constructed in deep underground shafts for several 5th and 6th Dynasty pyramids, including those of Userkaf, Niuserra, Djedkara Isesi, Unas, Teti, and Pepi II.

At Saqqara, 18 quartzite columns appear in a temple court of the 6th Dynasty pyramid complex built for Pharaoh Pepi II (c. 2246–2152 B.C.).[19] Among the hardest types of rock, quartzite is entirely too dense to cut with copper, bronze, iron, or flint tools. In quartzite, quartz grains are bound together with natural cement that makes the rock incredibly dense. Quartzite is composed almost entirely of quartz, which can be shaped with topaz, corundum, or diamond. Egyptologists do not believe that the 6th Dynasty Egyptians had any of these three materials.[20] The first undoubted reference to diamond during antiquity appears in Roman literature of the 1st century A.D.[21]

Quartzite is also extremely tough. Using today's technology, it is a very slow and difficult process to drill through a bed of quartzite with a modern tungsten carbide bit, with 950 pounds of pressure on the drill bit's shaft and a drill strength of 5,000 to 10,000 pounds per square inch. The tungsten carbide bit is next in hardness to diamond.

While impressive quartzite items date from the earliest times in Egypt, experts have no viable suggestions as to how the Egyptians quarried quartzite, and shaping

28. THE IMAGE ABOVE IS FROM *ANCIENT EGYPTIAN CONSTRUCTION AND ARCHITECTURE*, BY SOMERS CLARKE AND REGINALD ENGELBACH. THEY INFORM US: "REMAINS OF THE CASING AT THE ENTRANCE TO THE PYRAMID OF UNAS AT SAQQARA. THE PART A-B, THOUGH NOW BROKEN, CONSISTED OF ONE BLOCK. (PHOTOGRAPH BY CECIL FIRTH, ESQ.)" BEFORE IT BROKE THE BLOCK WAS 29½ FEET LONG.

29. SECTION FROM A BLOCK MADE OF RED QUARTZITE. THE CUT SURFACE IS CURVED, SHOWING THAT THE REGULAR CUTTING LINES WERE MADE WITH A TUBE DRILL, THE DIAMETER OF WHICH WAS ABOUT 20 INCHES. IT IS IN LONDON'S PETRIE MUSEUM.

PHOTO PROVIDED BY JOHN REID

huge objects with this material raises unresolved problems. Some have suggested that quartz sand must have been the cutting medium, because it was plentiful. A piece of quartz will indeed scratch another piece of quartz with considerable difficulty, because they are of the same hardness. But imagine scratching quartz against quartz to create finely sculpted, inscribed statuary over 60 feet high! Indeed, explaining the creation of Egypt's inscribed, finely sculpted 60-foot-high quartzite statuary without the unfathomable task of scratching quartz sand against quartzite is the one of the objectives of the volumes of this book.

The mundane task of scratching quartz against quartz certainly fits within the technological abilities of ancient people. We can imagine a sculptor spending his years creating a single vase or statuette with this method. But it is logical to suggest that quartzite colossi over 60 foot high alert us to the existence of a more sophisticated technology. Extraordinary claims demand extraordinary proof, as Carl Sagan used to like to say. In this case, asserting that quartz sand was used to sculpt 60-foot-high quartzite colossi is an extraordinary claim, and it is not backed by any proof—just assumption.

W.M.F. Petrie was astounded when he discovered the exquisitely made 80-ton monolithic quartzite sepulcher in the 12th Dynasty pyramid of Pharaoh Amenemhet III, at Hawara. To find the sepulcher, Petrie had to squeeze through a dark, water- and mud-filled maze of blind alleys, designed to confound anyone who might enter the substructure of the pyramid. The passageway was so narrow that he had to remove his clothes to squeeze through it. Petrie reported:

> The workmanship is excellent; the sides are flat and regular, and the inner corners so sharply wrought that—though I looked at them—I never suspected that there was not a joint there until I failed to find any joints in the sides.[22]

He simply could not fathom how such an item could be made in one piece. This monolithic quartzite sepulcher is box-shaped, with no lid. It measures about 22 x eight x six feet. If we were to assume the construction means proposed by Egyptology to be correct, its flat, regular surfaces would vastly compound the enigma of its production.

A large sarcophagus and a second smaller one, each made of quartzite, were found inside of the sepulcher itself. Three four-foot-thick quartzite slabs, placed side by side, sealed the sepulcher. Protecting the sepulcher from above are two stress-relieving chambers covered by two sloping limestone beams. These beams form a pointed saddle roof and weigh almost 50 tons each.

Among the other sarcophagi made with quartzite are those found in the Valley of the Kings, in southern Egypt, in the tombs constructed for the later 18th

**30-31.** THE PREVIOUS TWO PAGES SHOW THE GREAT COLOSSUS OF RAMSES II AT MEMPHIS: AFTER MOHAMMAD ALI MADE A GIFT OF THE COLOSSUS TO THE BRITISH MUSEUM, THE DIFFICULTY OF MOVING IT PREVENTED ITS EXPORTATION. INSTEAD, A MUSEUM WAS BUILT AROUND THE FALLEN COLOSSI TO PROTECT IT. PHOTOGRAPHS BY JON BODSWORTH

Dynasty Queen-Pharaoh Hatshepsut, Pharaoh Tutankhamun, and Pharaoh Amenhotep II. In 1817 the Italian archaeologist Giovanni Belzoni found the tomb of the 19th Dynasty Pharaoh Ramses I in the Valley of the Kings. The tomb included a huge sarcophagus made with red quartzite.

The long-destroyed 12th Dynasty Labyrinth, one of Egypt's most remarkable structures, was associated with the pyramid of Pharaoh Amenemhet III. In 1843 German Egyptologist Richard Lepsius, one of the most eminent 19th century Egyptologists, identified and explored the Labyrinth site.[23] Although the Labyrinth no longer exists, Lepsius was able to determine that the structure was about 585 feet long and 520 feet wide.

The Labyrinth amazed both the ancient historian Herodotus and Strabo the geographer. Herodotus acclaimed the Labyrinth as beyond description. He reported that it had 12 roofed courts and 3,000 galleries, half of which were subterranean and not accessible to visitors:

> The Labyrinth has 12 covered courts - six in a row facing north, six south. Inside, the building is of two storeys and contains 3,000 rooms, of which half are underground, and the other half directly above them. I was taken through the rooms in the upper storey, so what I shall say of them is from my own observation, but the underground ones I can speak of only from report, because the Egyptians in charge refused to let me see them, as they contain the tombs of the kings who built the Labyrinth and also the tombs of the sacred crocodiles. The upper rooms, on the contrary I did actually see, and it is hard to believe that they are the work of men; the baffling and intricate passages from room to room and from court to court were an endless wonder to me, as we passed from a courtyard into rooms, from rooms into galleries, from galleries into more rooms, and thence into yet more courtyards. The roof of every chamber, courtyard and gallery is, like the walls, of stone. The walls are covered with carved figures, and each court is exquisitely built of white marble and surrounded by a colonnade. . . . It is beyond my power to describe. It must have cost more in labour and money than all the wall and public works of the Greeks put together - though no one would deny that the temples of Ephesus and Samos are remarkable buildings. The Pyramids too are astonishing structures, each one of them equal to many of the most ambitious works of Greece; but the Labyrinth surpasses them.[24]

Strabo described it as equally as marvelous as the pyramids although only a one-story building. The interior of the Labyrinth was a maze of confounding, winding passageways. Once inside, anyone unable to comprehend its structure could not find his or her way out without a guide. The architectural design itself incorporated deep religious significance, perhaps akin to the mazelike patterns depicted on the floors of some medieval churches.[25]

Strabo described the Labyrinth's giant wall blocks and great monolithic pillars. He was astounded when he witnessed the ceilings of the rooms, which were monolithic slabs of extraordinary size.

One of Egypt's most praised construction works, built in the 18th Dynasty, is the twin Colossi of Memnon. These statues, made with quartzite, are over 60 feet high. Despite their name, given to them by the Greeks, they were statues of Pharaoh Amenhotep III (c. 1391–1353 B.C.) constructed under the supervision of his architect Amenhotep-son-of-Hapu of Athribis. They stand at the approach to the now-vanished Mortuary Temple of this pharaoh. Made with quartzite, the weathered colossi have endured deliberate damage and natural disasters. Quartzite is the hardest and toughest type of stone used in making Egyptian colossi. During this historical period, iron was rare and very precious because of its hardness. Nevertheless, iron tools are not capable of sculpting quartzite. As mentioned, modern drill bits almost as hard as diamond can penetrate a bed of quartzite only with a great amount of pressure, and the task is considerably difficult.

Aside from the problem of transporting and raising 60-foot-high colossi, anyone who has ever tried creating a work of art out of quartzite using any means appreciates the severe problem posed by carving quartzite objects this massive. Keep in mind that experts who try to explain away such objects have not actually created anything comparable and can point out no modern team or company that has.

These remarkable colossal statues were originally monoliths, until the Roman Emperor Septimus Severus (A.D. 193–211) restored the earthquake-damaged southern statue with large blocks.

Including their pedestals and crowns, the colossi each measure about 63 feet high. The third fingers of the hands each measure 4½ feet. The widths at their shoulders measure 20 feet. Each statue weighs some 750 tons and rests on a 556-ton quartzite pedestal.[26]

In the 19th Dynasty, the gold-gilded Mortuary Temple that the Colossi of Memnon once guarded was exploited for building material by Pharaoh Menerptah (c. 1224–1214 B.C.), a son of Ramses II. A stele that Menerptah expropriated bears a description of the temple:

> . . . an everlasting fortress of sandstone, embellished with gold throughout, its floor shining with silver and all its doorways with electrum [an alloy of

> silver and gold]. It is wide and very long, adorned for eternity, and made festive with this exceptionally large stele. It is extended with royal statues of granite, of quartzite and of precious stones, fashioned to last forever. They are higher than the rising of the heavens, their rays are in men's faces like the rising Sun. . . . Its magazines have stored uncountable riches.[27]

We can only imagine the splendor of the interior of this Mortuary Temple.

During the 19th Dynasty the administration of Ramses II (c. 1290–1224 B.C.) erected an enormous limestone colossus of this pharaoh to adorn a great temple of the god Ptah in Memphis.[28] The Ptah Temple complex, one of the largest in Egypt, extended a third of a mile in length and a quarter of a mile in breadth. It was located near the central quarter of old Memphis, Egypt's first capital. The Temple was founded within the so-called "White Walls" associated with the founding of Memphis in the 1st Dynasty (c. 2920 B.C.). The splendor of Memphis is said to have been beyond belief. Even in the 12th century A.D., the ruins of Memphis were reported to be a collection of such marvelous beauty that the intelligence is confounded, and the most eloquent man would be unable to adequately describe them.

For the Greeks, the now-vanished Ptah Temple of Memphis epitomized Egyptian architectural genius. Some modern linguists believe that the Greeks named the land of Egypt after it.[29] The Greek word for the Ptah Temple is transliterated as *Aegyptos*, which in English is Egypt.

Today only the Temple's enormous colossus of Pharaoh Ramses II remains. Although it has fallen, the colossus, originally about 40 feet high, is so extraordinary that it remains one of the most famous features of Egypt. It is one of the most outstanding of Ramses II's statues. Stuart M. Edelson is a sculptor who worked in the Conservation Department of the Metropolitan Museum of Art, in New York. His deep appreciation for this statue arises from his own work with similar limestone for more than 20 years:

> Anyone who has never carved stone might marvel most at the quarrying of the many-ton block, and then at the task of roughly hewing it into shape, tasks which must have been gargantuan. Of course, this impressed me, but the drudgery of rough carving spoke to me of an effort that could have been achieved by any gang of workers sufficiently numerous, supervised, and driven. Persistence on this grand scale is not uncommon. The distinction of the Ramesses colossus lay elsewhere.
>
> The essence of this great statue lies in the many square yards of carved surface. Faced with a task of such magnitude, a cold sweat would form on the brow of any modern worker in stone. I scrutinized a ten-foot-long portion

of the royal leg. Along its entire length no flaw distracted from the grace and power of the sinewy, kingly stride, and I knew something of the difficulty with which such perfect surfaces could only be achieved.

Among the many problems presented by this stone, it likes to chip unpredictably to the terror of the sculptor who would shape it. The stone was familiar to me. I had worked on a small piece of similar but softer material the year before, and the twenty years' experience that went into my small sculpture provided an insight into the true greatness of the colossus before me.

I had spent countless hours vainly trying to grind out by machine the countless ripples that had formed in the carving process—on a much smaller expanse of softer stone. Only after much experimentation with various abrasives and finally with different rhythms of sanding was I able to produce the smooth surfaces essential to the overall impact of the work. Even on the small scale the effort involved was enormous.

When modern, mechanized marble yards cut smooth and polish stone the size of Ramesses, the shapes are either flat or they are featureless columns. It is done with power tools the size of houses and even then the work is painstaking, time-consuming and risky. Here, the ancients achieved perfection with hand-held stones and crushed abrasives applied to sticks. And the shapes wrought were the complex, subtle forms of the human anatomy.

How these master carvers achieved perfect surfaces on this scale with simple tools was beyond my comprehension. My own twenty years' experience provided no clue. But clearly this was not the work of slaves. This forty-foot length of stone could only have been brought to life through the sensitive hand and watchful eye of a master sculptor, and with a great deal of loving care.

Unlike so many works on a Herculean scale, this Ramesses allowed for no imprecision in areas the sculptors knew could not be seen. The hidden places were equally finely finished. There were no technical concessions to the many near-insuperable problems that had to be faced. Looking at the supreme craftsmanship that went into the body's hidden recesses as well as its conspicuous visible areas, it was clear to me that all involved in making this image had the integrity and wisdom worthy of the god and the great king it was meant to represent.[30]

32. THE ENORMOUS STATUE OF RAMSES II BUILT IN FRONT OF THE GREAT PTAH TEMPLE IN MEMPHIS: THE ABOVE SHOWS DETAILS OF THE KILT AND WAIST. THE FALLEN STATUE LIES FLAT; THE IMAGE HAS BEEN ROTATED FOR VIEWING HERE. PHOTOGRAPH BY JON BODSWORTH

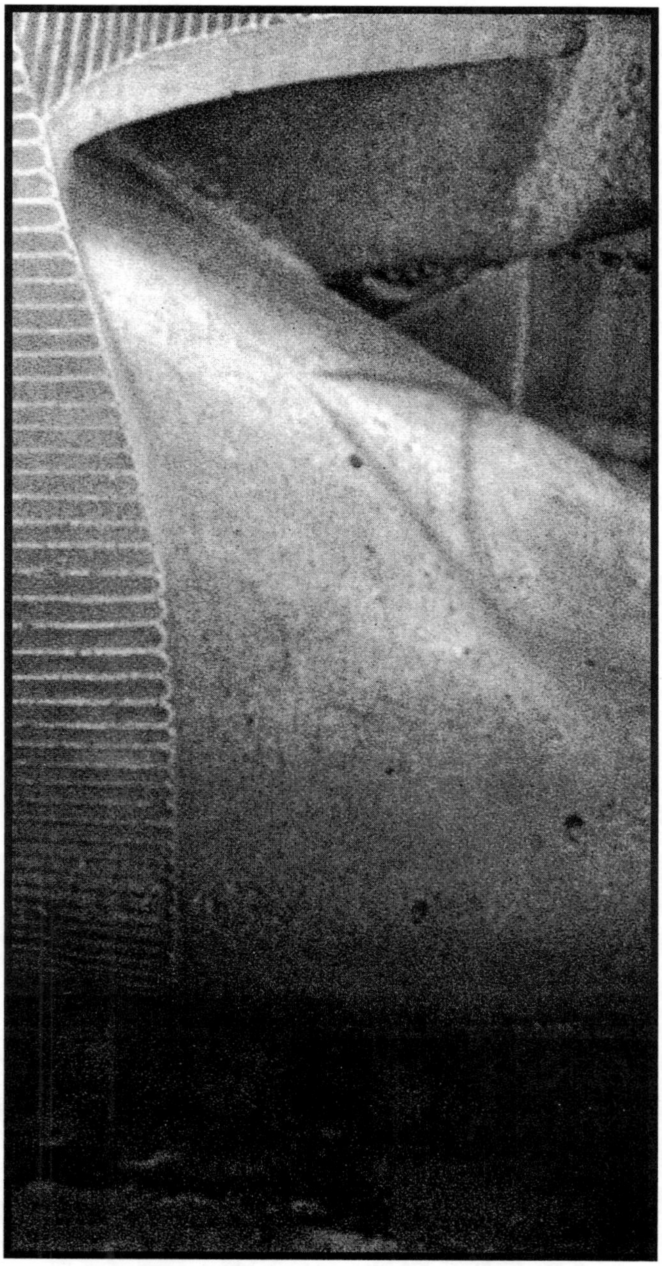

33. The image on this page is an extension of the one on the opposite page. They show details of a royal arm and hand of Ramses II, along with his kilt and a Lower thigh.

Enormous monoliths of Ramses II stood until the early Christian era in northern Egypt. In the 4th century AD, the Abbess Aetheria passed through a ruined city called "Ramses" and witnessed two colossi.

Photograph provided by Jon Bodsworth

Today a museum surrounds the statue, because it proved to be too large to move from Memphis to London after being donated to the British Museum.

The Greeks called a remarkable underground tomb in the necropolis of Memphis the Serapeum. Built upon an older site, the Serapeum was greatly expanded during Pharaoh Ramses II's reign. Several heavy sarcophagi are situated within the niches that form rows against the walls. The sarcophagi weigh about 65 tons each.

The problem of moving a 65-ton monolith can be better realized with the help of a famous ancient Egyptian tomb scene dating from about 1850 B.C.[31] It shows 172 men pulling a 60-ton colossus of the nobleman Djehutihotep along lubricated, flat ground. The tomb scene may be impressionistic, given that Egyptologist Henri Chevrier performed an experiment showing that 400 men are required to pull 60 tons on a flat surface. In any case, the hallway leading to the niche in the Serapeum is long and wide. It can accommodate a long train of men. Egyptologists believe that long rows of men slowly maneuvered the heavy, exquisite sarcophagi down into the niches in the Serapeum. However, in certain other tombs, heavy sarcophagi rest at the bottom of narrow sloping tunnels where there is not room for numerous laborers.[32]

Moving forward to the 20th Dynasty, the New Kingdom Pharaoh Ramses III (c. 1194–1163 B.C.) died and was buried in the Valley of the Kings, in the Theban necropolis. M. Costaz, a scholar of the Napoleonic Egyptian Expedition, found Ramses' sarcophagus after entering the Valley of the Kings through its only road. Costaz wrote:

> The gate through which one enters the valley is the only opening in its entire contour. As this opening is man-made, the valley must previously have been shaped in the form of an isolated basin which could only be reached by climbing the steep mountains. It was perhaps this remoteness which gave them the idea of placing the royal sepulchers there to make them safe from robbery, which the ancient Egyptians so much feared. . . . High mountains crowned with rock are hemmed in on all sides from the horizon, allowing only part of the sky to be seen. Towards midday, when the bottom of the valley has been in the sun for a few hours, the heat becomes concentrated and excessive. Any tempering wind can find absolutely no way into this enclosure. It is like an oven. Two men from the escort of General Desaix died from suffocation. I do not think that it would be possible to remain there for 24 hours without the shade provided by the catacombs which offer protection from the overwhelming heat.[33]

In the numerous tombs, Costaz encountered plundered and destroyed sarcophagi. Only the one belonging to Pharaoh Ramses III was still intact. Costaz made a compelling observation:

> Imagine a long oblong chamber made of pink syenite granite, ornamented inside and out with hieroglyphics and paintings. Its dimensions are such that a man standing inside can hardly be seen by everyone outside. A blow with a hammer makes it ring like a bell . . . The sarcophagus must previously have been closed by a cover that has since disappeared. . . . The cover would have formed a considerable mass that was very difficult to move. . . . A comparison between the dimensions of the sarcophagus to those of the entrance of the valley yields a big surprise and a new example of the Egyptians' taste for difficult tasks. The entrance of the Valley of the Kings is not wide enough to allow the sarcophagus through, so that the huge mass must have been hoisted with a crane or pulley up the hills that surround the valley and then brought down along their sides.[34]

Costaz's account becomes all the more compelling given the placement of Khufu's sarcophagus in the Great Pyramid 13 centuries before. No matter how Khufu's sarcophagus is oriented, it is too wide to fit through the doorway of the King's Chamber and its adjoining hall. Egyptologists believe that placing it involved the risky and frightening task of hoisting the sacred object halfway up the pyramid for installation, before the ceiling of the King's Chamber was built. Removing this and other sarcophagi intact requires dismantling tremendous amounts of stone structure in order to enlarge associated exit routes. We next consider why Egyptology is beginning to abandon its most fundamental ideas about how the Great Pyramid was built

# Chapter 7

# It Staggers The Imagination

Egyptology is abandoning a long-held, central tenet of pyramid construction. Since the inception of Egyptology, Egyptologists have asserted that copper chisels and saws were used to prepare several million pyramid blocks. Findings over the past few years are prompting Egyptologists to propose that primitive stone tools were used instead for almost every masonry task—without any explanation of how the extraordinary masonry feats might actually be achieved with these tools. Dieter Arnold, in his *Building in Egypt,* acknowledged trials in the 1980s that established a new dividing line between the types of rock that can and cannot be cut with copper chisels:

> For some time, the observation of ancient tools, their traces on the stone surface of unfinished monuments, and occasional tests of the hardness of Egyptian copper or bronze tools made it clear that Egyptian masons and sculptors were able to cut softer stones with copper tools but had to use stone tools for dressing hard stones. The line distinguishing the two was between limestone, sandstone, and alabaster on one side and granite, quartzite, and basalt on the other.
>
> A series of tests carried out recently by Denys Stocks seems to lower this border line drastically.[1]

The finding drastically affects the viability of the accepted theory of pyramid construction. Arnold continued:

> We know that hard stones such as granite, granodiorite, syenite, and basalt could not have been cut with metal tools. The tests conducted by Stocks seem to indicate that even hard limestone, sandstone, and alabaster would fall into this category.[2]

Most of the limestone blocks in the Giza pyramids and temples are medium hard to hard. In the 1980s geologists from Waseda University conducted a geological survey of the Great Pyramid. They provided this brief, general description of the limestone blocks:

> . . . hard and highly viscous.[3]

Their finding is logical, because the monument would have collapsed from its own weight long ago if its blocks were not sufficiently hard. The level foundation on which the Great Pyramid stands is hard enough to support the superstructure. A large percent of the blocks of the Great Pyramid, its main building blocks, are made up of fossil shells. Experimenters have only cut limestone of comparable hardness with hard bronze chisels, tools not available when the Great Pyramid was built. These fossil shells make those pyramid blocks that are fossiliferous limestone difficult to carve. As mentioned, when Egyptologist G. Goyon climbed the Great Pyramid with a precision instrument, he recorded the pyramid tier height measurements for all 73 different heights making up the 200 tiers to be exact within less than a half centimeter! Blocks had to be prepared so that they fit into tiers of the desired height and shape, and a myriad of the blocks are shaped so that they actually correspond to the shape of blocks they touch on all sides. Some blocks had or still have mortar between them (mortar helps cushion masonry against earthquake stress), so that they may only correspond to surfaces of blocks above and below them.

A copper arsenate alloy, considered bronze, was known in Egypt during early times. But this is not a hard metal. It is unsuitable for making stonecutting chisels, and so it was used to make statues instead. The type of bronze capable of cutting the medium-hard to hard limestone pyramid blocks is an alloy of copper and tin, the material tested by Antoine Zuber many years before the experiments of Denys Stocks.[4]

Using a cold hammering process, Zuber made chisels of bronze alloyed with eight to 12 percent tin. Using these chisels, Zuber successfully cut limestone closely comparable in hardness to pyramid blocks. But bronze hard enough to cut this limestone became available in ancient Egypt at about the end of the Middle Kingdom, about 800 years after the Great Pyramid was built.

To solve the problem of how stones harder than copper were cut, Egyptologists long theorized that a lost art of tempering copper made it hard. Hammering will harden a copper tool to a certain extent, but not enough to allow it to render hard limestone, granite, schist, diorite, basalt, quartzite, or other varieties of hard rock into the objects perfected in ancient Egypt. Too much hammering makes copper more brittle. While examples of harder (hammered) copper are mentioned in Egyptological literature, the vast majority of copper tools found in Egyptian tombs are nothing more than typical soft copper.

Given that bronze was unavailable, and that copper chisels are too soft to shape hard fossil-shell limestone blocks, and tools found are mostly soft copper, Egyptology is starting to advocate that stone tools were used to perform most of the masonry tasks of pyramid construction. But how could stone tools achieve the intricate perfection found in so many monuments and artifacts made of hard rock?

There is another reason that copper chisels, or copper saws combined with abrasive sand, could not have been used to cut the millions of limestone blocks. Shaping the 2.3 million blocks of the Great Pyramid would consume a staggering amount of copper. The Second Pyramid at Giza, built for Pharaoh Khafra, is almost as large as the Great Pyramid. The two large pyramids of Pharaoh Snofru, who preceded Khufu, collectively contain more limestone than the Great Pyramid. Dieter Arnold calculated that the major pyramid complexes of the 80-year Pyramid Age, the golden age of pyramid construction, contain 12 million blocks. Known copper mining and/or importation does not account for this phenomenal demand. Besides, sawing with copper and sand would produce regular surfaces, whereas form-fitted pyramid blocks

34. THIS UNFINISHED GRANITE BOWL IN THE CAIRO MUSEUM WAS STARTED WITH THE USE OF A TUBE DRILL. ALL OF THE HOLES MADE WITH THE TUBE DRILL SHOW PARALLEL GROOVES THAT ARE OF REGULAR DEPTH AND SPACING. THE HOLES OVERLAP AND THEIR GROOVES REMAIN REGULAR, AND THIS IS NOT WHAT WE WOULD EXPECT FROM SLOW GRINDING WITH A COPPER TUBE DRILL USED IN CONJUNCTION WITH ABRASIVES. THE FEATURES SUGGEST RAPID CUTS. PHOTOGRAPH BY JOHN REID

exhibit wavy joints.

In his *Atlas of Ancient Egypt* (1985), Egyptologist John Baines provides a brief overview concerning the copper supply:

> Sinai is also a source of copper, and copper mines contemporary with the Egyptian 18th–20th Dynasties have been excavated at Timna near Eilat. These were probably worked by the local population under Egyptian control; there is no evidence that the Egyptians themselves mined copper anywhere in Sinai.[5]

Mining native copper reached its peak in the New Kingdom, about a thousand years after the Great Pyramid was built. In the New Kingdom, the amount of copper produced annually was about four tons. Copper can also be obtained from the more labor- and energy-intensive process of reducing copper ores like azurite and chrysocolla, but it seems unlikely that the Pyramid Age Egyptians went through this process, because native veins of copper ore remain available in the Sinai.

An amount smaller than four tons annually is insufficient for cutting eight or nine million cubic meters of limestone for the Fourth Dynasty pyramids. Cutting granite consumes much more copper than does cutting limestone, and Joseph Roder estimated that about one million cubic feet of granite was incorporated into the monuments of the Old Kingdom.

In short, Dieter Arnold recognized that copper consumption would have been too great. The Great Pyramid is estimated to have been made with 93.5 million cubic feet of limestone, and other pyramids collectively consumed more than triple this amount. Dieter Arnold concluded, therefore, that the Egyptians used stone tools for most masonry tasks:

> These observations would again be in accord with the assumption that even "soft" stones were not only dressed but also quarried mainly with stone tools, an assumption that would not deny, of course, that metal chisels existed and were occasionally used for special purposes.[6]

Egyptology has determined a far greater reliance on stone tools for all types of masonry work than previously recognized. Arnold deduced that stone tools were more abundant than metal ones from the earliest times to the days of the New Kingdom and perhaps later. Arnold added:

> First, no marks of metal tools have been observed on these stones [hard limestone, hard sandstone, alabaster and other harder rocks]. Second, all known types of copper chisels do not—even after cold hammering—have any effect on these stones; in fact, the tools suffer so much damage that

they could not have been used for that work. In addition, near the pyramid of Senwosret I, layers of stonecutters' debris could be studied, and the presence of granite dust indicated that the material was worked there. In these layers, no traces of greenish discoloration from copper could be detected.[7]

Thus, the question is clear: How did the ancient Egyptians produce the

35.

A VIEW OF THE TIERS OF THE GREAT PYRAMID: ALTHOUGH MUCH OF THE MASONRY HAS BEEN REMOVED OR REPOSITIONED, PETRIE'S SURVEY SHOWED THE ORIGINAL ACCURACY OF THE ROUGH FACES OF THE GREAT PYRAMID. THE MEAN OPTICAL PLANE THAT TOUCHES THE MOST PROMINENT POINTS OF THE BLOCKS SHOWS AN AVERAGE VARIATION OF ONLY 1.0 INCH.

PHOTO COURTESY OF JON BODSWORTH

unparalleled features of the Great Pyramid, and the remarkable features of other objects described in these pages, mostly with stone tools? Egyptology has not answered this question in a manner that will withstand even the most rudimentary scrutiny.

The 1992 Nova film *This Old Pyramid* tested a copper chisel on a block of very soft Tura limestone that had been preshaped with a steel tool. Just as the copper tools Dieter Arnold mentioned were immediately ruined during testing, a few strokes badly

35.1.
THIS IMAGE IS AN EXTENSION OF THE PREVIOUS PHOTOGRAPH. THE GREAT PYRAMID WAS MADE OF OVER 200 TIERS ALL CONFORMING TO ABOUT 73 TIER HEIGHTS, WITH A MARGIN OF ERROR OF LESS THAN ½ CENTIMETER. TIER 201 IS NOW MISSING, BUT IT WAS INTACT DURING NAPOLEON'S TIME, WHEN IT WAS CAREFULLY MEASURED. TIER 201 WAS TALLER THAN TIER FOUR NEAR THE BOTTOM.

blunted Nova's copper tool. The Nova crew did not attempt to produce a level miniature pyramid tier or even one level block with copper tools. The Nova presentation used modern steel tools to quarry and shape all blocks when building its miniature pyramid.

Nova's pyramid blocks were covered with crude tool marks made by modern steel tools. The film shows a quarryman working and standing so that one of his legs is in a deep trench he made, with a heavy modern steel tool, in the soft limestone bedrock. Although the film's opening narration states that the Nova crew would use only ancient means, the ring of steel resounds in the film. Nova's quarrymen used steel adzes and steel pry bars. They used heavy steel pickaxes to cut trenches. They would not have made their rate of progress with copper chisels, stone pounding balls (because of the tendency of limestone to crack), stone pickaxes, or by cutting blocks from the quarry by trying to use copper saws combined with abrasive sand, the only tools Egyptologists have determined to have been available to the Egyptians of the Pyramid Age.

To separate blocks from the quarry floor, Nova's stonemasons drove steel wedges beneath the blocks and hit these wedges with heavy steel sledgehammers. Comparably, in 1965 Joseph Roder showed that wedges (which fit into rectangular slots made in the stone) were not used in Egyptian quarrying before the Saite Period (c. 500 B.C., when Greek stone working methods had been introduced).[8] The wedge holes were made to accept iron wedges; therefore, the technique dates to the Iron Age.

Despite this use of modern means, the film concluded by saying that the experiments of the Nova crew had solved the problems of pyramid construction. Likewise, the fairly large blocks used for Waseda University's 34-foot-high experimental pyramid were cut with modern steel tools.

Mark Lehner simply ignores the new Egyptological standard on stone masonry, Arnold's *Building in Egypt* (1991), and other presentations showing that copper tools are not useful for cutting blocks for huge medium hard to hard limestone structures. In *The Complete Pyramids* (1997), Lehner wrote:

> The many acres of fine Turah limestone which cover the pyramids were dressed using chisels only c. 8 mm (1/3 inch) wide.[9]

This kind of incorrect information otherwise appears in the older, out-of-date Egyptological sources.

When limestone is freshly quarried, it is softer than after being exposed to air. But this does not mean that ancient pyramid builders were able to take advantage of its initial softness. Dieter Arnold recognized that quarried blocks would have dried out and hardened by the time workers could have hauled them to construction sites for custom shaping:

> Blocks intended to be built into foundations and core masonry, which did not need further dressing, could be left waiting, sometimes up to three years, until they were used. The other blocks that needed dressing could not be left too long, for the stone would dry fast and its hardness would increase considerably. . . . Because some time might have elapsed between extracting the stone from the quarry and the final dressing of the surface, the stone would probably have dried out and become more difficult to work.[10]

Arnold's statement implies that the majority of quarried blocks would not need shaping. But fossil shell limestone blocks cannot be quarried so that they are automatically suitable for forming a level foundation or corresponding, well fitted tiers that form an enormous pyramid shape. Accuracy is critically important for building the perfect pyramid shape. The Great Pyramid has great stability, because its 13-acre foundation is almost perfectly level, off only 7/8 inch from corner to corner. Top surfaces of each pyramid course had to correlate with the next tier to be built. Here we can review the important point Systems Engineer Mike Carrell contemplated, because it bears repeating:

> Among the remarkable features of the great pyramids are their great weight and the levelness of the tiers. At Giza, the pyramids rest on a hard limestone bedrock, which must have been chosen because it is reasonably level. The first tier of blocks must transmit their weight and the weight of all above them to the bedrock. To do this there must be exact conformity of the lower surfaces of the blocks with the actual surface of the bedrock. Any misfits will concentrate the burden on a smaller area, increasing the stress, and possibly resulting in a fracture.
>
> The same considerations apply to the horizontal interfaces between each successive layer. They must mutually conform to transmit stress, and they must be level, lest errors accumulating from one tier to the next cause distortions in the shape of the pyramid. Producing these necessary features in hard limestone with the tools available, within the recorded time, presents a seemingly insurmountable task.

Clearly, blocks required some sort of shaping so that they would fit with the scheme of surrounding masonry. It is not realistic to think that blocks for producing 73 tier heights, exact in height to within a half centimeter, will come neatly out of a craggy fossil shell limestone quarry to form a pyramid of over 200 tiers without shaping being a requirement; this is a critical consideration that Arnold does not address. Indeed, a great deal of accuracy appears in the foundation and the corresponding tiers, rough as the latter may look today.

Observations by Petrie show more accuracy in the building blocks, and this also shows that all blocks required some kind of shaping. He partially surveyed the Great Pyramid, using reference points at both corners of each face:

> The form of the present rough core masonry of the Pyramid is capable of being very closely estimated. By looking across a face of the Pyramid, either up an edge, across the middle of the face, or even along near the base, the mean optical plane which would touch the most prominent points of all the stones, may be found with an average variation at different times of only 1.0 inch.[11]

In short, we have seen that the idea that pyramid builders took advantage of the initial softness of moist, freshly quarried limestone does not hold. Dieter Arnold acknowledged that by the time blocks could be moved from the quarry to the construction site, they would have dried and hardened. The glaring problem cannot be minimized by stating that most blocks did not require shaping. All blocks had to be shaped, and a myriad are custom-shaped, to fit the grand plan. Thus, the problem remains: How did the Egyptians shape 12 million blocks to produce well formed pyramid complexes during the Pyramid Age?

We have seen above that Dieter Arnold did not recognize the full weight of the block-cutting problem, because he assumed that most of the 12 million pyramid blocks did not require shaping. Thus, to solve what he recognizes as the block-cutting problem, Dieter Arnold (as do some other Egyptologists) proposes that the Egyptians must have relied on stone pounders! Arnold wrote:

> The picture is completed by the presence of huge quantities of spherical balls of dolerite and elongated mauls or axes all over Pharaonic construction sites . . . By bouncing the dolerite balls, which weighed up to 6 kilograms [13 pounds] or more, at a certain angle and rhythm, the surface of a stone like granite was bruised and ground down to powder.[12]

If we follow Arnold's logic, then many millions of pyramid blocks would have to have been shaped to conform to tier heights and other specifications with pounding balls! The pounding balls Arnold had in mind were made of very tough greenish-black dolerite (any of various coarse basalts) or other hard rocks. It defies logic to think that the Great Pyramids could have been built by such means.

Arnold's suggestion suits Pyramid Age technology, and, given enough time, pounding rocks can produce results. A team of masons could build a wall this way.

Even the giant 60-foot-high Sphinx at Giza, which is relatively small compared with the Great Pyramid, might be sculpted by very gently pounding away at areas of limestone and grinding the created surfaces to their finished shape with abrasive sand. The body of the Sphinx is made of a soft grade of limestone, and no tight fitting joints or flat surfaces or tiers had to be achieved. No massive blocks had to be lifted and fitted to sculpt the Sphinx. But the scale and perfection of the Great Pyramids cannot have been achieved with pounding balls.

It would be impossible to use pounding balls to produce a level 13-acre foundation or 115,000 massive, beautifully sloped casing blocks that custom-fit as closely as 1/500 inch or in perfect contact. Remember that Petrie measured a flatness of .01 for a length of 75 inches up the face of the Great Pyramid where casing remains, accuracy equal to modern optician's straightedges. While we cannot assume that all casing block faces were that accurate (because most of them have been stolen), we cannot deny the strong possibility in light of the overall accuracy of the Great Pyramid and the existence of much flatter surfaces on other artifacts. Ancient historians marveled over the many tiers of smooth casing blocks covering the Great Pyramid. The top of Khafra's Great Pyramid at Giza still exhibits such casing blocks. Tight fitting, beautifully angled casing blocks appear on many monuments, and provide us with an idea of how those covering the entire Great Pyramid were fit. The four faces of the Great Pyramid were covered with 2,379,842 cubic feet of casing stones. Dieter Arnold admitted to serious problems with the use of pounding balls:

> It is difficult to imagine, however, how this method was applied to inclined, vertical, or even overhanging planes. . . . We do not know exactly how the masons achieved two corresponding and neatly fitted planes on two neighboring blocks.[13]

We see that Egyptology's last option, stone tools, is unworkable. Something is fundamentally wrong with the standard paradigm of pyramid construction.

Precise, intricate features are not simply the product of men working with stone tools. Fancy joints are common in Old and Middle Kingdom architecture. Some joints are L-shaped, and many exhibit oblique masonry angles. In some Old and Middle Kingdom structures, 30 percent of the joints are oblique.

Somers Clarke and Reginald Engelbach carefully studied these fancy joints and developed drawings and models. They tried to demonstrate that the Egyptians assembled the blocks on chains of so-called rockers.[14] These researchers reasoned that a temporary positioning of blocks on movable rockers would help workers pull blocks close together for adjustment. This awkward procedure requires a tremendous increase in work and is incompatible with the rapid construction rate reckoned for the Great Pyramid. Dieter Arnold doubted that the rocker system was used:

. . . the evidence for the use of such an instrument is rather weak.[15]

Most pyramid blocks bear no tool marks, making it difficult to determine what means were used to shape them. But very telling tool marks are apparent on the back of a number of Old Kingdom statues and on sarcophagi made with granite. Tool marks appear on basalt slabs east of the Great Pyramid, which formed a platform that originally covered more than a third of an acre. Egyptologists think that the platform is the flooring of a destroyed Mortuary Temple. About ten percent of these basalt

**36.** BASALT SAMPLES: AT GIZA, W.M.F. PETRIE FOUND THESE BASALT FRAGMENTS, NOW IN THE PETRIE MUSEUM. ONE WAS SAWN ON BOTH SIDES AND CUT NEARLY IN HALF. SAMPLES LIKE THESE ARE THE SUBJECT OF DEBATE BECAUSE NEITHER POUNDING BALLS NOR PYRAMID AGE COPPER SAWS CAN PRODUCE THEM. SOME BASALT SLABS AT GIZA EXHIBIT PLUNGE CUTS, WHICH ARE NOT THE PRODUCT OF SLOW GRINDING. PHOTOGRAPH BY JON BODSWORTH

37. THIS BASALT FRAGMENT FROM THE PAVEMENT EAST OF THE GREAT PYRAMID SHOWS PARALLEL SAW MARKS. LARGE BASALT PAVING SLABS HAVE UNDERSIDES THAT CORRESPOND TO IRREGULARITIES IN THE BEDROCK BELOW. PETRIE FOUND THIS SPECIMEN, WHICH IS NOW IN THE PETRIE MUSEUM. PHOTOGRAPH BY JOHN REID

slabs remaining today exhibit saw-mark striations between them that prove they were not made with stone pounding balls or diorite axes.[16] Basalt is too hard to perfect even with iron saws. Remember Arnold's statement: "We know that hard stones such as granite, granodiorite, syenite, and basalt could not have been cut with metal tools."

Some of the above-mentioned basalt slabs in the platform east of the Great Pyramid have notched corners for fitting adjacent blocks. Robert Moores, of the Black & Decker tool company, observed plunge cuts on two of the slabs.[17] According to Moores, the plunge cuts he observed indicate the definite action of a saw blade. Moores indicates that these plunge cuts eliminate any possibility that slowly shaping the slabs with abrasives made the saw striations. In other words, the plunge cuts suggest a much more rapid cutting process than using abrasive sand.

During W.M.F. Petrie's research in Egypt, many of these slabs were being sawed or broken up for the purpose of exploiting the thin layer of fine limestone below for lime production. But these hammering and sawing efforts of the local Egyptians would not produce the plunge cuts or other signs of rapid cutting that Moores observed. Nonetheless, it is important to sort out the tool marks on these slabs so that ancient rapid cuts are not confused with modern hammering or sawing performed to tear up the slabs. Signs of rapid and/or precision cutting are common on Old Kingdom artifacts, whereas modern cutting methods do not produce these same features.

Similarly, many intricately cut artifacts made with hard stone bear definite tool marks, and some of the features have prompted certain contemporary machinists to defy the historical record and assert that advanced machining must have existed during Egyptian antiquity. However, such machines were not needed with the highly efficient technology I explain in Volume 2 of this book.

To address the quandary of the basalt slabs, in 1991 Robert Moores designed a giant fixed copper drag saw that he theorized might cut basalt. He did not build a prototype to prove his system, but only sketched his design. His sketch shows a notched blade about 13 feet long, requiring nine men to operate. He imagined the huge copper blade suspended by ropes attached to its two ends. Other attached ropes would be used to pull the blade back and forth, producing saw strokes. The cutting medium is quartz sand, poured onto the blocks at the point of the sawcut. Moores reckons that either the blocks would have to be cut underwater or a slurry of water and sand must constantly be applied to the cut. The blocks must be guided by bearings to keep the cutting edges in exact alignment. A block would also have to be rotated, given that the blade's angle of attack was altered several times on a slab Moores examined at Giza. Moores does not postulate why the Egyptians would have undertaken this additional work, which would complicate an already cumbersome operation.

Moores does not explain how such a device would produce the compelling plunge cuts. His saw does not fit with the known tools of the Pyramid Age. The Pyramid Age is not characterized by machinery. The drag saw itself is not thought to have been invented until some two thousand years after the Great Pyramid was built. Ancient Egyptian tomb paintings and texts do not depict or mention the use of any sort of large machinery or anything similar to a drag saw. Egyptology knows only of copper handsaws, suitable for cutting wood. These tools were used in the Pyramid Age to make wooden furniture.

Ancient Egyptian tools were very rudimentary.[18] Needles, knives, handsaws, chisels, hoes, adzes, and picks with wooden handles date from early periods. The heaviest copper tools were the adz, ax, and hoe blade.

Ancient Egyptian chisels have a broad, flat cutting edge, making their shape appropriate for block cutting. But Dieter Arnold indicated that a heavy blow with a mallet would drive such a chisel deep into its wooden handle, causing it to split. Ancient Egyptian chisels are not suitable for cutting good-quality stone. Tomb paintings show chisels in the hands of leather workers and carpenters.[19]

Returning to Moores' drag saw, a wealth of evidence proves that the Egyptians did not cut the pyramid and temple blocks with giant drag saws. The pyramids and temples exhibit innumerable examples of perfectly fitting mosaic and wavy joints. On both the interior and exterior, the Great Pyramid exhibits a tremendous number of highly irregular joints, which are very closely fit. For instance, blocks lining the interior vaults above the Great Pyramid's King's Chamber are form-fitted, like so much of the rest of the structure. Such blocks hug one another very closely along their whole joints, even though the joints deviate from being purely straight up and down.[20] Such close, wavy jointing is common in pyramid complexes, and this feature is not the product of a giant drag saw. The back-and-forth motion of a saw blade will instead produce far more regular surfaces.

Some form-fitted blocks are very crudely shaped. The ceiling and other areas of the entrance passage of the Great Pyramid show examples. The ceiling of the burial chamber of the collapsed pyramid at Meidum, built for the 3rd Dynasty Pharaoh Huni (c. 2599–2575 B.C.), is a stunning example.[21] The ceiling units are so crudely shaped that they cannot be considered blocks. But all fit tightly together along their oddly shaped joints, bringing to mind a finished jigsaw puzzle. A huge reciprocating (back-and-forth motion) drag saw does not produce the wavy, custom-fitting joints. Clearly, the pyramid blocks are not the product of machine tools that make regular planes or anything similar to Robert Moore's drag-saw design.

Casing blocks on the three main pyramids at Giza emphasize this point: The casing blocks conform to one another on each touching surface, and they also conform to the irregular faces of backing stones behind them.[22] Experts who have examined some of Khafra's form-fitting casing blocks observed that they fit together with tongue and groove joints. These configurations defy the use of a drag saw. Arnold described Giza's form-fitting casing blocks:

> . . . the connection of the casing with the backing stones is very close and would have to be carefully prepared. The best examples are the close joints between casing and backing stones at the three main pyramids of Giza. The backing stones were frequently dressed exactly to the shape of the rear face of the casing blocks. . . .[23]

Casing blocks made with granite and measuring up to ten feet long on Khafra's Pyramid are form-fitted, as are the granite casing blocks on Khufu's Pyramid. The rear of the granite blocks are highly irregular, yet they fit exactly into the irregularities of the front faces of the limestone blocks behind them. The conforming fit cannot result from working with either a drag saw or stone pounding balls, flint picks, or stone axes.

Paving blocks fit tightly, and at all sorts of fancy angles. Their notches receive the corners of adjacent blocks. Dieter Arnold described these blocks:

> In the huge limestone buildings of the Old Kingdom, a pavement of granite is not uncommon. In a few cases, even basalt was used. Since both stones were much harder to work than the underlying limestone, the undersurface of the limestone foundation was chiseled out in a way that allowed the protuberances of the pavement to fit into it. This could be done only by frequently setting and lifting the pavement blocks, a procedure that had to be carried out in any case to fit the mosaic-like blocks together.[24]

Dieter Arnold's proposal is illogical. The 13-acre pavement-foundation of the Great Pyramid and the irregular bedrock under it are hard and strong enough to support this massive monument. What kind of tools were used to achieve the flawless correspondence between the foundation slabs and the bedrock? If we follow Arnold's method, then hundreds of thousands of giant casing blocks on the exterior of the Great Pyramid would also have to be repeatedly lifted and reset until they conformed to the shape of all adjacent blocks. The aforementioned paper-thin cement would have to be applied in the process. It is much easier to cut regular blocks so that joints will automatically be close without constant reshaping and resetting until a peerless fit is achieved to create giant pyramid faces measuring five acres each.

Those who advocate the notion of the construction of the Great Pyramid with stone or copper tools repeatedly ask us to believe the unfathomable. Fancy, mosaic basalt and granite pavement slabs, and fancy joints separating enormous blocks and beams, cannot be the product of working with no technology other than crude stone pounding balls, stone axes, soft copper tools, and abrasives. Given the masonry features already described in these pages, common sense tells us that some elusive technology existed that allowed Pyramid Age tools to be highly effective.

Tall monolithic temple columns, made with granite or limestone, have decorated capitals and are sometimes round shafts with cross sections that are true circles.[25] Some columns taper. These cannot be the products of artisans working with pounding balls or drag saws or giant lathes. When explaining 36-foot-high monolithic granite columns, Egyptology can only address simple tasks like measuring roundness. As for the production of such columns, Arnold admitted that Egyptology simply lacked an explanation:

> The dressing of a monolithic column certainly was more difficult, and we have no information about the methods used. . . . Achieving accuracy was difficult, however, if we consider that granite columns nearly 11 meters long had to be manufactured. On a portion of a 6.30-meter-long shaft of the granite columns of Sahure, the mean diameter tapers 11.4 centimeters, with an error of only 8 centimeters. . . . By viewing such column shafts, one can see that their diameter is not always a true circle. This observation, the heavy weight of such column shafts, and the missing drill holes for inserting a fulcrum-shaft axle rule out the possibility that the column shafts were hung in a horizontal position and rotated.[26]

We see that the idea that giant lathes were used to make these columns is out of the question. Such a tool would have been very large, powerful, and sturdy machinery, and would defy all of the findings of archaeology. No one has demonstrated that huge temple columns that are round can be made by sanding with abrasives. The ancient means presented in Volume 2 of this book solves the problem and fits with the Late Stone Age level of technology.

# Chapter 8

# Iron Is Not The Solution

Iron tools are not hard enough to cut hard stones like basalt, diorite, granite, greywacke (schist), or quartzite. Egyptologists used to suggest that masons might have had iron tools for quarrying and shaping the millions of limestone pyramid blocks. An example of this out-of-date opinion appears in an older book, Ahmed Fakhry's *The Pyramids* (1969 ed.):

> Both in quarrying and building, workmen used copper chisels and possibly iron tools, as well as flint, quartz and diorite pounders.[1]

Ahmed Fakhry's assumption probably arises from the observation of a minority of blocks in the pyramid complexes exhibiting tool marks, such as chisel marks. Some of these tool marks are known to date to later periods. For instance, during the 19th Dynasty, when iron was available on a small scale, pyramids were restored. In the Middle Ages some pyramid blocks were hacked at or partially cut up by treasure hunters and builders. Although tool-mark classifications have been established for quarries, no comprehensive study has dated the various tool marks on blocks. Some pyramid blocks exhibit rectangular wedge holes, made to accept iron wedges, that match those in the Aswan granite quarries dating to after 500 B.C. The evidence at Giza, therefore, suggests abandoned attempts to cut up pyramid blocks in the Iron Age. Among other evidence of Greek and Roman activity at Giza, a considerable village dating to Greco-Roman times has been known since the early days of Egyptology, having been reported by both W.M.F. Petrie and Howard Vyse.

The overwhelming majority of pyramid blocks exhibit no tool marks. When the standard paradigm of pyramid construction is applied, one of the mysteries of Egyptology is why masons would erase all traces of tool marks on the majority of blocks, blocks that were supposed to remain forever hidden from view by multiton casing blocks. A myriad of blocks directly behind the casing and deeper into the interior are highly irregular, and so we must ask why masons would leave these blocks rough and yet rid them of tool marks.

Although iron chisels are not suitable for cutting mosaic basalt paving slabs (or plunge cuts in basalt such as observed by Robert Moores) or sculpting quartzite or

38. BASALT PAVEMENT SAW CUTS: THE LARGE BASALT SLABS AT GIZA EXHIBIT ANCIENT PLUNGE CUTS AND OTHER SIGNS OF RAPID CUTTING, AND PERHAPS ALSO MUCH LATER ABANDONED ATTEMPTS TO CUT THEM UP. IN W.M.F. PETRIE'S DAY, MANY WERE BROKEN UP AND REMOVED FOR THE PURPOSE OF OBTAINING THE FINE LIMESTONE LAYER BELOW THAT WAS BURNED INTO LIME. PHOTOGRAPH BY JON BODSWORTH

other varieties of hard rock, the use of iron seemed to some Egyptologists to be the best way around the problem of making pyramid blocks.

In 1837 Col. Howard Vyse found a fragment of sheet iron wedged between two blocks at the south air channel of the Great Pyramid's King's Chamber.[2] The piece of iron had been there for a long time, as shown by rust on it in the shape of a nummulite fossil shell.

Egyptologists have pondered the question of the Arabs' having left the iron centuries ago. Treasure hunters looking for secret entrances repeatedly pried at blocks over the ages, presumably on both the interior and exterior of the Great Pyramid. The

Great Pyramid's interior was penetrated by the caliph Ma'moun in the ninth century.[3] A related account states that an expedition of men encountered a chamber containing a sarcophagus.

Treasure hunters were scouring the Great Pyramid's interior in Abd el-Latif's time (A.D. 1162–1231), when travelers were allowed to go into and out of the monument.[4] An account by Murtada ibn al Khafif, an Arabian writer thought to have lived in the 13th century, collected stories for his *A History of the Marvelous Things in Egypt*.[5] One account tells of a troop of 20 men who entered the Great Pyramid carrying provisions for two months. They had with them iron plates and bars. There is no telling how much tampering with the masonry might have taken place over the centuries.

In the 19th Dynasty, when iron was available, the administration of Pharaoh Ramses II restored several pyramids, as attested to by inscriptions. Egyptologists suspect that the inscriptions on the Great Pyramid read to Herodotus might have been among those left by Ramses' restoration crews. The plate of iron could be a remnant of a restoration project.

Even if the sheet iron were original to the construction of the Great Pyramid, then the idea that iron tools were used to cut the blocks does not hold. Excavators have found no iron tools inside of other Old or Middle Kingdom tombs, suggesting that iron was extremely rare. Dieter Arnold offered some clarification:

> The question of the date when iron came into general use in Egypt is much disputed. Specimens of early iron are reported from predynastic dates on. Fragments supposedly of chisels from Saqqara are said to belong to the Fifth Dynasty, and pieces of a pickax found at Abusir and broken tools from Dahshur are said to be of the Sixth Dynasty. Since the circumstances of these finds are extremely vague, the dating of the tools may be questioned, and they could as well have been used by stonecutters of a much later period. A later date for these tools is also suggested by the fact that iron objects from the [18th Dynasty] tomb of Tutankhamun were of poor quality and were considered to be so valuable that they were set in gold.[6]

No paintings or papyri support the use of iron during the Old Kingdom, when the Great Pyramid was built, or earlier times in Egypt. Sealed tombs of these periods have yielded only wood, copper and stone tools. However, it is possible that the iron found by Vyse, which exhibited traces of gold, was brought to Egypt as a gift by a foreign embassy when the Great Pyramid was being built.

The iron found by Vyse is statistically insignificant, because the amount of iron required for building the Great Pyramids would have been enormous. Iron-bearing meteorite fragments could not have met the demand. There would be an abundance of archaeological evidence of mining and smelting if the Egyptians smelted iron on even a modest scale in early times. In short, with the archaeological evidence lacking, Vyse's discovery does not support the notion that pyramid builders shaped blocks with iron tools.[7]

Iron probably came into use late because of the difficulties of smelting the ore and reducing it to a state of malleability. The metals available since early times—gold, copper and silver—are found in the native state in the mountain and river channel environs. This is not true for iron, and iron is not easily fused. It must undergo two laborious heating processes to gain strength.

Only from the end of the 18th Dynasty does a gradual increase of iron objects become apparent. By the 26th Dynasty (664–525 B.C.) iron was in common use in Egypt. During the 26th Dynasty workers conducted restoration and other activities at Giza and elsewhere. These activities may account for the iron fragment found on the inside of the Great Pyramid and around the outside of other old sites Arnold mentioned.

No trace of steel has been found, and there is no evidence that steel was known. Egyptologists have accounted for all of the ancient Egyptian words for metals, and none of the words can mean steel.

Notwithstanding actual trials, ancient literature mentions the difficulties of cutting hard stones with metal tools. In *De Lapidibus*, the Greek philosopher and natural scientist Theophrastus (c. 372–278 B.C.) briefly mentioned stones too firm to be cut with iron.[8] Diorite, basalt, and quartzite are examples. The use of iron cannot solve the dilemma facing Egyptology regarding the pyramid blocks.

Even modern and ultramodern tools cannot duplicate the features of some ancient stone artifacts. It bears repeating that drilling into a solid bed of quartzite is quite a task with a tungsten carbide bit, with 950 pounds of pressure on the dill bit and a drill strength of 5,000 to 10,000 pounds per square inch. Heavy-duty, high-strength steel hammer peens and picks are ruined when used to hammer diorite.

No combination of ancient tools can solve the problem. Iron, steel, and hard abrasive powders (the latter used in combination with stone drills) are not adequate for making many examples of Egyptian stonework. Among many dramatic examples, Egyptologist John G. Wilkinson was astonished by crisp, detailed two-inch and deeper hieroglyphic intaglio in granite obelisks.[9]

Comparably, during the 1997 PBS Nova film *Secrets of Lost Empires: Obelisk*, stonemason Roger Hopkins remarked as follows about hieroglyphs on an obelisk of Ramses II:

> Even with modern tools and . . . diamond wheels and all that, we would have . . . a tough time getting it [the hieroglyphs] to this kind of perfection.

The Nova film did not reproduce such hieroglyphs.

A granite sarcophagus greatly impressed Wilkinson, because the pharaoh's image is raised up to nine inches above the surface. In other words, Wilkinson was astonished by the idea of a sculptor's successfully cutting away nine inches of granite across the lid so that he could then sculpt the raised image of the pharaoh.

The sarcophagus found in Menkaura's burial chamber (and later lost at sea), in the Third Pyramid of Giza, is basalt. The etchings on the sarcophagus were recorded before the object was lost in the Mediterranean en route to England. Deep etchings form a beautifully decorated palace facade style that covers the sarcophagus. Other examples that defy explanation are the large colossi, temple columns, sarcophagi, corridor plug blocks, and pavement slabs all made of quartzite. They have defied trials with primitive stone-working techniques. Egyptology offers no satisfactory explanation for the production of these and a myriad of other hard-stone objects.

With regard to iron, Mark Lehner, in his *The Complete Pyramids* (1997), bases his pyramid-building estimate on modern work done with so-called iron tools. His premise is, therefore, invalid. His estimate of the time it took to perform ancient quarry work is useless, as we see by his following description:

> To build the Great Pyramid in 23 years . . . 322 cu. m (11,371 cu. ft) of stone had to be quarried daily. How many quarrymen would this require? Our NOVA pyramid-building experiment provided a useful comparison: 12 NOVA quarrymen produced 186 stones in 22 days' work, or 8.5 stones per day. But though they worked barefoot and without power tools, they had the advantage of a winch with an iron cable to pull the stones away from the quarry face. An additional 20-man team might have been needed for the task in Khufu's day.[10]

Lehner added that his "figure can be expanded further to compensate for other advantages of iron tools." In other words, with this last statement, he admits, in a very subdued manner, that his estimate is not based on the use of Pyramid Age tools. Studies have shown stone axes and copper chisels to be incapable of quarrying limestone suitable for construction. No number of additional men working with copper and stone tools will compensate for the advantage afforded by iron or the modern steel tools Nova's crew used to cut the softest limestone at Tura.

In addition, Lehner's *The Complete Pyramids* (1997) repeatedly states that the Nova team used iron tools to quarry and cut Tura limestone. Joseph Davidovits witnessed the construction of Nova's miniature pyramid in Egypt and photographed the operation. Joseph Davidovits insists that the tools were made of steel, which is logical because steel was being used at Tura when Somers Clarke and Reginald Engelbach studied the quarries in the early 1900s and before. Steel is iron that contains up to about 1.7 percent carbon, which is essential to form the alloy. Lehner's use of the word iron may sound more ancient, but steel cannot accurately be referred to as iron. Steel is tougher than iron and has greater overall strength, making it much better than iron for stone cutting. Joseph Davidovits' photographs of the Nova pyramid project show the use of heavy modern tools, and modern tools are made of hardened steel. These same tools appear in the Nova film.

Here is a summary of the Egyptological dilemma: Attempts at cutting limestone comparable to the blocks of the Great Pyramid immediately ruin copper chisels. Large quantities of iron were not available when the Great Pyramid was built, and iron will not cut basalt, and certainly did not produce the plunge cuts Robert Moores observed in basalt paving slabs in the flooring next to the Great Pyramid. The Egyptians used thousands of tons of basalt in Old Kingdom monuments, mostly as paving slabs in pyramid complexes.

The Egyptians could not have cut the pyramid blocks with copper tools if such tools were suitable, because the amount of copper needed for trimming and dressing the 12 million blocks produced in the Pyramid Age would have been far too great. Hard bronze, which is suitable for cutting pyramid blocks, was not available until about 800 years after the Great Pyramid was built, and iron came even later. Stone tools cannot achieve the refinement incorporated into the pyramid complexes. The problem is not solved by the softer consistency of freshly quarried limestone, because limestone blocks will dry out and harden by the time they can be transported and shaped to fit with existing masonry. Most copper implements found in ancient Egyptian tombs are made of typical copper, not special, hardened copper. The overwhelming majority of blocks in the pyramid complexes exhibit no signs of tool marks. How were pyramid blocks prepared? Although many Egyptologists assume that the methods used to construct the Great Pyramid are sufficiently understood, in reality Egyptology is faced with a real mystery.

# Chapter 9

# How Was It Possible?

In addition to limestone, researchers have tackled the hardest rock varieties using replicas of ancient Egyptian tools. The same bronze tool that Antoine Zuber used to cut limestone blocks had no effect on granite.[1] A Nova experiment yielded similar results. Michael Barnes, producer of Nova's *This Old Pyramid,* wrote the following in private correspondence dated April 25, 1995:

> . . . our limited financing did not allow us to make enough bronze tools to work the stones. However, we demonstrated that bronze chisels are effective at cutting limestone (but bronze is not hard enough to cut granite).

Sir John G. Wilkinson, an early pioneering scholar of Egyptology and the first British Egyptologist of distinction, found a nine-inch-long bronze chisel in southern Egypt at Thebes.[2] It dated to hundreds of years after the Pyramid Age. The chisel was in an excellent state of preservation. Its cutting edge measures 7/10 of an inch at its greatest width, and the metal contains 5.9 parts tin per 100. When Wilkinson tested it, he found it altogether incapable of cutting granite.

Unlike limestone, granite is very hard within the bedrock. Freshly quarried granite will harden more after being exposed to the air. Even freshly exposed in the quarry, when it is at its softest, most moist state, a steel tool is required to cut granite. The steel tools, however, will be so badly damaged that the method is not practical. Diamond drills are typically used today to cut granite. After very long exposure to the atmosphere, granite and other igneous rocks begin to soften from weathering. But the weathering process affects the rocks only after periods ranging from thousands of years to hundreds of thousands of years, depending upon the climate. In other words, there was no taking advantage of a softer material during Old Kingdom rock extraction, when only soft metals were available. Nonetheless, as mentioned, Joseph Roder estimated that during the 450-year-long Old Kingdom, a little less than 1.6 million cubic feet of granite was consumed for incorporation into monuments! Given the tremendous effort required to quarry granite, such statistics invite us to consider the existence of a special, highly efficient technology.

Tests show how poorly bronze chisels perform when used to try to cut hard rocks. In the 1980s Denys Stocks produced bronze chisels of different grades of hardness by using ancient casting methods. He tested his chisels on nine different types of stone, ranging from soft sandstone to hard granodiorite. The latter is an intermediate between granite and quartz-containing diorite. Stocks found that he could easily cut soft sandstone with bronze chisels. He cut soft limestone with infrequent sharpening of his bronze chisels. He cut hard alabaster with frequent sharpening. Hard limestone and the other hard rocks immediately ruined his bronze tools. Stocks wrote:

> All the copper and bronze chisels suffered expected severe damage against both granites and grano-diorites. The granular structure of rose granite and diorite literally tore away the cutting edges of the chisels. . . . I will mention the test use of a modern engineer's chisel, manufactured of hardened and tempered steel, upon a smoothed surface of grano-diorite. A groove 0.5 mm deep and 1.3 cm long was cut into the surface by utilizing both corners of the chisel edge. It sustained such severe damage, caused by pieces of steel being torn away, that only considerable sharpening would allow any further cutting.[3]

Stocks concluded that hard stones must have been dressed with stone tools and abrasives. But stone tools and abrasives cannot account for quarrying and cutting all of the masonry that has gone into creating the grandiose scale and design complexities of the Great Pyramid and other Old Kingdom monuments.

A brief description of ancient tools makes it clear that they are inadequate for producing the impressive hard-stone artifacts experts have pondered. Museums have many stone tools from ancient Egypt, and all are very rudimentary. Flint knife blades date from the middle of the 1st Dynasty, as do wooden sickles with flint cutting edges. Flint is a strong material equal in hardness to quartz, and flint will fracture so as to produce sharp edges. But flint is very brittle. Flint tools easily break when struck with a wooden mallet. Pointed flint is useful for hunting and domestic chores, and flint was abundant in ancient Egypt. But flint is useless for detaching and shaping massive granite and hard limestone blocks.

Ancient Egyptian stone tools fall into four main groups: grinding stones, picks, pounders, and rammers. Actual tools and weapons, and ancient drawings of them, demonstrate the level of implement making before, during, and long after the Pyramid Age. Limestone ax heads dating from the 18th Dynasty (c. 1550–1070 B.C.), 1,000 years after the Great Pyramid was built, are crude slablike chunks of stone. Stone pickaxes were made of granite, chert, basalt, quartzite or hard limestone. The ax heads were tied to wooden handles with leather strips.[4]

A drawing of a stone hammer from the tomb of Ti depicts an egg-shaped rock.[5] A quartzite ax was found with its original handle, which consists of two sticks and banding chord for affixing the ax head. This ax dates between the 22nd and 26th Dynasties, more than 1,500 years after the Great Pyramid was built.[6] A diorite ax head found at Pharaoh Amenemhet I's pyramid at el-Lisht, in Middle Egypt, is believed to date to either the Middle or New Kingdom. Egyptology has established that it was left at the el-Lisht work site at least 500 years after the construction of the Great Pyramid.[7] This ax is like the one replicated and used by Mark Lehner for his futile stone-cutting efforts behind the scenes of the Nova presentation (witnessed by Joseph Davidovits). Ancient Egyptian axes look like the sort we envision being carried by cavemen (see Figure 62 on page 200).

How can we believe that primitive tools, combined with no other technology, produced the features of the Great Pyramid? These include its level, 13-acre platform-foundation; more than 200 tiers made of blocks that conform to the shape of blocks above and below them, and sometimes to all surfaces they touch; the accuracy of the 73 remaining tier heights to within ½ centimeter; the near-perfect planes of the rough core masonry; its four carefully bowed faces; the masonry patterns we have explored; its precise right angles on a massive scale; the estimated 115,000 form-fitted casing blocks that fit as closely as 1/500 inch or in perfect contact; the angle of casing blocks, which produced its four flat sloping faces each covering five acres; its tall edges that met perfectly at a point at the top; and its magnificent interior features, including giant, beautifully corbelled walls, and exquisitely rendered granite walls and ceilings.

Antoine Zuber conducted a demanding experiment with stone tools.[8] It took him 12 days just to cut six crude holes in a granite quarry so he could detach a small chunk of granite with wooden wedges. He was testing the now-abandoned assumption that rough granite blocks were quarried with wooden wedges.[9] A wedge tapers to a thin edge, which can be used for splitting certain kinds of rocks. Presumably, water was poured onto the wedges, causing them to swell and produce enough pressure to split the bedrock along a seam.

Egyptologists long debated the lengthy chains of cavities in the Aswan granite quarries of southern Egypt, since most experts believed water-swollen wooden wedges to be incapable of breaking out granite.[10] Zuber did manage to break out his granite chunk with sycamore wedges after constant wetting for one day and one night.[11]

Given the difficulties Zuber encountered, one might assume that relatively little granite would appear in construction work. But, as mentioned, Joseph Roder estimated that during the 450-year-long Old Kingdom a little less than 1.6 million cubic feet of granite was removed from the Aswan quarries![12]

Other than limestone, granite is the most common rock found in Old Kingdom architecture, and its use in construction work started during the 1st Dynasty. Evidence from tombs, including paintings and papyri, does not show that Egyptians quarried

39. The entire Great Pyramid was originally covered on all four sides by tight-fitting casing blocks like those shown here. Despite earthquake damage and displacement, the close, custom fit remains largely intact.

The casing blocks were all originally very white and smooth according to ancient reports. W.M.F. Petrie measured their accuracy as equal to a modern opticians' straightedge. A stunning feature of the casing blocks is their custom jointing on all of their sides, including their backs.

Photograph by Jon Bodsworth

**40. OPPOSITE PAGE: THE ABANDONED GRANITE OBELISK AT ASWAN WAS NEVER DETACHED FROM THE BEDROCK BELOW. PHOTOGRAPH BY JON BODSWORTH**

granite with wedges. Joseph Roder studied the open quarries at Aswan and showed that no wedge holes dated before the 26th Dynasty (c. 500 B.C.).[13]

Having abandoned the wedge theory, Egyptology now holds that, during the Old and New Kingdoms, workers used loose boulders to make blocks. That is, Egyptologists think that workers bashed out granite blocks with pounding balls. With long, hard use, these tools can be used to bash deep trenches in the quarry floor until blocks are formed.[14]

Mark Lehner reports spending five hours hammering the quarry floor at Aswan. During those five hours, he produced an approximately 12 by 12 inch patch that was four-fifths of an inch deep.[15]

In the 1920s Reginald Engelbach produced similar results. Even without further trials, there is ample proof that stone pounding balls were used at Aswan, at least in the New Kingdom or later. In 1921–22 Reginald Engelbach cleared the granite quarry at Aswan, where a huge, unfinished granite obelisk rests. Deep trenches appear around it, and the distinct, rough impressions of pounding balls are pronounced on the obelisk itself. The obelisk cracked a number of times while it was being pounded, and each time its design was reduced. Finally, the obelisk was abandoned when a huge crack split down the interior. But although this example shows that granite can be quarried by breaking up the bedrock with stone pounding balls, the puzzle of quarrying of pyramid blocks is not solved by this.

As already discussed, if crude pounding balls, alone or in combination with stone pickaxes, were used to extract pyramid blocks, then the Giza quarries should be much larger.[16] There should also be millions of cracked and broken blocks at Giza, and much more waste rock should exist. There should be evidence of the use of pounding balls in the large quarries associated with the Great Pyramid. But these quarries, and other Old and Middle Kingdom, exhibit an entirely different kind of tool marks, the marks of pointed picks. There should be bruising and or pounding-ball marks all over the pyramid stones, but these features are absent. In contrast, pounding-ball marks on the Aswan obelisk are very distinctive channels made by continuous heavy downstrokes.

More than an ability to bash out trenches is required to explain the construction of the pyramids and inscriptions in granite that are of better quality than can be achieved with today's diamond drills. A different ancient technology is required to produce them and the many thousands of superb artifacts made with very hard rock. The problems are very challenging to experts. For example, a team led by Denys Stocks expended a great deal of effort to cut a round core out of Aswan granite with a bow drill and abrasive sand. As would be expected, the core exhibits striations all merged together that do not match ancient cores.

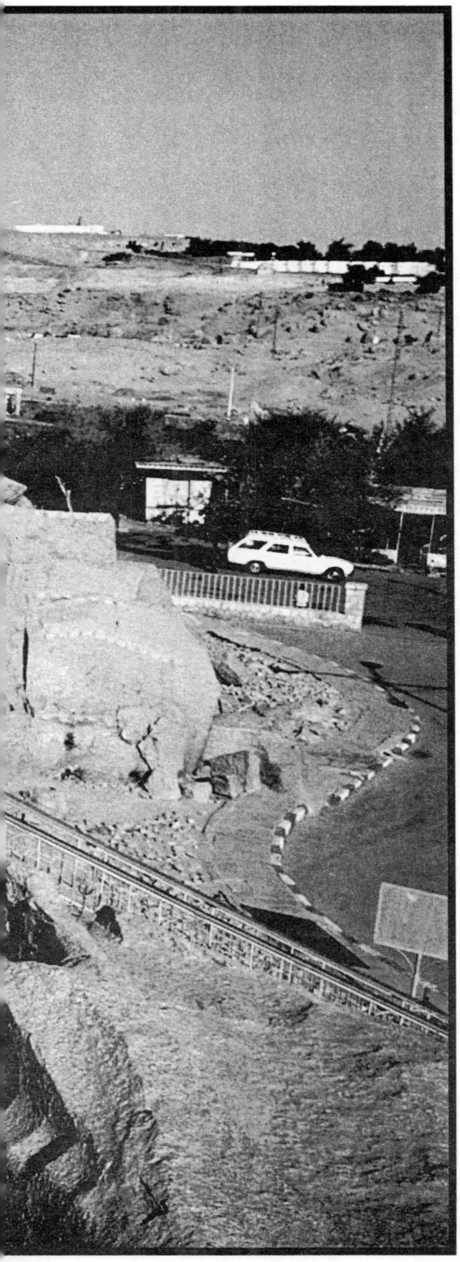

**41. The unfinished obelisk at Aswan was abandoned because of a huge crack made with the pounding ball masonry method.**

Although both limestone and granite are more moist (less brittle) when they are freshly quarried, Giza limestone is much weaker and more prone to cracking during masonry work than is Aswan granite. Hitting limestone with pounding balls greatly increases the chances of producing cracks in the stone. The pounding ball method is inadequate to produce the millions of limestone pyramid blocks.

Photograph by Jon Bodsworth

42. The vertical channels on the rock face at Aswan show the distinctive marks of pounding ball activity. A number of different techniques for obtaining rock were used at Aswan over the ages, including the Pyramid Age method, pounding balls, Iron Age wedges, and the steel tools and dynamite of modern times.

Thousands of Iron Age wedge marks appear at Aswan. By the 26th Dynasty iron was in common use in Egypt. The granite structures of Alexandria, made after 332 B.C., were most likely made with blocks detached with iron wedges.

Photograph by Jon Bodsworth

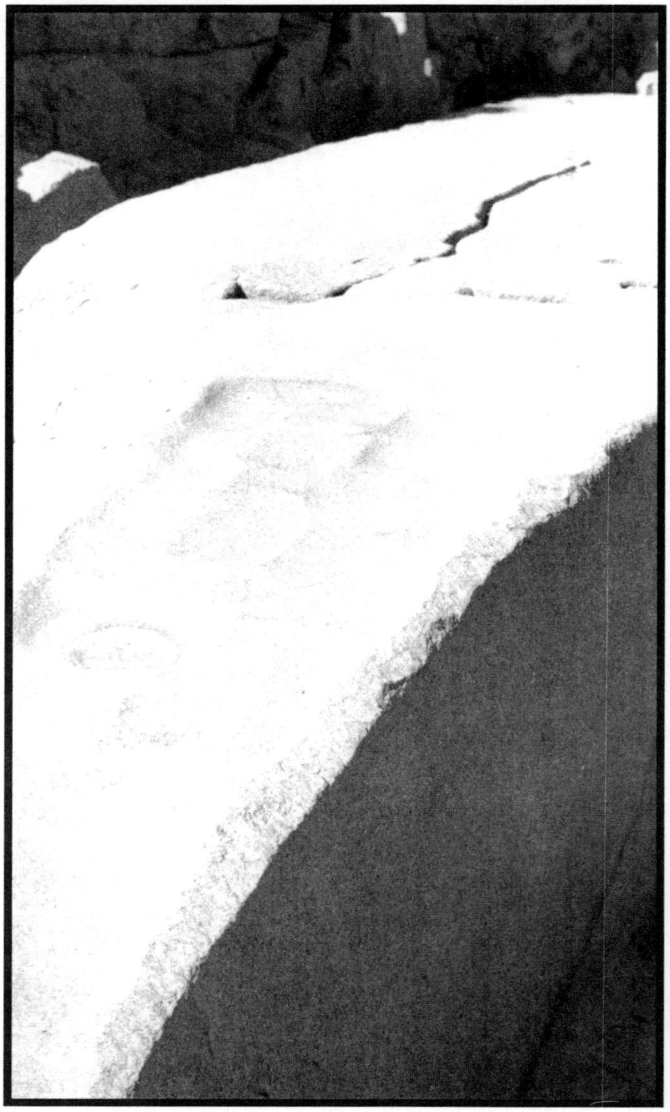

44.

BELOW. POUNDING BALLS MARKS APPEAR ON THE ENCLOSURE PIT OF THE UNFINISHED OBELISK AT ASWAN. POUNDING BALLS MARKS APPEAR ON THE SIDES OF THE OBELISK AND ON ITS PYRAMIDION TOO. PHOTOGRAPH BY JOHN REID

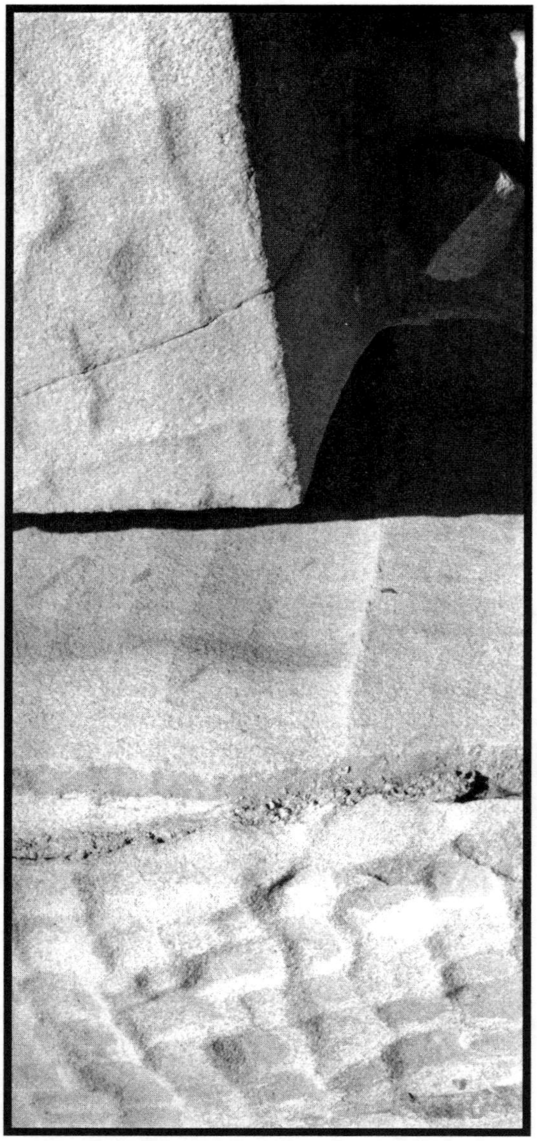

43.

ABOVE. POUNDING BALL MARKS ARE APPARENT ON THE OBELISK AT ASWAN. IN SHARP CONTRAST, TOOL MARKS ON THE WALLS OF THE GIZA QUARRIES WERE MADE WITH POINTED PICKS. EGYPTOLOGY HAS NOT EXPLAINED HOW MILLIONS OF PYRAMID BLOCKS COULD BE SHAPED AND DETACHED WITH POINTED PICKS. PHOTOGRAPH BY JOHN REID

45.
On the previous page: a photograph of the pillars of Khafra's Valley Temple. Made with granite, they are located at Giza.

46.
The photograph to the right shows a view into the interior of Khafra's Valley Temple: Blocks curve around corners and custom-fit with neighboring blocks.

Photographs by Jon Bodsworth

For instance, a granite core (# 7) found at Giza by W.M.F. Petrie exhibits a very clean helical cut. The cut is a continuous helix with some interruptions that were continued along the same average helical path. Machinists who worked with Petrie, and in recent years expert machinist Christopher Dunn, deliberated about this core long and hard, because their training tells them that the cut is amazing and significant. We can understand why Petrie said that modern cores made with diamond drills look like smudged work compared with the ancient cores.

On a larger scale, there are the granite crypts in the pyramid Egyptologists have determined to be Egypt's first, built for Pharaoh Zoser at Saqqara. The crypts of the main and southern tombs feature granite ceiling beams with round holes in them. These holes were sealed with matching round granite plugs that are up to six feet long and weigh three tons each. The ancient texts show nothing that would indicate a giant bow drill of the size needed to cut these large cores. There is no direct evidence of the existence of a bow drill during this Old Kingdom period, and the instrument would not be useful for producing the cores that puzzled Petrie and the aforementioned machinists. A much more sophisticated method than using stone pounding balls and bow drills with abrasives is required.

There are a great many more examples. Some monuments incorporate a large amount of granite, and some examples are particularly exquisite by design. Granite blocks cased the exterior of some pyramids. Six pyramids have one or more exterior courses of granite casing blocks.[17] The unfinished 4th Dynasty Pyramid of Djedefra, at abu Roash, about five miles north of the Great Pyramid, was all or mostly cased on its exterior with granite.[18] The casing blocks were carefully produced to conform to the pyramid's slope, producing beautifully made planes for this superstructure.

A beautiful example appears in Khafra's pyramid complex. The limestone interiors of the Valley and Mortuary Temples in Khafra's complex are cased with granite. Khafra's Valley Temple measures 147 feet from east to west and similarly from north to south. It rises to 43 feet and is faced inside and out with beautifully made granite ashlars. The exquisite, flat interior walls of Khafra's Valley Temple are made of courses of smooth, form-fitting granite ashlars that interlock at various angles. Some merging joints deeply interlock, with spectacular blocks that curve right around the corners of walls before interlocking with neighboring blocks. Massive, square granite columns were built to support the flat granite roof of this exquisite building.[19]

Within the Mastabat el-Fara'un at Saqqara, an arched granite ceiling covers the burial crypt of Shepsekaf, the last pharaoh of the 4th Dynasty.[20] An arched granite ceiling also covers the crypt in the 3rd Pyramid at Giza, built for Pharaoh Menkaura of the 4th Dynasty.[21] In the 5th Dynasty reign of Sahure, enormous halls in Mortuary Temples, about 17 feet wide by 69 feet long, were constructed with arched granite roofing made of enormous blocks. There is also an arched roof above one of the queens' crypts of Pharaoh Senworset III's 12th Dynasty pyramid at Dahshur. Dieter

Arnold mentioned some examples of crypts with spectacular arched roofs:

> Good examples [of burial chambers with arched roofing] are also the vaults of the crypts of Senwosret III and Amenemhet III at Dahshur (with sixteen more rooms vaulted this way). In the princesses' gallery of the pyramid of Senworset III and in the pyramid of Amenemhet III at Dashur, we also find examples of elaborate methods of joining the two sloping beams at the top. Here the joints are not straight but run in a zigzag line, with correspondent mortises and tenons on each block. The direction of the zigzag joint alternates from one block to the next. The system has prevented the saddle roof in the chambers of Amenemhet III from being pushed in, despite the heavy pressure from above.[22]

Dieter Arnold thinks that workers made these ceilings by first leaning beams against one another at their tops, and then cutting away at their undersides. Dieter Arnold assumed that the ancient workers had achieved this astonishing feat with nothing more than primitive tools. As mentioned, Arnold also proposed that the Great Pyramid, with all of its grandiose features, was made with pounding balls (and other stone tools)—although he could not account for the actual features of the monuments with the use of these implements: We recall that Arnold asserted that even soft stones were dressed and quarried mainly with stone tools, with metal chisels occasionally used for special purposes, until the New Kingdom and perhaps later.

Good scholarship requires careful examination of such assumptions. But Egyptologists often cite the monuments themselves as proof of method.[23] The monuments exist, the ancient tools are known, and so Egyptology assumes that a myriad of examples of masonry that cannot be duplicated with the best modern tools must have been made with nothing more than primitive tools.

Given the inadequacies of metal tools, some theorists propose that even the most extraordinary masonry work was carried out with abrasives combined with stone drills or copper saws. Recent experiments, which we will explore next, show that these instruments fail to replicate complex features of artifacts. Ancient Egyptian drawings show finishing touches being put onto statues, so that Egyptology is left to speculate about how ancient sculptors beautifully and routinely captured the subtle contours of the human body in complex statuary made with granite, diorite, quartzite, and other varieties of hard rock.

# Chapter 10

# Standard Masonry Theory Disproved

47. Masterpiece statue of Pharaoh Khafra in the Cairo Museum. Photograph by John Reid

A larger-than-life-sized statue of Pharaoh Khafra (made of a hard rock that is sometimes called "Chephren diorite") is very exquisitely detailed. Curators consider it a great masterpiece, and it is one of the most famous ancient statues. Excavations at Giza have unearthed a myriad of fragments of hard-stone objects dating from the Pyramid Age, including great numbers of fragments of finely executed diorite objects.

Egyptology has long advocated that hard-stone statues and other objects were fashioned with sharp pieces of broken flint, and combinations of implements like copper saws and abrasive sand. So far, tests of the types of implements available to the ancient Egyptians have not reproduced the complex features of artifacts made with hard stone.

Fairly recent experiments have disputed a long-held theory about how certain features might be made with abrasives and simple tools. For some 35 years, W.M.F. Petrie and Alfred Lucas debated the enigmas of various objects made with hard stone. Knowing that the metal tools available in ancient Egypt cannot produce the features of these objects (such as those made with granite, schist, basalt, diorite, and quartzite), Lucas argued that quartz sand was used as an abrasive in conjunction with a copper tool to produce them. Lucas proposed that the action of rubbing forced the sand into the copper, making the embedded sand behave like small cutting teeth.

Petrie responded by arguing that only drills with fixed teeth, made of diamond, corundum, or emery (an impure variety of corundum) gems could make the cuts in artifacts he collected. Petrie had shown these samples to machinists, who agreed that nothing but fixed points could have produced their features. Here is Petrie's retort to Lucas' idea about quartz sand behaving as cutting teeth:

> . . . It seems physically impossible that any particle of a loose powder could become so embedded in a soft metal by the mere accidents of rubbing that it could bear the immense strain needed to plough out a groove of any considerable depth in such a hard material as quartz. . . . Modern diamond drill cores are clumsy and smudged work when compared to the Egyptian cores.[1]

Lucas responded by pointing out that cutting gemstones into teeth and then setting those teeth in copper so they can endure the strain of hard use was totally unrealistic and unworkable. Diamond, the hardest substance known (aside from crystals recently produced by materials scientists), has a hardness of ten on the Mohs' scale,* and corundum and emery have a hardness of nine. Lucas asserted that the idea of the ancient Egyptians having shaped these hard materials into gemstones produces more problems than it solves.

*THE MOHS' SCALE OF RELATIVE MINERAL HARDNESS (WHICH IS STRICTLY A RELATIVE RATHER THAN A PRECISE SCALE) IS NAMED FOR GERMAN MINERALOGIST FRIEDRICH MOHS (1773–1839). HE DEVISED THE FOLLOWING LINEAR HARDNESS SCALE, UTILIZING TEN MINERALS ARRANGED IN ORDER OF INCREASING HARDNESS. THE MINERALS ARE EACH ASSIGNED A NUMBER: 1) TALC, 2) GYPSUM, 3) CALCITE, 4) FLUORITE, 5) APATITE, 6) ORTHOCLASE (FELDSPAR), 7) QUARTZ, 8) TOPAZ, 9) CORUNDUM, AND 10) DIAMOND. EACH CLASSIFICATION WILL SCRATCH THE ONE PRECEDING IT, E.G., DIAMOND WILL SCRATCH CORUNDUM.

THE RELATIVE HARDNESS OF ANY PARTICULAR MINERAL IS DETERMINED BY WHICH MINERAL WILL SCRATCH A SPECIMEN. GALENA, FOR INSTANCE, WITH A HARDNESS OF 2.5, SCRATCHES GYPSUM AND WILL BE SCRATCHED BY CALCITE. THERE IS A MUCH GREATER GAP BETWEEN THE HARDNESS OF DIAMOND AND CORUNDUM THAN BETWEEN ANY OTHER OF THE TWO MINERALS LISTED. DIAMOND IS FOUR TIMES HARDER THAN CORUNDUM AND SIX TIMES HARDER THAN TOPAZ.

Furthermore, industrial quantities of gemstones would have been required. But

Egyptologists do not believe that the gemstones that are useful as abrasives existed in ancient Egypt. There are no ancient Egyptian drawings or written descriptions of cutting teeth made of gems. These factors, and the inability of ancient Egyptians to shape the gems, rule out the existence of jewel-tipped saws.

Besides, gemstone teeth would fracture under the great pressure Petrie proposed was needed to force them through granite or other hard rock. Moreover, the Egyptians converted many thousands of tons of hard rock into a myriad of form-fitting blocks and engraved and finely sculpted obelisks, columns, colossi, sarcophagi, statuary, stone dishes, and other items. The surviving artifacts, including building ruins, are a small fraction of the masonry work produced in ancient Egypt.

Numerous dishes and other vessels, made of varieties of hard rock, are Predynastic, dating from a time when it was even more unlikely that gemstone abrasives were imported. The Egyptians had to overcome the natural, protective barriers of their land before the importation of materials became viable. Dangerous, deafening cataracts border Egypt in the south. The parched Libyan Desert stretches out west of Egypt. The formidable Mediterranean Sea is situated to the north, and the vast, barren Sinai Desert borders Egypt to the east. In early times these geographic features isolated and protected Egypt, but these same barriers prevented the mass importation of goods.

According to Petrie and other experts, artifacts exhibit detail more crisp than artisans can achieve with modern diamond drills. Petrie was amazed by Khufu's granite sarcophagus, which still rests in the King's Chamber of the Great Pyramid.[2] A groove cut along the sides of the top of the sarcophagus accommodated a sliding lid, which was long ago removed from the Pyramid. Dowel holes allowed pins to affix the lid. Petrie was astonished when he examined cutting lines on the north end of the sarcophagus.

These lines show that when the sarcophagus was being made, the saw blade ran askew, slanting into the side of the sarcophagus. The artisan had backed his saw out so that he could rectify the angle of his cut. A second cut ran askew two inches lower, showing that the mason had again backed his saw out. These cuts astounded Petrie because they clearly proved to him that the mason sliced through the granite at an extraordinarily rapid rate.

In other words, Petrie recognized that no one could make this kind of a mistake when slowly grinding away at granite with a copper saw and an abrasive. Copper is 3.5 to 4 on the Mohs' hardness scale; Aswan granite is 6-8. Pouring on a constant supply of sharp sand will not produce a rapid wayward cut, given the amount of time and grinding (and continual renewing of sharp sand grains) that is required. The feature clearly goes against the assumptions of Lucas (which are now accepted by Egyptology). Petrie bolstered his argument with his collection of stunning artifacts with features made with sharp, pointed tools that showed no sign of dulling during cutting! Petrie marveled, for instance, at etchings with fine cross sections, measuring a mere 1/100 inch, indicating that the tool that created them had to have ploughed through the granite in a single pass.

We can get a sense of Petrie's amazement by comparing the exhaustive work of the team that operated Denys Stocks' bow drill at Aswan in 2001 to cut a granite core.[3] We can also compare with a 1999 experiment by Stocks involving sarcophagus manufacture.[4] Using tube drills and a great deal of sand, he producing drill holes with considerable effort, and the holes are shown in his report in the sort of even rows expected from such an operation. On the other hand, wayward drill marks showing characteristics of rapid cutting astonished Petrie as he pondered Khufu's sarcophagus.

In another experiment in the 1950s, it required 12 days for Antoine Zuber to cut six crude holes in a granite quarry so he could detach a small chunk of granite with wooden wedges.[5] Other examples are the minor removal of granite, after pounding the quarry floor at Aswan for hours, in the aforementioned experiments performed first by Reginald Engelbach and later by Mark Lehner.

We can also gain an appreciation of Petrie's point of view by considering an eleventh century report by Theophilus concerning how a crystal was cut with an iron lapidary saw:

> If you wish to cut crystal, fix four wooden pins on a bench, with the crystal lying firmly between them. These pins are so arranged that they are joined together in pairs, above and below, so closely that the saw can hardly be drawn between them and can nowhere be deflected. Insert the iron saw and, throwing on sharp sand mixed with water, have two stand by to draw it and to throw on the sand and water without stopping. This is continued until the crystal is cut into two parts.[6]

Returning to Petrie's observations, on the interior of the east side of the sarcophagus, he identified a three-inch-long mark made by a circular drill. He insisted that only a jewel-tipped saw could make this mark, which signified a rapid cut. At Giza and elsewhere, Petrie found cores left over from the drilling of hard stone. Some cores are the leftovers of helical cuts.

Petrie was amazed by the amount of pressure he reckoned must have been applied to the drills to cut through rock so rapidly:

> The great pressure needed to force the drills and saws so rapidly through the hard stones is very surprising; probably a load of at least a ton or two was placed on the 4-inch drills cutting in granite. On the granite core, No. 7, the spiral of the cut sinks 1 inch in the circumference of 6 inches, or 1

> in 60, a rate of ploughing out of the quartz and feldspar which is astonishing.[7]

In his discussion of Khufu's sarcophagus, Petrie proposed the use of jewel-tipped saws some eight feet long to make a clean slice 90 inches long though granite. In recent years machinist Chris Dunn calculated that much more pressure was needed to force a drill through Khufu's granite sarcophagus.[8] He also asserts that much more advanced machinery must have existed, of the type just now beginning to be developed. Dunn and the machinists with whom he consulted find no other way to account for many items, and they prefer this method for making Petrie's granite core number seven, from Khafra's Valley Temple. Notwithstanding the severe historical problems associated with Dunn's proposal, we will consider his work after reviewing the problems with Lucas' proposed abrasion method.

Alfred Lucas argued relentlessly for abrasion methods. He asserted that sand was used to grind down rock. He reckoned that the Egyptians used the sand in conjunction with small hand-held pieces of softer materials, like copper, wood, horn or rope, which were frequently replaced because of wear and tear. Lucas speculated that the repeated grinding of rock surfaces would wear them away until cuts were made.

Lucas' *Ancient Egyptian Materials and Industries* (revised by J.R. Harris) is an Egyptological standard; therefore, his proposed method became more popular than those Petrie proposed. Besides, Lucas' methods are more acceptable to Egyptology because they suit the primitive technological level and materials of ancient Egypt, and even diamond teeth would crumble under the great force Petrie proposed. But Petrie collected many examples that defy the use of abrasives.

The diorite bowls Petrie collected at Giza are examples. As Petrie showed, these bowls bear 4$^{th}$ Dynasty inscriptions made by sharp, pointed instruments:

> These hieroglyphs are incised, with a very free-cutting point; they are not scraped nor ground out, but are ploughed through the diorite, with rough edges to the line. As the lines are only 1/150 inch wide . . . it is evident that the cutting point must have been much harder than quartz; and tough enough not to splinter when so fine an edge was being employed, probably only 1/200 inch wide. Parallel lines are graved only 1/10 inch apart from centre to centre.[9]

Diorite is one of the most difficult types of rocks to cut. It is extremely hard and incredibly tough. The most common variety of diorite used for bowls of the type Petrie described contains feldspar and black hornblende, such that large quantities of corundum (which is similar in hardness to tungsten carbide) is needed to scratch it. Lucas did not believe that the Egyptians of the Pyramid Age or before imported corundum.

There is also the clean helical cut on Petrie's granite core number seven, which he described as follows:

> On the granite core, broken from a drill-hole (No. 7), other features appear, which also can only be explained by the use of fixed jewel points. Firstly, the grooves which run around it form a regular spiral, with no more interruption or waviness than is necessarily produced by the variations in the component crystals; this spiral is truly symmetrical with the axis of the core. In one part a groove can be traced with scarcely an interruption, for a length of four turns. Secondly, the grooves are as deep in the quartz as in the adjacent feldspar, and even rather deeper. If these were in any way produced by loose powder, they would be shallower in the harder substance—quartz; . . . and further, inasmuch as the quartz stands out slightly beyond the feldspar (owing to the latter being worn by general rubbing), the groove was thus left even less in depth on the feldspar than on the quartz. Thus, even if specimens with similarly deep grooves could be produced by a loose powder, the special features of this core would still show that fixed cutting points were the means here employed.[10]

As mentioned, a team led by Denys Stocks operated a bow drill and used abrasive sand to very gradually cut a core from Aswan granite. The results do not match the features of Petrie's core number seven, which shows a groove running a few rotations around the core and equaling three feet of cutting with no wear on the tool. It is to be expected that a team laboriously operating a bow drill and continuously applying a large amount of quartz sand will not produce a helical grove that looks like it was cut with a few clean turns of a drill.

Quartz is an essential component of granite, the latter of which was used on a massive scale in ancient Egypt. Quartz sand and/or sharp quartz shards can be used to gradually abrade quartz. A pointed quartz shard can be used to sheer across a piece of quartzite to gradually wear away the quartzite. A problem with the system is that the worn quartz shard must be constantly replaced. Another problem is that quartz must be crushed to obtain sharp shards, and the process of crushing will produce microfractures that will cause many of the shards to break during the scribing process. The milky or cloudy form of quartz, which allows one to see fractures, is full of a multitude of small air cavities and moisture that produce the opaque appearance. Petrie may have considered the structural weaknesses inherent to producing quartz shards, because he did not include them on his list of potential cutting points. Quartz shards will not reproduce the features Petrie collected, showing the rapid advancement of a pointed tool. The system is not practical for producing 60-foot-high monolithic statues and tall, monolithic temple columns.

Quartz shards rapidly abrade when cutting quartz, so the shard quickly becomes rounded off and is no longer sharp. Cutting teeth must be far harder and remain sharp to be effective, as Petrie asserted. The Egyptians possessed flint, which is harder than quartz. In 1956 Antoine Zuber showed the problems with using flint shards, which are brittle and break when hard blows are applied. Cutting with flint shards leaves raised ridges when the edges of the shards chip. Flint shards do not produce the clean tool sweeps, like those on artifacts described below, which show no evidence of the tool chipping or becoming dull although the cut can extend up to 20 feet long!

Petrie collected a number of fragments of artifacts exhibiting distinct saw cuts. His collection includes fragments from the aforementioned large basalt platform east of the Great Pyramid. Petrie collected a slice of diorite exhibiting equidistant and regular grooves running in circular arcs that are parallel to one another. In other words, masons cut this sample with a circular saw.

One of Petrie's impressive specimens is part of a drill hole in diorite 14 inches in circumference. Seventeen equidistant grooves look like successive rotations of the same cutting point. Thus, what looks like a single cut through diorite is 20 feet in length! Clarke and Engelbach attended a lecture by Petrie in 1883 at the Anthropological Institute and described three of the most impressive artifacts. They described this particular cut:

> The second specimen is part of a drill-hole in diorite. The hole has been [cut] 4½ inches in diameter, or 14 inches in circumference. As seventeen equidistant grooves appear to be due to successive rotations of the same cutting-point, a single cut is thus 20 feet in length.[11]

Here is the way Clarke and Engelbach described another striking artifact:

> The third specimen--a piece of diorite—shows a series of grooves, each ploughed out to a depth of 1/100 inch at a single cut without any irregularity of or 'starting' of the tool.[12]

They also contemplated Petrie's granite core number seven, which they observed shows that ". . .in one part a single groove may be traced around the core for a length. . . equal to three feet." Petrie had pointed out to them that there is no difference in quality in the cut, as there would be if the cutting point had started to get dull or fail.

Petrie and Lucas debated the manufacture of these and other matters over their long careers, with the result being that, in general, Egyptology accepted Lucas' abrasion method for cutting artifacts. Many Egyptologists have grown accustomed to accepting that many artifacts may remain unexplained. Some other Egyptologists try to explain them away even though the items have not been replicated using the means proposed by Egyptology. Others take the scientific approach of remaining neutral, because they lack appropriate technical training to make a determination.

Denys Stocks has created some stone objects with simple tools. For instance, Stocks created a limestone vessel. He has not made one of diorite, and diorite vases with uniformly thick walls make them extremely challenging items to re-create with any kind of grinding equipment.

The results of some other drilling experiments did not work in favor of Lucas' proposal about grinding with abrasive sand.[13] Experiments by L. Gorelick and J. Gwinnett showed that flint drills and quartz sand did not reproduce clean, concentric cutting lines, a series of circular lines that are all parallel with a common center. The interiors of shallow hard-stone bowls in museums exhibit such clean, concentric cutting lines. These crisp, circular cuts represent places where the angle of the cutting tips changed as the items being made were turned during production.

Gorelick and Gwinnett tested a variety of abrasives to establish which were capable of making clean, concentric lines on granite objects. For example, some sarcophagi have a hole at each end, probably used for attaching lids. Gorelick and Gwinnett made casts of the concentric cutting lines on the holes in the two-ton lid of an Old Kingdom granite sarcophagus in the Brooklyn Museum thought to have belonged to a prince named Akhet-Hotep.

They used a slab of similar red granite for their drilling experiment. They tested with and without lubricants, using a copper rod and a copper tube along with abrasives. The abrasives they tested were beach sand and a variety of crushed materials, including quartz, silicon carbide, garnet, emery, corundum, and diamond. Their drill operated at a constant rotation speed of 1,000 r.p.m. They also did some drilling with a brace and bit, moving in an oscillating manner. Similar to the experiments by Denys Stocks, Gorelick and Gwinnett tested with a bow drill, as well.

In all of their tests, the abrasives known in ancient Egypt failed on the hard granite they used. Quartz sand did not produce clean, concentric cutting lines, when used wet or dry. Lucas' idea that sand will attach to copper and behave as set teeth did not hold up in their experimentation. Chipped flint, fashioned sandstone and quartzite failed to produce clean, concentric lines when used both wet and dry.

Their experiments showed that the extent of cutting was negligible with the sandstone and quartzite drills, although quartzite is very hard rock. A flint drill was also ineffective on granite.

The only abrasives that produced comparable concentric cutting lines in the granite were powders of emery, corundum, and diamond. Egyptologists do not believe that these materials were available in ancient Egypt.

Egyptologists do not think that opal, ruby, or sapphire were available, either. Emery (corundum) was found in Nubia and on the Grecian Islands, but Alfred Lucas always opted for quartz sand as an effective abrasive, because he did not think that emery/corundum was imported. He indicated:

> Although it is often stated that emery was employed in ancient Egypt as an abrasive with drills and saws for working hard stones and, although some abrasive powder must have been used, it has never been proved that the material was emery, which in my opinion was most improbable.[14]

No word for emery appeared in the Egyptian vocabulary until Ptolemaic times (the ancient Greek word for emery was "smeris"). Emery is indigenous to the Grecian Cycladic islands in the Aegean Sea, appearing mainly on the island of Naxos. However, no emery from Naxos or anywhere else has ever been found in the ruins of ancient Egypt. Also, the use of emery cannot explain artifacts that exhibit rapid cutting, including sharp-point etchings in diorite.

Lucas was right to think that quartz sand would abrade granite. Denys Stocks showed that long, hard labor can produce some results with sand used in conjunction with tube drills. But producing and publishing results that can be shown to match artifacts made of granite and harder stones is an entirely different matter. Petrie's words come to mind: "Modern diamond drill cores are clumsy and smudged work when compared with the Egyptian cores."

Granite beams with zigzagged joints, granite statuary, granite colossi capturing the subtle curvatures of the human body and weighing over 1,000 tons, granite obelisks with crisp intaglio of better quality than can be achieved with diamond drills, arched granite ceilings over crypts, tall, round, monolithic temple columns made with hard rock, hard-stone vessels with walls of uniform thickness or that taper to a paper-thin edge all invite us to consider a more sophisticated technology.

The experiments by Gorelick and Gwinnett and those by Denys Stocks help illuminate this masonry quandary. Gorelick and Gwinnett showed the problems of re-creating a feature that is much easier to achieve than some Petrie collected and many thousands of others. Denys Stocks' crew ground long and hard into granite in an attempt to show how ancient Egyptians made sarcophagi and other objects. However, the features produced do not match the striking examples—like the rapid cuts through granite Petrie observed in Khufu's sarcophagus or the cores he and machinists have pondered. The paradox is clear and unanswered by experiments conducted with standard rock-cutting methods.

# Chapter 11

# Artifacts Defy Modern Reproduction

In the 1980s Denys Stocks performed experiments showing that both ancient and modern metal chisels are unsuitable for working certain types of hard stone.[1] With this in mind, Stocks theorized that the ancient Egyptians must have used stone tools to dress hard rocks. He proposes that the ancient masons used tubular copper drills with large amounts of abrasive sand and a tremendous amount of labor to hollow out granite sarcophagi. Stocks experimented with rose-granite sarcophagus manufacture and theorized that the sarcophagus in the Great Pyramid was made with the kinds of tools he used. But the abrasive method is extremely slow. The method Stocks used fails to address the cutting lines on Khufu's sarcophagus, which astonished Petrie because the granite was cut through extremely rapidly. These cutting lines, and those Petrie showed were made with sharp points, demonstrate that Old Kingdom Egyptians did not use the slow methods employed by Stocks. Instead, the highly efficient Late Stone Age means used afforded rapid cutting. It stands to reason that the rapid cutting was possible only because of the recovered ancient technology I explain in Volume 2 of this book. When all of the facts are considered, nothing else makes any sense.

Stocks' masonry theories sharply contrast with those of machinist Christopher Dunn.[2] Stocks has considerable experience working with simple tools and abrasives. Dunn has long experience in advanced manufacturing methods, including laser processing and electrical-discharge machining. In 1995 Dunn examined a number of Egyptian sarcophagi dating from the Old and New Kingdoms. His cursory examination left him stunned and unshakably convinced of the existence of advanced machining in ancient Egypt.

Arriving at Giza, Dunn set to work, but the King's Chamber of the Great Pyramid was too crowded for him to examine Khufu's sarcophagus. Undaunted, he went to Khafra's pyramid nearby, which attracts less tourist traffic. Dunn was able to enter its granite sarcophagus. He had with him a flashlight and a parallel, a tool used to test the flatness of a surface. It is a piece of steel ground extremely flat, measuring roughly a quarter of an inch thick and six inches long. Inside Khafra's sarcophagus, Dunn was amazed. At his GizaPower Web site he describes what he found:

> The first object I inspected was the sarcophagus inside the second (Khafra's) pyramid on the Giza Plateau. I climbed inside the box and, with a flashlight and the parallel, was astounded to find the surface on the inside of the box perfectly smooth and perfectly flat. Placing the edge of the parallel against the surface I shone my flashlight behind it. No light came through the interface. No matter where I moved the parallel, vertically, horizontally, sliding it along as one would a gage on a precision surface plate I couldn't detect any deviation from a perfectly flat surface.

Although he would not be able to determine whether or not the surfaces he was measuring are bowed with his six-inch parallel, he says that the several internal and external areas he measured exhibited extreme flatness to within .0002 inch.

Dunn recognized that it would not be possible to perform this masonry work by hand on hard rock. The task would be complex and difficult even with modern machinery. This sarcophagus is not the product of the techniques used by Denys Stocks. Stocks would not likely be able to achieve flatness of .0002 inch over a radius of more than a few inches.

Dunn was more wonderstruck by a sarcophagus he was able to measure in the Serapeum. The Serapeum, located at Saqqara, is a remarkable subterranean tomb enlarged during the New Kingdom by the administration of Pharaoh Ramses the Great. Its many large granite and granodiorite (an intermediate rock type between granite and quartz-containing diorite) sarcophagi contained the funerary remains of Apis bulls, the male counterparts of the sacred Isis cows. A few of the sarcophagi are limestone. These great stone sarcophagi weigh at least 65 tons each. The added weight of their lids brings the total to about 100 tons per sarcophagus. They each stand about 11 feet high, 13 feet long, and 7½ feet wide. When French Egyptologist Auguste Mariette (1821–1881) discovered and excavated the Serapeum, he recorded 24 sarcophagi still in position.[3] The heaviest weighs about 70 tons. Each sarcophagus sits in its own sunken rock-cut niche, and these niches form rows along the bedrock walls.

Christopher Dunn reported that the surfaces he was able to examine are extremely flat. He moved his parallel in many positions against the stone surfaces. When he shined a flashlight against his parallel, no light came through to its other side. Dunn was able to make a careful comparison between a sarcophagus and its lid. He found both to be perfectly flat. With its heavy lid in place, the air between the two stone surfaces was pushed out, producing a very effective seal. Dunn's mind was staggered as he reckoned the technical difficulties of producing both a lid and a sarcophagus to fit in this ultraprecise, conforming way (the conforming fit brings to mind the blocks making up the King's Chamber of the Great Pyramid and many other examples). He reckoned the task to be vastly more difficult than producing the

48.

W.M.F. PETRIE FOUND THIS BASALT CORE, WHICH IS NOW IN THE PETRIE MUSEUM IN LONDON.

SOME ANCIENT CORES WERE VERY LARGE. THE CRYPTS OF TOMBS AT ZOSER'S 3RD DYNASTY STEP PYRAMID AT SAQQARA DISPLAY CEILING BEAMS MADE WITH GRANITE, WITH ROUND HOLES IN THEM. THESE MATCHING ROUND GRANITE CORE PLUGS ARE UP TO SIX FEET LONG AND WEIGH THREE TONS EACH. THERE IS NO EVIDENCE OF A BOW DRILL OF ANY SIZE FROM THIS PERIOD, AND CORES SHOWING ONLY LONG, CLEAN TOOL SWEEPS DEFY THE USE OF SUCH INSTRUMENTS.

PHOTOGRAPH BY JON BODSWORTH

surfaces of the sarcophagus itself.

With an appreciation that could only come from a long career in advanced machining, Dunn examined with amazement a number of ancient Egyptian ruins and artifacts during his trip that are taken for granted by Egyptologists these days. Dunn found several that defy the conventional explanations.

49.

Granite Core No. 7 discovered by W.M.F. Petrie and now in the Petrie Museum, in London. The groove can be traced for three feet around the core. Petrie pointed out that there is no difference in quality in the cut, as there would be if the cutting point started to get dull.

Petrie, who worked with machinists to try to understand artifacts that puzzled him, observed that, "Modern diamond drill cores are clumsy and smudged work when compared to the Egyptian cores."

Photograph by Jon Bodsworth

After returning home, Dunn conferred with four different manufacturers in the U.S. that precision-cut granite. None possessed equipment capable of producing a comparable monolithic sarcophagus. They could not make a custom-fitted lid with a comparably tight fit, either. The best the companies could offer was granite slabs bolted together to form a box. This is an example of an artifact that defies modern replication, just as are the Colossi of Memnon and the 1,000-tons and heavier statues of Ramses II and long, clean sweeps through artifacts with no sign of dulling of the tool used. As mentioned, by comparison, the sarcophagus worked by Stocks does not exhibit extreme flatness of .0002 inch along large wall areas, and he did not attempt to produce a custom lid that would render his sarcophagus airtight.

Dunn interested some of his peers in the machine industry in contemplating the enigmas posed by Petrie's granite helical-cut core sample number seven, described above in Petrie's own words. After considerable pondering, Dunn and his peers concluded that highly advanced machining must have existed in ancient Egypt.

Petrie's granite core number seven mystified these machinists, particularly the great speed at which the drill had to have penetrated the granite. Donald Rahn, of Rahn Granite Surface Plate Company, in Dayton, Ohio, who works with diamond drills, offered some information. He advised Christopher Dunn that diamond drills rotating at 900 r.p.m. penetrate granite at a rate of one inch in five minutes. With this information, Dunn calculated that the ancient Egyptian masons drilled Petrie's granite core sample number seven at a feed rate that is 500 times greater!

After much contemplation, Dunn came up with an explanation for the enigmatic features of Petrie's granite core number seven from Khafra's Valley Temple. Knowing that Egyptologists frown upon ideas that defy the established history of Egypt, Dunn hoped to gain supporting opinions from his peers. Dunn continually challenged them with aspects of the problem.

Finally, one of them suggested the same method Dunn had in mind for producing the features of Petrie's artifact. The method they envisioned (ultrasonic machining) did not exist in Petrie's day. They reckoned that *only* an ultrasonic toolbit can tear away at granite rapidly enough. The ultrasonic toolbit vibrates at 19,000 to 25,000 cycles per second, and its use satisfies this anomaly of Petrie's sample.

Dunn subsequently engaged in a debate with an opponent named Ralph Ellis, after which Dunn suspended his assertion that only ultrasonic machining could have produced Petrie's core number seven. However, Dunn still favors ultrasonic machining over any other method. He also recognizes that there are a great many artifacts, like the sarcophagus in the Serapeum with the airtight lid, that are far more difficult to explain than Petrie's core number seven.

Petrie, who also worked with machinists to try to solve the enigma of the production of certain artifacts, described some with details more crisp than can be achieved with diamond drills. Petrie's words merit repeating: "Modern diamond drill cores are clumsy and smudged work when compared with the Egyptian cores." Although Dunn's theories defy ancient Egyptian history as carefully established by Egyptology, we cannot ignore the calculated rate (calculated by measuring the pitch of points on a descending straight line that intersects the helical groove on the core at 1/10 inch per revolution) of descent of the tubular drill that cut core number seven:

Dunn calculated that an Egyptian artisan cut through the granite at a feed rate 500 times greater than possible with today's diamond drills.

Despite the attempts by detractors to explain away Petrie's core number seven, Dunn maintains that the helical groove cut into it is significant and amazing. Dunn set up an appointment at the Petrie Museum in London and carefully examined the core firsthand. He observed that the cut is indeed a continuous helix with some interruptions that were continued along the same average helical path.

The surfaces Dunn measured on interior and exterior sarcophagi walls, flat to .0002 inch, pose a real challenge to the simple methods Stocks has tested. Stocks recognizes that the instruments the ancient Egyptians possessed could test flatness only to .01 inch. I interviewed a number of stone cutters about the problem, and they all advised me that producing a flatness of .0002 inch along a few inches can be achieved with a great deal of work. However, because of their appreciation for the problem, they were all astonished when I explained to them that Dunn reports large areas of wall surface on granite sarcophagi to exhibit the extreme flatness of .0002 inch.

Although primitive tools—in combination with no other technology—are inadequate for producing the pyramids and a myriad of smaller artifacts, the real means of production negates the need for advanced machining in ancient Egypt. In short, we need not defy the technological level established by Egyptology to explain the remarkable artifacts described in these pages. Thus, assuming Dunn's calculations of the rapid rate of granite cutting are correct, the ancient Egyptians possessed a simple means of making their impressive artifacts that is 500 times more efficient than cutting hard granite with today's granite cutting technology. Assuming Dunn's flatness measurements are correct, the Egyptians were also producing a degree of extreme flatness over large surface areas that far surpasses today's industrial standard.

Indeed, a myriad of artifacts dating back to the Archaic Period (c. 3000–2649 B.C.) exhibit features that challenge modern stone-cutting means. Egyptologist Walter B. Emery presented stunning pieces in his *Archaic Egypt: Culture and Civilizations in Egypt Five Thousand Years Ago*. Among them was a leaf-shaped schist dish dating to the middle of the 1st Dynasty. An inscribed schist statue belonging to the 2nd Dynasty Pharaoh Kha-sekhem is from Hieraconopolis. Kha-sekhem was rendered seated on his throne wearing his ceremonial robe and the crown of Upper Egypt. Its base depicts rows of slain enemies.

Among other examples, a cup made of schist, with a pink limestone base, is from the 1st Dynasty tomb of Queen Her-nit at Saqqara. A diorite spoon dates to the middle of the 1st Dynasty. Fragments of a leaf-shaped schist dish date to the middle of the 1st Dynasty. This wonderful dish is incised in relief, exhibiting the delicate raised pattern of the veins of a leaf. An exquisite schist dish shaped as a reed basket dates from the 2nd Dynasty. Although hard, schist is brittle and will easily break along its foliations into thin, flaky plates. But the intricate dish is marvelously detailed. All the

**50. PRINCESS NOFRET: THE CRYSTAL EYES IN THIS STATUE OF PRINCESS NOFRET ARE MASTERPIECE EXAMPLES OF THE 'FOLLOWING-EYE' EFFECT. PHOTOGRAPH BY JON BODSWORTH**

symmetric details of a reed basket appear in high relief. It has perfectly formed, delicate carrying handles.[4]

The Petrie Museum in London exhibits a sawed fragment of a diorite palette with a beveled edge and engraved line. The piece (Museum Number UC2529) dates to the Neolithic Period and was found in the Faiyum. The Petrie Museum exhibits an engraved diorite fragment (number UC6560), perhaps part of a 12$^{th}$ Dynasty statue, found at Lahun, a town located at the entrance of the Faiyum. Another diorlte piece found at the same site (Petrie Museum number UC6539) dates to the Dynastic Period and exhibits a hieroglyphic etching. A diorite fragment from a bowl is inscribed with the name "Khufu" (Petrie Museum number UC11758).

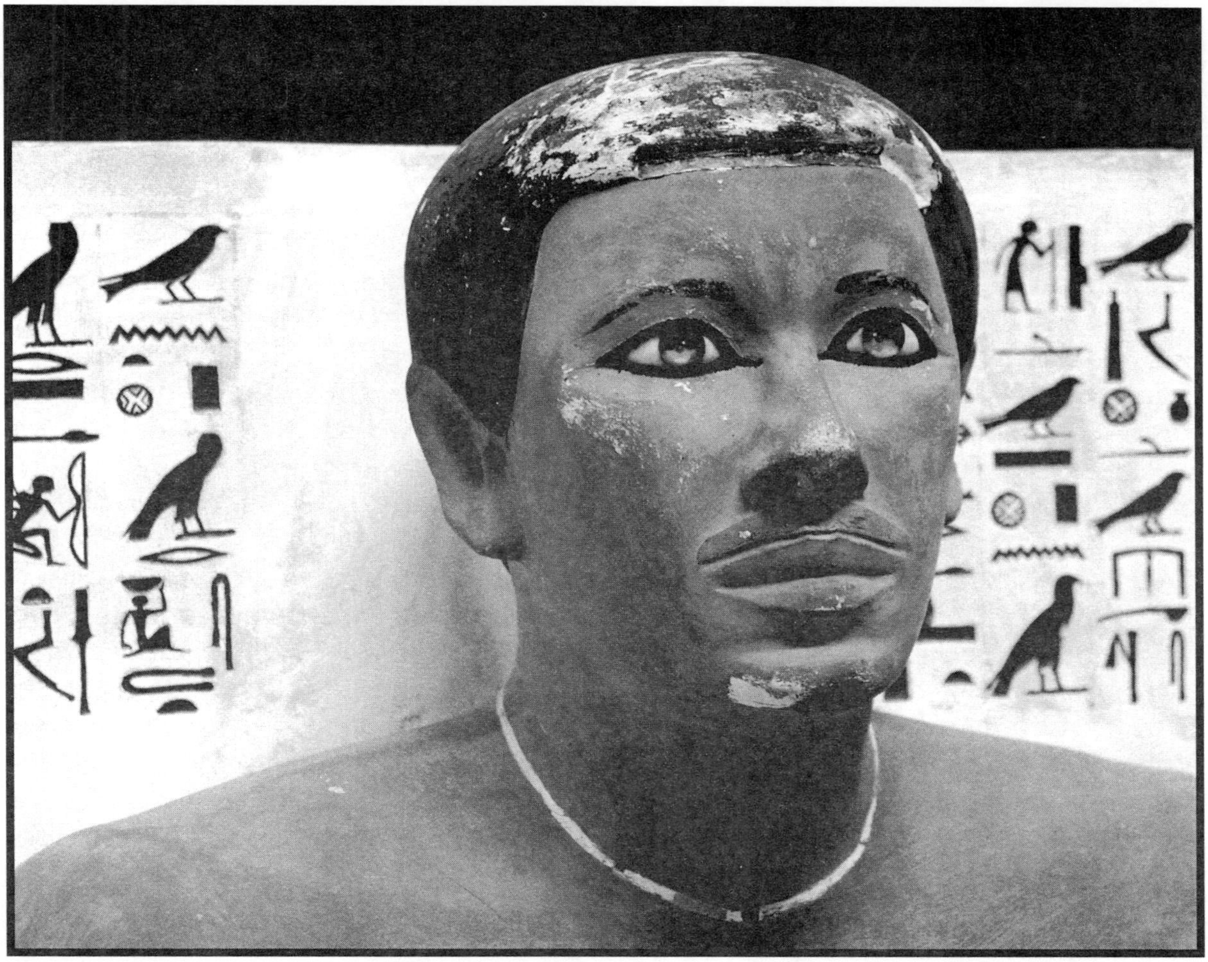

51. PRINCE RAHOTEP: THE LIFE-SIZE STATUE OF PRINCE RAHOTEP EXHIBITS MASTERPIECE EXAMPLES OF THE 'FOLLOWING EYE' EFFECT. THE EYES ARE MADE WITH STUNNING, CLEAR CRYSTAL LENSES. PHOTOGRAPH BY JON BODSWORTH

A small black diorite statue of a Theban priest of Amun dates to the end of the 25th Dynasty. Less than 20 inches high, it is now in the Boston Museum of Fine Arts. In the Louvre in Paris a statue of the god Amun and Pharaoh Tutankhamun (now better known as King Tut) dates to about 1347–1337 B.C. This statue is seven feet tall and made of diorite.

In the Cairo Museum, stone beads dating to the Middle Kingdom (c. 2040–1640 B.C.) have remarkably small threading holes.[5] Some stone beads measure as small as 0.023 inch in diameter, with smaller threading holes. The smallest bead holes produced by Denys Stocks are much larger, measuring 1 mm.

I corresponded with a beadmaker at the top of his field. Although he does not want to be named or involved in the controversy over enigmatic artifacts, because so many wild claims have been made, he felt confident that he could reproduce the .023 beads with smaller holes if he could use modern means. But he was not willing to take up the challenge assuming he could use only ancient methods. The best ancient Egyptian beadmaking drill was flint. In short, while drilling beads is feasible with flint drills, certain examples, like those tiny beads mentioned above, suggest the use of a different technology. Any drill used to cut into rock like carnelian or lapis must be tough enough at the tiny hole size (less than .023 inch) not to splinter or fracture.

Certain Old Kingdom statues exhibit remarkable examples of eyes so realistic and ingeniously crafted that they give the impression of following the eye movements of the onlooker. Striking examples are the eyes of the 4$^{th}$ Dynasty statues of Prince Rahotep and his wife Princess Nofret (c. 2600–2575 B.C.), found in their twin mastabas near the Meidum pyramid. Like most others with this extraordinary form of eyes, they are ka statues (the ka having been considered the body double that lingered on in tomb statuary or otherwise inhabited the tomb).

An analysis was conducted on a number of such uncanny eyes by optical specialist Jay Enoch, of the School of Optometry at U.C. Berkeley, who consulted with several other specialists for his research project. The specimens investigated included the masterpiece eyes of the famous 4$^{th}$ or 5$^{th}$ Dynasty seated scribe (E-3023) in the Louvre. The lenses appear to be polished rock crystal (they are considered to be either alpha silica or fused silica). All of the finest examples are beautifully constructed and demonstrate very good knowledge of the anatomy of the human eye. Jay Enoch was astonished by the complex technological achievement dating to such early history. The early dynastic, unique schematic eyes capable of the "following movement" are unprecedented in all of ancient and modern history.

# Chapter 12

# A Technological Riddle

During the Pyramid Age, before hard metal tools were introduced in Egypt, grandiose structures abounded, all made of massive medium-hard to hard blocks. But as the centuries passed, and as better tools were introduced, art and architecture fell into a serious decline that worsened as time passed. There are impressive exceptions, like the 60-foot-high quartzite Colossi of Memnon, built during the 18th Dynasty, but they are relatively few in number. Egyptologists cannot explain this paradoxical architectural apex and decline.

The overview I present here illustrates the scope of this riddle. When only primitive stone tools and abrasives were available, the most ancient masons made great quantities of superb objects. In some cases, the best modern tools will not enable their replication. In Predynastic times, artisans used extremely hard rock types to fashion many thousands of the most perfect vessels in history.[1]

In the 1st Dynasty, the first stone pavement appeared in the tomb of Pharaoh Den at Abydos, in northern Upper Egypt.[2] It is made of slabs of granite, each a little more than eight feet long and only about five inches thick.

After the 2nd Dynasty, numerous hard-stone pavements were made of hard limestone, basalt, granite, or quartzite. Granite pavements are fairly common in Old Kingdom buildings.[3]

At the apex of Egyptian architecture, master pyramid builders of the 4th Dynasty used medium-hard and hard rock on an unprecedented scale. They built the only remaining wonder of the world: the Great Pyramid.

After the Pyramid Age, pyramids were built increasingly smaller, although Egypt was very prosperous in the 5th Dynasty. Egypt's economy remained stable until the end of the 6th Dynasty.[4] By the 12th Dynasty, the last Egyptian pyramids were built. They are made of mud-brick rather than stone. Most are mounds of rubble today.[5]

By 800 years after the Great Pyramid was built, a hard form of bronze became available in Egypt. Even so, the monuments of this period pale in comparison with the Great Pyramids. Architecture prospered during the New Kingdom, especially during the 18th and 19th Dynasties. But most constructions were built of relatively small, soft sandstone blocks. Masons also made some temples by hollowing out very soft sandstone cliffs, rather than moving large building blocks. Some large statues were made in situ by sculpting soft sandstone cliffs so that the large statues did not have to be moved at all.

The severe architectural decline that set in long before, after the Pyramid Age, was steadily worsening. As mentioned, the quartzite Colossi of Memnon made during the New Kingdom are exceptions to this trend, as are the 1,000-ton and heavier statues of Ramses II. Egyptology has no explanation for the continuing architectural decline. The Egyptians had bronze and even iron, but with few exceptions, the Theban monuments do not compare to the fabulous monuments built a millennium earlier.

We arrive at a dramatic statistic when we compare the volume of stone consumed by the Old and New Kingdoms. Pyramid Age workers used millions of massive blocks in a single monument. Khufu's Great Pyramid, consisting of about 2.3 million blocks, was followed by that of Khafra, the Second Great Pyramid at Giza. Khafra's pyramid incorporates about two million blocks and is about 50 feet shorter than the Great Pyramid. Pharaoh Snofru was the most ambitious builder, using more stone for his two pyramids collectively than are incorporated into Khufu's Great Pyramid.

Compare the collective volume of these pyramids with New Kingdom constructions: Pharaoh Ramses II's grandiose architectural presence appears at about half of ancient Egypt's habitation sites. For his great many architectural accomplishments, works intended to renew Egypt's splendor, he was one of the few pharaohs deified during his lifetime.[6] But the total amount of rock used during Ramses' ambitious 65-year reign pales in comparison with the amount found in the Great Pyramid.

During the 18th Dynasty, Pharaoh Amenhotep III glorified Thebes, giving it the monumental beauty of a great capital city. He, too, was deified during his lifetime for this accomplishment.[7] Some other pharaohs also have impressive building records. But all of the Theban architecture from the New Kingdom down to the Roman occupation of Egypt—an expanse of about 1,500 years—incorporated less stone than the Great Pyramids. By contrast, the four greatest pyramids were built in only about 60 years. They include the Great Pyramids of Khufu, Khafra and two built for Snofru.

Rainer Stadelmann, director of the German Archaeological Institute in Cairo, estimated that 4th Dynasty workers consumed almost 318 million cubic feet of limestone to build pyramids.[8] Compare this figure with the approximate volume of stone in Theban constructions. According to geologist Francoise Michel de Roziere of the Napoleonic Egyptian Expedition, the total volume of Theban constructions must have amounted to about 141 million cubic feet of sandstone.[9] His estimate includes buildings and their foundations, floors and external architectural features, as well as roads, piers and watercourses. He excluded the extensive Nubian structures south of Thebes and demolished Theban constructions, because blocks of the latter group were likely recycled. All of the Theban sandstone constructions of the New Kingdom,

52. A LITHOGRAPH OF THE ABU SIMBEL TEMPLE MADE BY ARTIST DAVID ROBERTS (1796-1894) IN 1938, LONG BEFORE THE MONUMENT WAS CUT UP AND MOVED BY A TEAM FROM THE UNITED NATIONS.

Late Period, and Ptolemaic Period—together spanning 1,500 years—do not equal half the amount of stone used during the Pyramid Age (the 80-year span in which all of the Great Pyramids arose). The rapid construction of the Great Pyramid alerts us to a highly efficient technology that was gradually lost.

The dramatic paradox comes into sharper focus when we consider the materials and structural designs of New Kingdom Theban and later work. Middle and New Kingdom workers mostly used smaller building blocks than did their illustrious predecessors, with few exceptions. For instance, Ramses II added to the extensive Theban Temple at Luxor. The first pylon at Luxor he built is about 88 feet high, and its towers are 98 feet wide. But the bulk of the temple, and all of its external features, are made with interlocking sandstone blocks that are small compared with the blocks of the Great Pyramid. The Temple of Karnak, the most important in ancient Thebes, is adorned with 122 temple columns that tower 70 feet. These giant columns, like the bulk of the temple itself, are made of relatively small interlocking sandstone blocks.

The core masonry of pylons II, III, and IX of the Karnak Temple was built with blocks taken from earlier structures. New Kingdom workers often demolished Middle Kingdom temples to get blocks for building new temples. Builders even expropriated and recycled more ancient statues.

In later Ptolemaic times the Greek pharaoh Ptolemy XI (c. 112–51 B.C.) began constructing the imposing Hathor Temple at Dendera. The Roman Emperor Augustus Caesar later completed it. The Temple is almost 300 feet long and about 135 feet at its widest point. Its enormous portico is supported by 24 columns, each 50 feet high and more than 22 feet in circumference. But the structures are made of sandstone blocks that cannot compare in size to the large blocks in Old Kingdom superstructures.[10]

New Kingdom and later artisans built mostly with the soft sandstone of Egypt's southern quarries. The most commonly used variety, which is abundant in the Theban region, is soft enough to abrade with one's fingernails (which are 2.2 on the Mohs' hardness scale). The famous Abu Simbel Temple of Ramses II is a good example of this type of soft rock. His masons hollowed the Temple from a very soft sandstone cliff. Between 1964 and 1966 a United Nations team cut up and moved the Temple to save it from the rising waters of Lake Nasser. Their task was complicated by the tendency of the rock to crumble. Workers had to cut very deeply into the fragile cliff to obtain masses strong enough to tolerate transportation. It was necessary to inject the sandstone with resin to stabilize it so that they could cut the temple blocks into units weighing up to 30 tons each.[11]

Although there are extensive hard limestone mountains at two sites in the Theban area, few limestone buildings were erected in the vicinity. Instead of using this hard, local limestone, the Egyptians of this era transported the softest limestone of Tura, located hundreds of miles to the north.

Soft sandstone was the preferred material for construction, although a hard form of bronze was available in the New Kingdom. Even iron was available on a very limited scale.

Limestone casing blocks appear in only a few royal tombs of the early 18th Dynasty.[12] Most New Kingdom tomb interiors were coated with mud plaster.[13] Compare interior walls of Old Kingdom tombs. Made of limestone, they are generally fully or partially lined with hard granite. Old and Middle Kingdom temples, especially those of 4th and 5th Dynasty Mortuary Temples, were usually lined with hard stone.[14]

A description by Dieter Arnold provides a good idea of the poor quality of most New Kingdom Theban masonry work:

> Close jointing was frequently neglected, however, especially in the huge buildings of the New Kingdom, where the stone broke easily during

> handling or not enough time was left for more careful work. The results are gaping joints and crevices along the front faces of blocks, which had to be hidden by extensive use of mortar. In buildings of such irregular and neglected joining, one cannot see how the builders could have planned the joint position.[15]

The riddle of Egypt's severe and permanent architectural decline cannot be explained by a shortage of stone. Limestone and granite regions were never exhausted of suitable building stone. As mentioned, New Kingdom artisans did not take advantage of the hard limestone in their nearby Theban mountain ranges.

A labor shortage cannot explain the riddle. Large task forces are known to have existed, having carried out military campaigns and civilian programs during the New Kingdom and later. An example is the huge task force Pharaoh Ramses II organized for his military campaigns. Masses of foreigners crowded into Egypt's northern cities during Ramses II's reign and were drafted into his fighting armies and labor forces.[16]

We cannot assume that the answer is that far more men were set to work on pyramids than on later constructions. Densely packing workers produces highly counterproductive conditions, since people cannot work effectively when they are packed elbow to elbow. Teams of densely packed men pulling blocks up slick ramps would result in hazardous conditions. Because of friction and other factors, elevating massive blocks to great heights requires more manpower than building the smaller New Kingdom structures with relatively small blocks.

A shortage of wealth is not the answer. The 18th Dynasty began with the expulsion of the Hyksos invaders from northern Egypt. During the 18th Dynasty, Egypt evolved from a fractured, occupied nation to become a vast, mighty and exceedingly wealthy empire. Vassal countries paid tribute to Egypt with all kinds of treasures and goods to assure peace and acquire political favors. Nevertheless, soft sandstone monuments, made of relatively small building units, characterize this period of triumph in Egypt's New Kingdom capital city and its environs.

To summarize, the archaeological record clearly shows the problem. Stone Age tools afforded the world's greatest architecture and a myriad of hard-stone artifacts, many of which defy reproduction today. As history progressed, Egypt produced increasingly fewer masonry masterpieces. We should expect that architecture would have flourished with the advent of strong metal tools. But the Bronze and Iron Ages ushered in a long architectural era characterized by relatively small, soft sandstone blocks and limestone blocks expropriated from much earlier structures.

During the 18th Dynasty, artisans produced the Colossi of Memnon and several tall granite obelisks, but the amount of hard stone consumed to build these structures is vastly smaller than that of Old Kingdom constructions. During the 19th Dynasty, a number of pyramids were restored with limestone, and some impressive constructions were built in northern Egypt, perhaps by artisans who inherited the special ancestral knowledge that had given Egypt its architectural splendor in the distant past. But the Theban structures are characterized by relatively small sandstone blocks. When hard stone was employed, it was usually reserved for smaller objects like sarcophagi and other tomb furnishings.

How can we explain this technological riddle? The reasonable explanation is that some kind of highly efficient technology was known. Before Egypt became a nation, Neolithic people took advantage of this special technology to make basalt objects and diorite vessels. Its use gradually increased; therefore, by the time Egypt became more organized and prosperous, the labor force used it on an industrial scale to build the Great Pyramids. The use of this special technology gradually declined. This decline is quite apparent, as pyramids were less well built and increasingly smaller as time went on. The decline continued over the centuries; therefore, great masonry works became an exception. Eventually, the technology was lost.

# Chapter 13

# The Trouble With Ramps

To build the Great Pyramid, workers raised more than two million blocks by means of an enormous ramp that rose to nearly 500 feet—so the entrenched theory of pyramid construction holds. The ramp was supposedly made of stone rubble cemented with clay. To ease friction when elevating blocks, workers surfaced their ramps with clay. So states the ramp theory advanced by architect Somers Clarke and archaeologist Reginald Engelbach in their classic book titled *Ancient Egyptian Masonry* (1930). For more than a half century, this was the most authoritative book on ancient Egyptian building. For lack of a better system in keeping with the primitive technological level, ramp theories have been at the forefront of reckoning pyramid construction.[1] But Clarke and Engelbach cautioned that their deductions may require considerable modification.

Engineers have since advanced several problems with ramp theories, and these problems have never been resolved. Consequently, some Egyptologists are beginning to recognize that long-held ramp theories are not workable. Dieter Arnold mentioned some problems:

> . . . ramps could not always be used—for example, at the upper parts of pyramids the enormous quantities of materials consumed and the static problems due to such accumulations probably prevented their use.[2]

Arnold rejected the ramps theories proposed for building the Great Pyramid:

> The type of ramp used for the construction of the Cheops Pyramid has been the subject of countless studies. They rarely take into account, however, that we do not have the slightest indication of the kind of ramp or ramp systems used for this pyramid. These studies also forget that traces of such ramps have actually been recorded from other pyramids. . . . For these reasons, we have to dismiss all theoretical systems so far proposed as pure imagination.[3]

In the 1980s, English master builder Peter Hodges successfully argued that the Great Pyramid would not exist if its construction depended on using any kind of ramp. Hodges evaluated the short, straight ramp style:

> A ramp can be used either as a 'short' or as a 'long' ramp. The 'short' is one where only the load passes up the incline so that the hauliers can either stand or walk on a level area at the top of the slope.
>
> This is the most efficient method, whereas the 'long' ramp requires the whole train to walk up the slope together thereby wasting much energy in raising the weight of the hauliers themselves, a considerable factor as their combined weight will probably be more than that of the load itself. A short ramp may be invaluable in a permanent situation such as an incline out of a quarry, but for building a pyramid shape its use is restricted to the lower levels because the working platform becomes too small to accommodate the hauliers. No building theory is worth study unless it encompasses the placing of all the stones required and in particular those at the very top.[4]

Hodges also criticized the commonly held theory of a long, straight ramp:

> The long ramp is the one most usually depicted in books on Egyptology, when the drawing shows a pyramid, three-quarters built and serviced by a ramp with a gradient of about 1 in 3. This layout cannot be based on reason because it is a hard task just to walk up such a gradient and it would be impossible for hauliers to manage their work under these circumstances. However, it might be possible for a gradient of 1 in 10 to be used if the friction under the load could be reduced without impairing the foot-hold for the hauliers. No one would use this method for raising stones today so we cannot study the device in use; the nearest I can get to reality is to walk up a slope which exists near my home. The gradient is 1 in 10 and extends for 100 yards (whereas a ramp to the top of the great Pyramid would run for 1,600 yards), but it is a steady pull, and quite enough to confirm my views that the largest pyramids would never have been built if this were the only method available.[5]

Many theorists advocate that ramps, made of stone rubble cemented with clay, were used to build the Great Pyramid, because small ramps remain attached to some of Egypt's small pyramids. But the use of ramps for small pyramids is logical, because most pyramids consist almost entirely of blocks small enough for one or two men to carry up a ramp of low gradation. Such pyramids include those of the 3rd Dynasty and all of those built after the 4th Dynasty. It is mostly the height, volume and heavy blocks of the 4th Dynasty Great Pyramids, especially Khufu's Great Pyramid, that pose insurmountable problems with regard to ramps.

Hodges understood the serious danger of an earthen ramp's collapsing from its own weight. An earthen ramp cannot be expected to support massive blocks, according to Hodges. He deduced that any ramp must be as stable as the Great Pyramid itself, and that to have such stability, the ramp must be made of squared stones. At its greatest height, the ramp's volume would have been three times that of the Great Pyramid. If it had been built at a low gradient of 1:10, then the ramp would have been 4,800 feet long and 480 feet high.

It would have taken three times as long to build as the Great Pyramid.[6] Consequently, to complete the Great Pyramid during the 23- or 24-year reign of Khufu, workers had to set blocks much faster than experts have calculated.

Even if a ramp made of stone rubble cemented with clay would have been strong enough, then the practical problems of constructing and maintaining such an enormous ramp would be very serious. Clay requires a considerable amount of water to adhere and become pliable. Given that the Great Pyramid incorporates about 93.5 million cubic feet of limestone, constructing a clay-rubble ramp at least two or three times its volume would demand a great many millions of gallons of water carried up the Plateau from the Nile. A huge, constant supply of water would be needed to keep the ramp's surface slick, as well, so that friction would be reduced when moving blocks. A slick clay-surfaced ramp would require constant refurbishing because of the damage block raising inflicts on the ramp's surface. But the main problem that makes earthen ramps unworkable is that they would not be strong enough.

If a ramp must be made of squared stones, as Hodges advocates, then there would be an incredibly large residue of stone blocks left over once the enormous ramp was torn away from the Great Pyramid. If we exclude the masonry volume of the Great Pyramids, then the stone residue from such a ramp would rival the amount of rock found in all subsequent Egyptian architecture put together down to Roman times. The vast stone residue from such a huge ramp does not exist.

If we imagine that Khafra's builders recycled stone blocks from Khufu's ramp to build Khafra's pyramid and construction ramp, then there would still be an enormous residue of limestone blocks when Khafra's ramp was torn down. The subsequent pyramids put together are not large enough to have recycled this much stone.

Not only does the residue of a sufficiently large ramp (made of either limestone blocks or clay and stone rubble) not exist at Giza, but there is no evidence that a ramp was used to build the Great Pyramid. Egyptologists have found no ramp remains of any kind connected to the base of the Great Pyramid.[7] Only an earthen ramp was found leading up from the quarry to ground level, but it will not support the weight of the massive blocks, either. This ramp allowed men to climb in and out of the quarry more easily.

As mentioned, Mark Lehner partially measured the Giza quarries. Despite the unmeasured areas, the quarries cannot accommodate the removal of the vast amount of material required for a ramp made of solid masonry.

The size of any ramp depends upon its incline. The steeper the incline, the more difficult elevating blocks becomes. Some engineers have tried to reduce the problem by proposing that the ramp extended only part way up the Great Pyramid. In that case, the highest tiers of the Great Pyramid would have to be constructed by some other means.

In 1974 Danish civil engineer P. Garde-Hansen calculated that a ramp built to the top of the Great Pyramid would require 17.5 million cubic yards of material.[8] The amount he calculated for the ramp is several times the volume of the Great Pyramid itself. Garde-Hansen calculated that it would require 240,000 men to build such a ramp within Khufu's 23-year reign. Additionally, Garde-Hansen calculated that 300,000 men would be required to dismantle the ramp within eight years. The size of the Giza quarries would have to be much larger to supply rubble or squared stone for such a ramp.

In 1997 Egyptian civil engineer Moustafa Gadalla published a book recognizing that there is only one solution that can account for the absence of a huge construction ramp at Giza, for the incredible construction rate at which the Great Pyramid was built, for the absence of broken blocks and debris at Giza, for the absence of tool marks on most of the pyramid blocks, and for the many acres of enormous smooth, conforming casing blocks on the Great Pyramid that were described by ancient visitors to Giza who saw them. That one solution, of course, is the highly efficient means explained in these pages and other writings by Joseph Davidovits and myself, including our book *The Pyramids: An Enigma Solved* (Hippocrene, NY, 1988).

As a civil engineer, Moustafa Gadalla is qualified to critique issues concerning the number of blocks that would have to be set per minute if the kind of ramp Garde-Hansen calculated were actually used. Moustafa Gadalla wrote:

> Hypothetically, if we agree with Garde-Hansen's theories, try to visualize the staggering figures: . . . 6.67 blocks per minute! Imagine 6.67 blocks every 60 seconds! This rate is impossible to achieve. This is another reason to disregard the validity of the . . . ramp theories.[9]

Mark Lehner and others adhere to the standard theory and propose that a helical ramp was used to build the Great Pyramid.[10] Lehner argues that a wraparound ramp would better suit the topography of the site than would a straight-on ramp. He points out that an enormous straight ramp could not have existed on the south side of the Great Pyramid, because it would have covered the quarry area, and the large open quarries to the south of the Great Pyramid would not exist. The northern area could not accommodate a ramp because of a 120-foot drop in the terrain. Lehner also argues that structures to the east and west of the Great Pyramid prohibit the construction of a straight ramp. The monuments he has in mind include three small queens' pyramids situated to the east, and the field of tombs for Khufu's court members to the west.

No helical ramp has been found associated with any pyramid, however. Dieter Arnold pointed out serious problems with the helical ramp design:

> . . . one would even doubt their feasibility. In spite of the ingeniousness of such a device, spiral ramps would have created serious problems. During the whole construction period, the pyramid trunk would have been completely buried under the ramps. The surveyors could therefore not have used the four corners, edges, and foot line of the pyramid for their calculations. Furthermore, at a certain height the sides of the pyramid would no longer be wide enough to provide a ramp from one corner to the next.[11]

As the helical ramp rose, it would increasingly engulf the pyramid, burying its true reference points. The true reference points are the four corner stones at the base of the pyramid, the angle of the sides of the pyramid, and its baseline. Failure to make all measurements from these absolute reference points would introduce errors that would tend to compound themselves as the pyramid rose. Even the slightest measurement error would have compounded as workers took successive measurements from inaccurate reference points. The result would be a structure with irregular sides that would not form a proper pyramid shape. Neither Arnold nor Hodges could reckon a way around this serious problem.

Nova's *This Old Pyramid* proposed a helical cantilevered ramp winding up the pyramid.[12] Notwithstanding the fundamental problem of reference-point verification described above, the cantilevered design offers one great advantage: It requires dramatically less material to build. Nova displayed a very simplistic, three-dimensional computer-rendered image of a cantilevered ramp wrapping around a pyramid. By definition, a cantilever is a projecting beam or member supported only at one end. Viewed from the side, a cantilevered beam looks like a diving board in that it is supported only at one end. Nova's image showed such a projecting ramp, supported only at the end attached to the pyramid. Nova provided no engineering detail, engineering opinion, or field demonstration to try to establish whether such a ramp design might be workable.

Without a detailed construction design showing exactly how the ramp would be attached to and supported by the pyramid, we are left to speculate about how such a ramp could have been constructed. A cantilevered ramp involves very demanding engineering and construction techniques. Its strength would have to come from thousands of closely spaced, extremely long, thick, hard-rock support beams. Perhaps these beams would require interlocking joints. I seriously doubt that limestone would be strong enough at the needed beam lengths.

These special support beams would have to be built into the pyramid faces to meet complex engineering requirements. For instance, the beams would have to extend far enough into the core masonry to counterbalance the weight of their lengths extending out of the pyramid. Each beam must also have enough counterbalance to safely support the weight of its proportional load of the finished ramp, plus the proportional load of the heaviest anticipated weight moving along the ramp.

If the need for greater strength were anticipated, then engineers would have to stack the beams vertically, as well, in which case the beams would occupy a number of pyramid tiers. Another way to increase counterbalance is to secure the beams to adjacent core blocks with interlocking joints. Piling masonry onto the beams as the pyramid rises also helps with counterbalancing.

No evidence exists for beams that extended into the faces of the Great Pyramid—evidence that must be there for this alternative ramp design to be more than wild speculation on the part of Nova. Most tiers very high in the Great Pyramid are not tall enough to support the existence of cantilevered support beams of the immense size needed (see Appendix). No one has found evidence of special masonry joints capable of locking in a keyed ramp. In short, it is very unlikely that such a ramp existed.

A ramp must be strong enough to support its greatest anticipated weight. Huge girdle blocks encase large areas of the Ascending Passageway and granite beams forming the ceiling of the King's Chamber of the Great Pyramid measure up to 27 feet long and weigh up to 73 tons. Moving one of these long beams around the corner of a helical ramp would pose incredibly difficult problems. The ramp would have to be extremely wide, at least at the corners that wrap around the pyramid to the level above the King's Chamber. It is not likely that a 27-foot-long beam would have been moved with its long axis vertical, because the beam could too easily tip. All of this tells us that a cantilevered ramp system would be so demanding that it would dramatically complicate matters and adversely affect calculations for building the Great Pyramid. Theorists mostly work with an average block size of 2.5 tons, but they would need to factor in the elevation of thousands of enormous cantilevered beams for the ramp itself.

NOVA proposed that after the pyramid tiers were completed, masons lopped off the cantilevered support beams to form the outer faces of a number of pyramid tiers. The cutting operation would have had to achieve the accurate planes that Petrie reported. As mentioned, Petrie found that the mean optical plane that touches the most prominent points of the blocks of the Great Pyramid's rough core faces shows an average variation of only 1.0 inch. The concave faces would have to be achieved, too. Beams damaged by pounding balls—the block-shaping method preferred by Dieter Arnold and others—would not conform well and would have to be replaced with blocks made especially to fit into existing masonry. How can we believe that such a complex operation was accomplished with primitive tools? Given the overwhelming demands of the cantilevered ramp, it is very surprising that the award-winning science program Nova introduced the idea at all.

Nova conducted a limited block-pulling experiment on a partially constructed, noncantilevered miniature helical ramp. The Nova crew built the miniature helical ramp to the extent that it allowed blocks to pass around one corner of Nova's miniature pyramid. The operation was aided by a rope and a simple wooden post set up on the ramp's corner, a device used for turning the block around the corner of the ramp. This turning post allowed workers pulling a block to exert their force from around the corner of the ramp. They positioned the block slightly beyond the ramp's corner so they could reorient the block and then pull it higher up the ramp. They finally positioned the block with levers and the pulling force of the workers.

The Nova experiment did not represent the actual problem. Blocks weighing only one ton each were raised on Nova's miniature helical ramp. The weight of the blocks of the Great Pyramid is averaged at 2.5 tons, but many blocks high in the structure weigh much more. For instance, the blocks making up the King's Chamber walls weigh up to 50 tons each, and beams in the ceiling weigh up to an estimated 73 tons. The blocks in tier 35 are taller than those in tier two at the base. Because Nova's workers had little problem raising three or four one-ton blocks over a short distance, Mark Lehner concluded that the Great Pyramid's construction problems were solved. He concluded that building the Great Pyramid within Khufu's 23- or 24-year reign was feasible. But there are serious problems with this block-raising experiment that Nova did not mention or address.

Given that it is unlikely that a helical ramp was used for the Great Pyramid, the use of a turning post in the 4$^{th}$ Dynasty is suspect. A reason is that a turning post is a primitive precursor to the pulley, and, according to Dieter Arnold, the oldest true pulley found in Egypt dates possibly to the late 12$^{th}$ Dynasty. Even with a turning post, Nova fell far short of the construction rate theorized for the Great Pyramid. The Nova film stated its requirement: An average of one block was set in place every three minutes per day for the 23-year reign of Khufu. The problem Nova had meeting this requirement is evident in a letter from the film's producer Michael Barnes, dated April 25, 1995. Barnes responded as follows to a viewer who confronted him about building the Nova miniature pyramid with a front-end loader:

> Our film . . . is an attempt to demonstrate tools and techniques that the best archaeological evidence suggests were available to the ancient Egyptians. Because of constraints on our budget, we could only afford to have a film crew on location in Egypt for three weeks. Once we began work it quickly became clear we had a choice: if everything was done by ancient means we would probably only finish one or two courses of pyramid stones.

> Alternatively, if we employed a front-end loader to speed up the repetitive work of placing blocks we had a good chance of building to the top of the pyramid.[13]

If the Nova team could have kept up their planned construction rate, which was much slower than what they had theorized for the Great Pyramid, then they should have been able to place the 180 blocks for the miniature pyramid in three weeks without a front-end loader.

There is a basic methodological distortion in drawing conclusions from a miniature experiment. Engineering problems multiply in full-scale operations. The cumulative congestion on a ramp of the size required for the Great Pyramid would be extraordinary. Compare hundreds of blocks set per day, high in the Great Pyramid, with fewer than 200 smaller blocks set in three weeks in Nova's unfinished 18-foot-high miniature pyramid—almost all with the use of a front-end loader.

The front-end loader placed the heaviest blocks, weighing two tons, on Nova's miniature pyramid. The few one-ton blocks that the workers raised manually were put onto the miniature ramp by the front-end loader, which also brought these blocks from the quarry. This same machine placed a two-ton block on a concrete road, and Nova hauled this block on rollers for its roller experiment only after placing it on this strong modern surface. Unfortunately for the unsuspecting viewers, the film does not show the heavy construction equipment Nova used. The film never told viewers of it.

It is important to clarify this, because Nova's *This Old Pyramid* has convinced many people that there are no difficult pyramid construction mysteries. The WGBH Educational Foundation sells *This Old Pyramid* as an informal teaching aid to schoolchildren. The film is also used at the high-school and college level. Television station WGBH, in Boston, which produces Nova, is a Public Broadcasting affiliate. For the sake of schoolchildren learning about pyramid construction through this film and its companion book, it is important to distinguish between what *This Old Pyramid* says and shows and how the Nova miniature pyramid was really built behind the scenes.

At the beginning of the film, the narrator clearly states, "They'll [Nova's workers] use the methods and materials available to the Egyptians to build them [the pyramids]." The narration repeats the protocol when stating, "Roger wanted to lower these blocks in place with a fork-lift, but Mark has insisted on ancient methods." The entire film gives the impression that the Nova crew was building the miniature pyramid using strictly ancient means.

The Nova crew used steel tools to quarry and shape all the blocks, although Egyptologists insist that the Pyramid Age Egyptians had only relatively soft copper and crude stone tools. A front-end loader placed all but three or four pyramid blocks, those needed for the on-camera demonstration, onto the pyramid's tiers. Nevertheless, the film concluded by claiming that Nova's experiments solved all of the major problems of pyramid construction.

Because Congress oversees public television, I registered complaints with some congressional offices.[14] Consequently, some congressional staff assistants made telephone inquiries to *This Old Pyramid's* producer Michael Barnes. Barnes verbally promised them he would make a disclaimer or repackage *This Old Pyramid*, and his promise disarmed further inquires from congressional offices concerning scientific fraud at taxpayer expense. Barnes' promise appears in writing in a letter to viewer Charles Horton, of Fort Worth, Texas, who learned about Nova's methods from me:

> I am not sure what errors you are referring to as we feel the film was thoroughly researched and represents widely accepted knowledge of Old Kingdom Egypt and their methods of building pyramids. . . . With reference to the discussion with congressional staff I agreed to clarify the narration of the repackaged version of the film so that it clearly states that modern equipment was also used to build the NOVA pyramid. . . . But to avoid possible confusion, we will, when the program is rebroadcast in 1997, as part of a series on ancient engineering, add an additional line of narration to the effect that stonemason Roger Hopkins used a modern loader to help build the pyramid.

The repackaged 60-minute version first aired in February of 1997, as the lead film in Nova's series *Secrets of Lost Empires*. The revised pyramid film does not include the promised disclaimer or in any way admit to the use of modern equipment. Instead, it repeats the same old language, saying that Roger wanted to lower the blocks in place with a forklift, but that Mark Lehner insisted on ancient means. The film contains all of the elements that prompted my original complaints, first to top PBS and WGBH executives, then to Nova sponsor Johnson & Johnson, and when they all refused to air a disclaimer (after about two years worth of letter exchanges with me) I finally turned to my state congressmen.

The original 90-minute *This Old Pyramid* was repackaged and broadcast by other television programs, too, making them suspect as teaching aids as well. The British Broadcasting Corporation (BBC) aired the Nova film, and the Canadian Broadcasting Corporation (CBC) repackaged it for the science program *The Nature of Things*. CBC advertisements for the October 18, 1993 broadcast unwittingly stated that on the next *The Nature of Things*, viewers would see how the pyramids were built "without a forklift."

The *Nature of Things* host David Suzuki, in a letter to me dated November 23, 1993, stated:

> I was very surprised to learn from you of the extensive use of machines in

> the making of the pyramid. . . it is distressing to realize that the thrust of the show conveyed a totally false impression.[15]

Unfortunately for viewers, I was successful in informing Suzuki of the facts only after the show aired. The CBC ignored my previous attempts to warn against airing the show. After the show aired, Suzuki and top executives at CBC declined to air a disclaimer, despite my persistent requests. WGBH executives, who oversee the Nova show, refused to accept responsibility for CBC's accidental false advertising.

Long after the original version of *This Old Pyramid* aired over PBS broadcasting stations, those responsible were still refusing to issue a disclaimer for the Nova film or remove it from the educational market. I, therefore, finally issued a press release in the hope that the educational community would demand a disclaimer if the truth were exposed. But there was only one response from the media. When science writer Carlos Byars received my press release and learned of the front-end loader, he confronted Nova producer Michael Barnes.

Byars advised that "the viewer had better beware" in his article in the *Houston Chronicle* (Wrap-up, Saturday, November 13, 1993). The small article reads in part, "Although the use of modern machines is mentioned four times, Barnes said, the emphasis of the piece is on the use of tools and methods available to ancient Egyptians." "That is not quite the way it was," countered Byars, who had watched the film three times before interviewing Barnes.

Vague statements about machines in the film, if noticeable at all, lead viewers to assume the use of inconsequential devices. Instruments for checking leveling and vehicles for transporting equipment and people are acceptable for the experiment. Viewers who noticed the brief references to machines would naturally assume the use of these devices, because the film denies the use of heavy machinery. The film states, "Roger wanted to lower these blocks in place with a forklift, but Mark has insisted on ancient methods." As Byars aptly remarked, "One of the best and most award-winning science programs on television, Nova, has been caught with its front-end loader hanging out."

Some five years after *This Old Pyramid* originally aired, Lehner included a whisper of Nova's use of the front-end loader in *The Complete Pyramid* (1997). His book does not correct the problem, since the very wide, international television audience of Nova will not read it. Worse, Lehner's mention of the front-end loader in his award-winning *The Complete Pyramid* (1997) (Society for American Archaeology Award, 1999) presents even more misleading information about the front-end loader. Lehner wrote:

> And Roger brought in a front-end loader for shifting and setting the stones of lower courses so that we would have time to test different methods at

the top, where restricted space created special difficulties.[16]

With his statement, Lehner implies that the front-end loader only set stones in the lower courses, which is not correct. Joseph Davidovits watched the crew build the miniature pyramid in Egypt, and he provided a statement for me to include here:

> The front-end loader carried all stones from the quarries and placed them in the miniature pyramid from bottom to top, except for the pyramidion [the capstone], which was very small, and the blocks shown being moved manually on camera.[17]

As mentioned, only three or four one-ton blocks were moved for Nova's on-camera demonstration, and these blocks had been placed on the ramp by the front-end loader. Joseph Davidovits' above statement agrees with Nova producer Michael Barnes' letter to a viewer:

> Once we began work it quickly became clear we had a choice: if everything was done by ancient means we would probably only finish one or two courses of pyramid stones. Alternatively, if we employed a front-end loader to speed up the repetitive work of placing blocks we had a good chance of building to the top of the pyramid.[18]

Although they did build to its top with the front-end loader, they left the pyramid unfinished. With the scientific record necessarily corrected here, we can continue considering Nova's ramp experiment. The Nova crew affixed each one-ton block to a sled and transported the loaded sleds over log timbers embedded in the miniature ramp's clay surface. The workers poured water onto the timbers to reduce the friction between the blocks and the wooden sleds. In contrast, to build the Great Pyramid, on average, one block was incorporated every two or three minutes per ten-hour workday, according to the calculations of Rainer Stadelmann. The rapid operation requires a steady train of relatively closely spaced sledges and workers, and the frequent application of water to the clay surface of the ramp. Even in Egypt's arid climate, the frequent use of water would quickly cause the clay to become too slick and unstable. To avoid hazardous and impossible working conditions, the ramp would have to dry or be resurfaced before work continued. In other words, although not factored in by engineering studies, this problem must be considered when calculating the speed at which blocks could be raised for the Great Pyramid.

Raising one block on Nova's miniature ramp seriously damaged its clay surface. The ramp required refurbishing after the Nova crew raised one or two blocks. Because of the structural damage, Nova's building supervisor Roger Hopkins remarked that only a strong concrete ramp would be useful for experimentation. Egyptology assumes that a concrete ramp could not have existed and there are no remains of such a ramp at Giza. Thus, the remark by Hopkins complies with Peter Hodges' assertion that any ramp used to raise blocks for the Great Pyramid must have been solid masonry. As I have already stressed, such a ramp cannot be accounted for, because the quarries at Giza are too small and there are no such ramp remains at Giza. We see that, for many reasons, a huge construction ramp was unworkable for building the Great Pyramid. However, because no other block raising devices are known from the Late Stone Age, Egyptology adheres to the unworkable ramp method for constructing the Great Pyramid. Despite all of the authoritative literature claiming that pyramid blocks were raised on ramps, proper analysis shows that Egyptology has not solved one of the most fundamental problems of the construction of the Great Pyramid.

# Chapter 14

# Block-Raising Enigmas

Egyptology advocates that a 12th Dynasty tomb scene explains the method by which workers hauled blocks for pyramid construction. The scene is from the tomb of a nobleman of Hermopolis named Djehutihotep (1878–1841 B.C.), who lived about 800 years after the Great Pyramid was built [1]

The tomb scene shows 172 men pulling Djehutihotep's 60-ton colossus on a sledge. A liquid is being poured in front of the giant statue, which facilitated its transport along flat ground.

The colossus is small compared with some ancient Egyptian monoliths, which are so large that they are far too challenging for experimentation today. The 19th Dynasty Pharaoh Ramses II had a statue weighing about 1,000 tons built at his Ramesseum at Thebes.[2] In the ruins of Tanis, in northeast Egypt, fragments of either three or four granite colossi were uncovered that suggest that even heavier colossi were built for this pharaoh.[3] W.M.F. Petrie estimated one of them to have towered ninety-two feet from head to toe, and totaling 125 feet high with its pedestal. Petrie calculated the weight at 1,200 tons. It is the largest colossus known.

Some experts estimate that 1,000 men or 200 oxen are required to move a sledge carrying a 1,000-ton colossus on a slick, flat surface.[4] Engineers have not shown how such enormous numbers of men, or combinations of men and animals, could have worked in coordination in such a complicated and constrictive operation.[5] It is entirely possible to move monoliths weighing 1,000 tons and more along flat ground, but erecting a statue of this size presents a greater challenge than has been undertaken with modern stonework. To further vastly complicate matters, the 1,000-ton and heavier colossi rested on pedestals. We see that the scene showing the transport of the colossi of Djehutihotep does not put to rest—or, in reality, even begin to approach—the matter of how the ancient Egyptians put their heaviest obelisks and colossi in place or how millions of massive pyramid blocks could be raised on an incline.

We can get some idea of how many men would be required to raise Ramses' 1,000 ton colossi by comparing a calculation by Reginald Engelbach, who studied the problems associated with the famous unfinished obelisk at Aswan. Had this obelisk been completed, it would have weighed 1,168 tons. Engelbach indicated:

It may be mentioned here that to pull the obelisk over, on a level surface, would require some 13,000 men, which I am convinced could not be put on ropes in the constricted area of the quarry.[6]

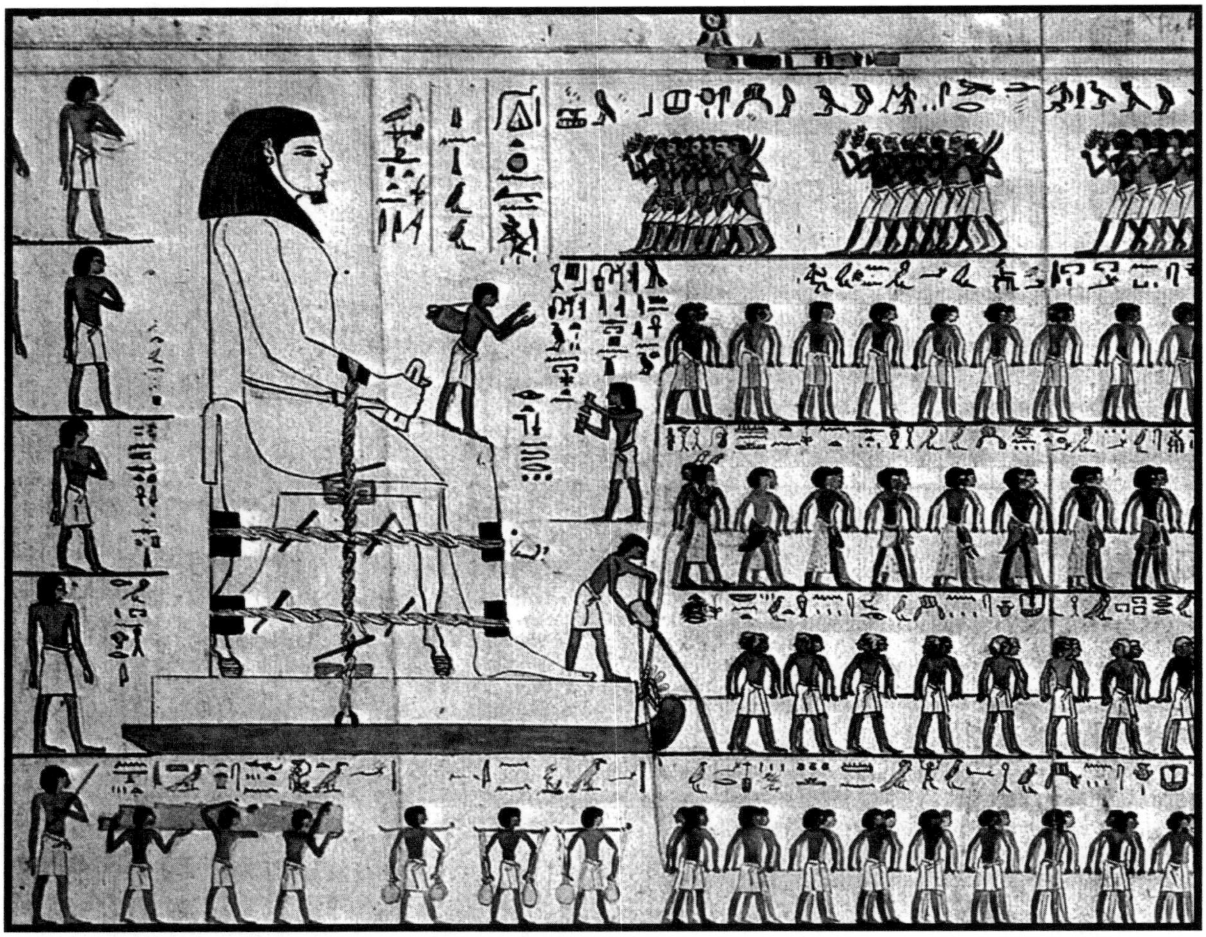

**53. A PORTION OF THE TOMB SCENE OF DJEHUTIHOTEP AT DEIR EL-BERSHA. PAINTING BY J.G. WILKINSON; PHOTO BY ELSEVIER**

Erecting Ramses II's colossi so that they would be upright on their pedestals would be a far more demanding operation than rolling them over on the ground. No modern obelisk-raising operation has moved an obelisk anywhere near the size of Ramses II's colossi each weighing 1,000 tons or more. Engelbach calculated that it would require 2,000 men just to pull the much smaller 227-ton obelisk at Luxor up a ramp.[7]

The ancient Egyptian obelisk called Cleopatra's Needle, now in London, weighs

150 tons, and the heaviest obelisk moved in modern times weighs about 330 tons. One of the largest obelisks in the world weighs between 445 and 510 tons, and it was moved to Rome in the time of Emperor Constantius (A.D. 317–361), the son of Constantine the Great. The obelisk was presumably brought to Rome and erected in one piece (in the 16th century it was excavated and found in three pieces). Also a fallen, broken obelisk was found at Axum, Ethiopia, that was 110 feet tall.

Raising enormous statues within the confined spaces of already existing buildings presents another conundrum. Engelbach pointed out that an obelisk built for the $18^{th}$ Dynasty Pharaoh-Queen Hatshepsut was positioned inside a preexisting court. The walls of the court measure less than the length of the obelisk! Engelbach carefully examined these court walls and was positive that workers had not torn them down or rebuilt them in any way to bring in the obelisk.[8] Thus, the manner in which this obelisk was brought in is unknown to Egyptology.

For monuments weighing 1,000 tons or more, and for tall obelisks in confined spaces within preexisting walls, calculations involving labor alone do not satisfy the questions. These examples are so extraordinary that they alert us to the existence of some kind of special technology that has nothing to do with the method used to move the 60-ton colossus of Djehutihotep.

Although most building units of the Great Pyramid weigh much less than Djehutihotep's colossus, the stele cannot legitimately be used to address the problems of raising pyramid blocks. French Egyptologist Henri Chevrier performed an experiment during his work at the Karnak Temple, in southern Egypt. His team pulled a sledge bearing a block weighing five to six tons along a lubricated track, the lubrication having greatly reduced friction.[9] He found that each man could pull 330 pounds on a lubricated, flat surface. Based on this figure, it would take 400 men, rather than 172, to pull the 60-ton colossus along the ground. The Stele of Djehutihotep was, therefore, probably not meant to be taken literally in terms of the number of workers. Instead, it was simply intended to convey the means of transport used for this particular project.

Based on Chevrier's experiment, hauling a typical six-ton block for the Great Pyramid along the ground would require 40 men. But on a ramp, the number would be much higher, increasing in proportion to the angle of the ramp's gradient.

The noted French Egyptologist Jean-Philippe Lauer studied the problems of pyramid construction for some 50 years. He suggested that workers used steep inclines of 3:1 and 4:1 when building the Great Pyramid. We recall Peter Hodges' more recent calculation, however. He remarked that slopes of 3:1 or 4:1 are entirely unrealistic and suggested a more workable low gradient slope of 1:10. In that case, any ramp would have to be 4,800 feet long and 480 feet high and made of squared stones, a scenario that puts an intolerable strain on the entire ramp theory.

If we calculate with the gradients Lauer suggested, then elevating one six-ton block would have required 140 to 200 men.[10] This also produces an impossible scenario, because to build the Great Pyramid during the 23- or 24-year reign of Khufu, hundreds of blocks had to be set daily. To meet this rapid rate, thousands of workers would have been required to maneuver the block-bearing sleds to great heights on the slick ramp. This scenario presents an engineering nightmare, because too many men would be working on the slick ramp at any one time.

Mark Lehner fails to recognize this fundamental fact when calculating the number of men required to elevate blocks for the Great Pyramid. Here is his calculation from his award-winning *The Complete Pyramids* (1997):

> . . . the famous scene from the tomb of Djehutihotep . . . depicts the moving of a large colossus . . . the statue would have weighed c. 58 tons . . . there are 172 men shown, each therefore pulling c. 1/3 ton. Modern trials confirm that this is possible on a fairly friction-free surface. By the same ratio (1/3 ton per hauler) a 2.5 ton block on a lubricated, level surface could be pulled by 7.5 men. If we assume that a division (20 men) moved 10 stones per day - allowing one hour to move the stone to the pyramid and return with an empty sledge - then 340 stones could be moved daily from quarry to pyramid by 34 divisions. There are points to note on both sides of this equation. More divisions work simultaneously in the lower levels, when there may have been many ramps, and therefore a higher hauling rate. Far fewer could work nearer the top, where there was less space and ramp gradients were steeper. Also, the stones of Khufu's pyramid are not all 2.5 tons - this estimate of the average block size is frequently quoted, but needs more study. Many stones, particularly near the apex, are smaller, while those of the core are by no means all neat, 2.5-ton cubes, and near the base many blocks exceed 2.5 tons. Perhaps one hour per stone is too demanding. . . .[11]

In his final estimate, Lehner allows for what he calls a "more realistic estimate of 1,360 haulers." His ridiculously low figure arises from fundamental flaws in his calculation. First, he inappropriately uses a calculation for moving blocks on level ground to calculate the number needed to elevate blocks on an incline. His error allows him to reduce the number of men by many thousands. Then, he rids the calculation of many thousands of men by mostly calculating with an averaged block weight of 2.5 tons. By doing this, he fails to acknowledge the special problems posed by raising the massive blocks situated at many levels of the Great Pyramid. Keep in mind that tier 35 was measured as taller than tier two at the base, and tier 201 at the top as taller than tier four (see Appendix). He says that the sizes need more study. But there are many size estimates, and tier heights have long been confirmed and published.

Lehner also calculated the number of men required to haul stones from the Giza quarry to the Great Pyramid:

> Let us assume that the stone haulers could move 1 km (0.62 miles) per hour en route from the quarry to the pyramid. The return journey was done with an empty sledge and so was much faster. The distance from Khufu's quarry to the pyramid, at c. 6° slope, could probably be covered in 19 minutes by 20 men pulling a 2.5 ton block. Certainly, this was well within the capacities of the NOVA team. . . .[12]

Again, Lehner used averaged weights of 2.5 tons. He did not address the sharp fluctuations in height increase in the pyramid tiers (including 127 cm. at tier 35, 100 cm. at 36, 196 cm. at tier 44, 100 cm. at tier 98, and 112 cm. at tier 201, the latter of which tier has been destroyed since measured by the Napoleonic expedition). In the masonry of the Great Pyramid, tier heights suddenly increase and diminish in nineteen sharp fluctuations (see my Appendix for the tier height measurements). Among the samples of heavy interior units, wall blocks in the King's Chamber, nearly half way up the Pyramid, weigh about 50 tons each. Ceiling beams weigh up to 73 tons. Enormous girdle blocks, 12 to 15 feet long, encase the Ascending Passageway. Both Herodotus and Abd el-Latif reported seeing a myriad of outer casing blocks 30 feet long.

To top off his argument, Lehner insinuates that the experiment of Nova validates his calculations. But the Nova team did not haul a single block from the quarry to the miniature pyramid. The front-end loader even hauled the three or four one-ton blocks raised manually for Nova's on-camera demonstration and put them onto the miniature ramp.

Compare Lehner's estimate with that of Petrie, who when taking into consideration the tier heights, calculated that 100,000 men per year were needed to build the Great Pyramid during Khufu's reign.[13] We have already considered the counterproductive congestion that having so many men working together would cause. As already discussed, Peter Hodges showed that the Great Pyramid would not exist if building it depended upon a ramp.

In 1997, in Tokyo, Japanese engineers tested an elevation method conceived of by Cambridge University engineer Dick Parry.[14] He rejected the theory that pyramid builders moved blocks up ramps on sledges, because he recognized that the number of men required would be too great.

Innovating upon the so-called rockers theorized by Clarke and Engelbach, Parry proposed that four rockers be arranged around a block to form a cylinder. Builders coiled a long rope around the cylinder to move it uphill.

When workers pulled on the rope from the top of the ramp, the rope uncoiled, causing the cylinder to roll up the ramp. Parry's ingenious operation reduces the amount of force needed to elevate blocks.

Parry's method was tested on 2.5-ton blocks. To push a 2.5-block on a level surface required only three men. To pull a block up a ramp with a one-in-four gradient required only 16 to 20 men. Workers pulled the 2.5 ton block up a 49-foot slope in only one minute.

Even this clever system fails, because it depends upon the use of an enormous ramp. We have already seen that building a ramp for the Great Pyramid would be too demanding. Parry's system calls for a very demanding ramp, because it must be either very wide or extremely strong. Consider the scenario when his cylinders have to raise beams up to 27 feet long for the ceiling of the King's Chamber.

A beam is most stable when positioned with its length perfectly horizontal. Imagine these beams up to 27 feet long rolling up a helical ramp. If the beams are hauled while horizontal to a height of about 160 feet, then the helical ramp would have to be constructed with extremely wide corners—wide enough to accommodate beams up to 27 feet long being turned around them. The ramp would have to be extremely strong, and most likely it would have to be keyed into the Great Pyramid's masonry with long, enormous support beams made of extremely dense rock.

Moving the beams while keeping them upright would not require such wide ramp corners. But the ramp would have to be extremely strong. When moving a beam in a vertical orientation, its weight is distributed over a smaller surface area of the ramp. In other words, the ramp must be quite strong, at least up to 160 feet high (higher for the relieving chambers), the level of the ceiling of the King's Chamber.

If the cylinders up to 27 feet long were moved up a straight-on ramp in a horizontal orientation, then this ramp, too, would have to be strong and solid. The ramp would require far more effort to build and tear down than needed to build the Great Pyramid itself. We see that the fundamental problem with Parry's theory relates back to the fact that the construction ramp itself is entirely unworkable.

Finally, if Parry's method existed, then we would expect that the Egyptians would have used the wheel for transportation from that point forward. However, the wheel did not come into use for transportation until much later, and known Egyptian wheels were not made to endure hard use (see Figure 55 on page 178).

Peter Hodges commented on mistaken ideas about ramps. He found systemic errors in logic throughout the standard Egyptological literature. He recognized that the errors could be corrected only by someone with a lifetime of experience in the building trade:

> An archaeologist has the talent of re-creating history from evidence left by another civilization but his background is one of scholarship rather than craftsmanship. It is not reasonable to expect an archaeologist to be an

> experienced manual worker in all the basic trades of living, from farming, building, husbandry, etc., through to embalming. . . . We send an archaeologist to search for history but for practical problems we really need an investigator who could, if need be, carry through the solutions himself on the basis of his practical experiences.[15]

Having recognized the irreconcilable problems with ramps and the proposed block-raising schemes, Hodges devised a levering system to eliminate the need for a ramp. In his book *How the Great Pyramids Were Built* (1989), Hodges proposed the use of his own specially designed levers.

Although they did not use Hodges' instrument, Nova's *This Old Pyramid* tested the levering system. The Nova crew levered a block into place in its miniature pyramid under the supervision of pyramid theorist Martin Isler. Workers pried the block up one end at a time, inserting wooden planks under it. They performed this process repeatedly until the block was slowly and tediously elevated a few inches at a time to the desired height. Workers placed each wooden plank under the edges of the block with great difficulty and trepidation. As the block rose, the wooden stack under it became unstable and difficult to manage, despite the even, planed surfaces of the planks. Once the block reached the desired elevation, the workers moved it carefully sideways onto the pyramid without disturbing the wooden stack. Otherwise, the block would have crashed to the ground. The workers had problems keeping the stacked planks stable, but they did manage to move the block safely.

It took five hours to raise the block onto the tiny Nova pyramid tier. The operation is too slow and hazardous to be practical on the scale of the Great Pyramid. Based on Peter Hodges' own trials with his special prying levers, he estimated that it would require about two days to maneuver the average block into place in the Great Pyramid. A 2.5 ton block might take about a day. Compare the rate of production established by Egyptology, an average of one block raised and set in place every two or three minutes per work day for the length of Khufu's 24-year reign.

Engineer Edward A. Murphy devised Murphy's Law, which says, "If something can go wrong, it will." With any levering system, some blocks would have gone crashing down. Just one block tumbling from a course high in the pyramid would cause terrible damage to the masonry below. Workers would have to raise new blocks to replace broken ones. Replacing blocks would have been especially difficult because of the problems of fitting them into existing tiers. Peter Hodges understood that fitting pyramid blocks is at least as demanding as raising them.

The tiers of the pyramid substitute for a ramp with Hodges' system. The tiers would suffer from the wear and tear of block raising. Fixing all of the damage raises the average number of blocks that had to be set per day. We see that the levering system is much too slow and dangerous to be viable for building the Great Pyramid.

Hodges' six-foot-long levers were fitted with angled ends like those of a pry bar. The design produces a lever equipped with its own fulcrum. His first trial used a lever of this design that had no metal reinforcement. It broke at the bend. His later model sandwiched the angled wooden pry ends between copper reinforcement fastened by rods. The design prevented its short end from tearing off when he pried blocks.

Notwithstanding his remarks about Egyptologists not being properly qualified to solve building problems, Hodges' own system is at odds with what Egyptologists understand from their training. Although Hodges' copper-reinforced levers are simple devices, they are more advanced than Old Kingdom tools. To explain why archaeologists have never found such lever tips, Hodges proposed that they were so highly treasured that they must have been stolen or deeply buried. But this would not have prevented drawings or written descriptions of them from being made. Excavators have frequently found highly treasured items in tombs, like gold and jewelry. Evidence of tremendous numbers of copper-reinforced lever tips would have to have vanished from history without a trace.

Reginald Engelbach commented on the use of simple levers of a size useful for prying large pieces of stone:

> The occurrence of levers is so rare that it has been doubted whether the Egyptians knew of them.[16]

Depictions of levers are unknown for the Old Kingdom, although scenes from that period are more scarce. Engineers and machinists have suggested devices to address the Great Pyramid's building enigmas. Egyptologists, however, understand the very limited technological frame of reference within which they must remain. They are very familiar with the tools and the tool-making capabilities of the ancient Egyptians. For this reason, Egyptologists do not invent new tools or simple machines to solve the mystery of the construction of the Great Pyramid.

The dilemma is clear. With their understanding of the lifting devices and tools and materials available to Khufu's workers, Egyptologists are highly reluctant to abandon the ramp theories altogether. Hodges, however, and other engineers have shown that ramps are not at all workable for building the Great Pyramid. Experiments show that levering systems are too slow, dangerous and cumbersome to be workable on an enormous scale. A combination of the two systems, ramps for lower tiers and levers for higher tiers, would be beset with the same problems already covered. Even a ramp built to the level of the King's Chamber (160 feet high) would be too demanding.

There is a dire need for a cross-disciplinary approach to the masonry and engineering mysteries. Only when Egyptological knowledge is combined with the correct scientific approach can the real solution finally be accepted.

# Chapter 15

# The Mystery Of Obelisks

Experts have not adequately explained how the Egyptians erected tall obelisks in confined spaces or situated colossi weighing over 1,000 tons on pedestals. Although ancient Egyptian documents indicate that obelisks were built during the Old Kingdom, surviving obelisks date to later times. There are more than 50 remaining Egyptian obelisks greater than 30 feet high.

The 18th and 19th Dynasty workers produced magnificent examples. The 19th Dynasty Pharaoh Ramses II ordered 14 obelisks constructed in Tanis, in northern Egypt. Artisans built at least 13 tall obelisks in ancient Thebes (now called Karnak), in southern Egypt. Pharaoh Seti I recorded building several in Heliopolis, in northern Egypt. Abd el-Latif, writing in the 12th century, reported that in Heliopolis (the city called On in the Bible) magnificent obelisks had gilded pyramidions. He indicated that they were surrounded by large and small obelisks too numerous for him to discuss individually. Today only one obelisk remains in Heliopolis (Egyptian: Annu). Tradition holds that the Virgin Mary rested at this obelisk with the infant Jesus during their flight into Egypt.

Reginald Engelbach, who served as chief inspector of antiquities of Upper Egypt early in the 20th century, studied the theories of the production and erection of obelisks. Egyptologists still consider his studies authoritative. One theory holds that ancient engineers positioned obelisks as high as possible on enormous embankments. Workers then caused obelisks to slowly descend into huge, sand-filled, funnel-shaped brick constructions. The theory holds that they carefully removed the sand, while others pulled the obelisks upright from the opposite direction with ropes. Engelbach recognized the serious problems with this theory, including the lack of archaeological evidence from ancient Egypt supporting its use. Archaeologists have found no traces of such brick constructions.

The operation that transported the 150-ton obelisk called Cleopatra's Needle to New York showed that there is nothing to prevent a massive obelisk from swaying out of control as workers pull it upright. When Cleopatra's Needle began to sway, the ropes tied to its upper portion could not control its motion.[1]

An obelisk to be placed within the confined spaces of a preexisting building complex presents more critical problems. Engelbach commented:

> The Egyptians could introduce obelisks inside courts whose walls were shorter than the length of the obelisk. Queen Hatshepsowet put hers between her father's pylons where there is no evidence at all that any of the walls had been removed or rebuilt; in fact I am certain that they were not.[2]

Modern engineers have not explained how the ancient Egyptians placed this obelisk.

One theory proposes that enormous levers were used to pry obelisks up. Engelbach pointed out a very serious problem with this idea:

> Some obelisks are so close to their pylons that there would hardly be room for the huge levers which would have had to be used.[3]

Engelbach reminds us that no large levers or depictions of them have been found:

> The occurrence of levers is so rare that it has been doubted whether the Egyptians knew of them.[4]

Engelbach described severe problems concerning lowering obelisks from huge embankments. The process involves moving the obelisk up a long, sloping embankment until it hangs over the edge. Workers would have to orient the obelisk with its trunk supported well above its balancing point to prevent it from falling over the edge of the embankment. They would then have to remove the earthen embankment from below until the obelisk was lowered down to the edge of its pedestal. Simultaneously, the workers would have to pull the obelisk upright with ropes. Engelbach showed this theory to be unworkable:

> a) It would be extremely risky business to cut earth from below an overhanging obelisk of 500 tons and upwards. Anyone who has seen earth undercut below a large stone in excavating work or elsewhere knows that the earth has a partiality for slipping sideways in any direction but the expected—preferably on to the heads of one's workmen.
>
> b) To make an obelisk settle down from a height on to a small pedestal by under-cutting would be an impossibility. Whatever method the Egyptians used, it was certain.
>
> c) After pulling the obelisk upright there is nothing to stop it from rocking about and getting out of control.[5]

Modern projects that moved heavy obelisks from Egypt and erected them in various cities of the world may not have been able to deal with ancient Egypt's heaviest monoliths, like the 1,000-ton colossi of Ramses. Consider Engelbach's remarks:

> Although the removal of obelisks from Egypt in recent times gives us very little information which might help us to understand the methods of the ancients, a brief account of them is of interest if only to the contrast; it makes us appreciate the work of the Egyptians the more, especially when we bear in mind that every method used in modern days for the lowering and erection of an obelisk—which has never exceeded 331 tons in weight—always taxed the strength of the tackle to the utmost; in each case it was only just strong enough. Every modern removal has been a nine days' wonder, and a ponderous tome has appeared about it, yet the Egyptians, we know for a fact, set up obelisks of over 550 tons, and—if we are to believe their records—of more than 800 tons, without troubling to put on record how they did it.[6]

There is no reason to doubt the ancient record of an 800-ton obelisk, given the 1,000-ton and heavier colossi of Ramses II, which were situated on pedestals.

The Roman naturalist Pliny the Elder reported a means of transporting an obelisk.[7] It concerns a 120-foot-high obelisk that was moved to Alexandria during the time of the Greek Pharaoh Ptolemy II Philadelphus (285–246 B.C.). Pliny recorded that workers dug a canal from the Nile to the spot where the obelisk rested. The obelisk was situated such that both banks of the river supported it. To get it afloat, workers loaded two large barges with heavy loads of rock beneath the obelisk. Workers unloaded the rocks until the barges floated up high enough in the water to receive the obelisk. The available evidence suggests, however, that the more ancient Egyptians did not use this method. According to Reginald Engelbach, there is no trace of a canal near the Aswan granite quarries, and I know of no canal leading to the Nile discovered since his time.[8]

As for how the surfaces of obelisks were finished and engraved, Engelbach reiterated the commonly held ideas about the use of abrasives and stone tools. A true scholar, he was reluctant to accept unproved ideas and qualified his remarks:

> I had intended to devote a chapter to the polishing and engraving of obelisks after they were set up, but our knowledge of the engraving of the hard rocks is so vague that it can be summed up in a paragraph. The details of the process, as given in the various works on the subject, are not clear to me—perhaps owing to my reprehensible habit of making experiments.[9]

In other words, Engelbach could not account for how the Egyptians engraved obelisks such that the hieroglyphics are more crisp than can be achieved with modern diamond drills. We recall the statement by stonemason Roger Hopkins, concerning an obelisk of Pharaoh Ramses II, in the PBS Nova film titled *Secrets of Lost Empires*:

> Even with modern tools and . . . diamond wheels and all that, we would have . . . a tough time getting it [the hieroglyphs] to this kind of perfection.

The unresolved problems of engraving and raising obelisks and 1,000-ton and heavier monolithic colossi, particularly when they are placed in confined spaces among preexisting building complexes, beckons us to consider the existence of some kind of special technology that was gradually lost.

# Chapter 16

# Proof From Ancient Texts?

Along with the tomb painting of Djehutihotep, ancient literature offers a number of documents that Egyptologists interpret to try to explain how the Great Pyramid was built. However, all of these documents postdate the Pyramid Age. None provides evidence for determining the construction method.

To explain how huge casing blocks were transported from Tura, some Egyptologists rely on a post-Pyramid Age bas-relief on the causeway of the 5th Dynasty pyramid of Pharaoh Unas (c. 2356–2323 B.C.), at Saqqara.[1] Causeways are long stone structures, made of individual blocks, which connect pyramids with their Valley Temples. The Unas causeway does not depict blocks being quarried or shaped, but it shows temple columns being moved along the Nile by barge. What is wrong with this scenario as it relates to building the Great Pyramids of the earlier Pyramid Age? A closer look at this scene reveals the answer, as follows.

In his *Building in Egypt*, Dieter Arnold indicated that workers had probably completed temple columns, including these, in the quarries before transporting them:

> That the production was carried out in the quarries can be gathered from reliefs showing the transport of finished columns from Aswan to Saqqara. . . . Thus the columns and cornices for the temple of Unas were sent in their final shape, if we may trust the wall reliefs in the Unas causeway.[2]

We cannot, however, take the reliefs on the Unas causeway at face value, because granite temple columns remain at the site today, and they are composed of half-ton units fit together by tongue-and-groove joints.[3] Thus, we readily see that they were not completed as whole columns at Aswan. It is fairly easy to haul half-ton units, especially when compared with transporting monolithic columns some 20 feet long.

Moreover, the Unas causeway relief does not relate to transporting blocks and beams for the Great Pyramids, for the following reasons: By the 5th Dynasty, the Pyramid Age had passed, and the Egyptians constructed only small, economically built pyramids. These structures were made largely of sand and rubble fill, and they were mostly or fully cased with blocks expropriated from earlier pyramids. Pharaoh Unas' workers removed building units from the pyramid complex of his predecessor

Pharaoh Djedkara-Isesi, located two miles away.

Unas' scribes probably rendered the columns as monoliths in the causeway reliefs as a matter of protocol. The reliefs were not meant to be taken literally, and instead they clearly document what was made from transported material.

Given that only a few half-ton units are involved, it is inappropriate to use the Unas' causeway relief to make a sweeping generalization about the water transportation of great numbers of truly heavy casing blocks. Remaining casing blocks on the Great Pyramid weigh 15 to 16 tons each, and both Herodotus and Abd el-Latif reported seeing a myriad of 30-foot-long blocks incorporated into the Great Pyramid's exterior casing. Collectively, at Giza there were once well over 200,000 massive casing blocks, according to estimates by Egyptologists (the estimate depends upon the average size of casing blocks, which is difficult to judge for all of the monuments, because most have been cut up and removed in chunks over the ages).

Other objects are too large to have been made in finished form and then transported hundreds of miles from Aswan and stood upon pedestals, such as the 1,200-ton colossi of Ramses II in Tanis along with others of nearly the same size. The chances are too great that the statues would chip or crack during transport and erection. Indeed, a special technology was required to produce such objects, and this special technology—explained in Volume 2 of this book—was also applied to casing and other pyramid blocks during the Old Kingdom. This special technology was in serious decline by the time the Unas pyramid was constructed, at least in part, with expropriated masonry work from miles away.

Another document Egyptologists use to explain pyramid construction is the Tura Stele. It was engraved into a limestone wall at the Tura quarries.[4] The stele vanished during the early days of Egyptology; therefore, only a copy remains. The Tura Stele depicted oxen dragging blocks from the quarries to the edge of the river. In his *The Pyramids* (1969 ed.), Ahmed Fakhry presented a drawing of the Tura Stele and related it to pyramid construction, He added:

> There is a scene showing the transport of blocks of stone from the quarries of Tura, in which we see the oxen dragging the sledges. This was not unusual.[5]

The problems of relating the Tura Stele to pyramid construction include its late date. The Tura Stele was engraved almost 1,000 years after the Great Pyramid was constructed, at a time when the special technology used to build the Great Pyramid was in severe decline. Moreover, the oxen are shown dragging the block on a horizontal surface. Thus, the stele cannot be used to explain the hardest problem: raising millions of pyramid blocks on an incline. Clearly, the Tura Stele does not hold the key to the mystery of pyramid construction.

54. THE TURA STELE SHOWS THE TRANSPORTATION OF BLOCKS FROM A QUARRY AT TURA

The wheel was in use by the time scribes engraved the Tura Stele in the 18th Dynasty. The Tura Stele suggests that the wheel was still not being used to haul blocks 1,000 years after the Great Pyramid was built.

Although the wooden roller is a precursor of the wheel, Egyptologists have largely abandoned the old idea that pyramid builders hauled blocks on wooden rollers. Conveying blocks from the quarries would have required strong, smooth roads, because wooden rollers cannot function in sand. The construction and maintenance of numerous strong, level roads would have demanded much more masonry work, adding greatly to the already overburdened construction rate estimated for the Great Pyramid.

Many years ago Hermann Junker performed experiments to test the idea that the dolerite balls found at ancient construction sites served as rollers for heavy stones.[6] There are many problems with this idea. Sturdy, smooth roads are required for this cumbersome method, raising the demand for squared blocks. One would expect wheeled carts to have developed from such an operation. Engelbach summarized the development of the wheel for transportation in Egypt:

> As far as is known, the wheel played a very small part in the life of the ancient Egyptian; the word for it is almost certainly of foreign origin, and it is not found applied to chariots or wagons until the New Kingdom, though this may well be because horses do not appear in Egypt much before that date. The wheels of the known Egyptian chariots are extremely flimsy affairs, and it is doubtful if any wheel built on lines similar to those which have come down to us would take any load or endure hard wear . . . all known evidence of the methods of transport for building materials used by the Egyptians indicates that the sled alone was used.[7]

Early Egyptologists assumed that paintings from the 18th Dynasty tomb of Rekhmira might explain the tools used to shape pyramid blocks.[8] These scenes, dating 1,300 years after the Great Pyramid was built, show workers carving blocks with chisels. During Rekhmira's time, bronze chisels were in common use. Today Egyptologists

55. THE CHARIOT WHEELS SHOWN ARE THE TYPE KNOWN FROM ANCIENT EGYPT AFTER THE INTRODUCTION OF THE WHEEL DURING THE SECOND INTERMEDIARY PERIOD (BEGINNING ABOUT 1640 B.C.). THESE TWO-WHEELED HORSE-DRAWN CHARIOTS WERE STRONG ENOUGH TO CARRY TWO ARMED SOLDIERS INTO WAR, BUT THEIR WHEELS ARE NOT STRONG ENOUGH TO ENDURE MOVING MULTITON BLOCKS. THE ABOVE SHOWS PHARAOH RAMSES II LEADING HIS ARMY IN THE BATTLE OF QADESH DURING THE 19TH DYNASTY: IMAGE BY D. BARNARD, LONDON, BASED ON RICHARD LEPSIUS AND WOLFGANG HELCK DOCUMENTATION

recognize that a hard form of bronze, needed to cut the medium-hard to hard blocks of the Great Pyramid, was not available until about 800 years after the Great Pyramid was completed. The location of Rekhmira's tomb, in southern Egypt, suggests that the blocks depicted were sandstone. Sandstone soft enough for us to abrade with our fingernails was abundant in the south, called Upper Egypt. Most New Kingdom structures built in the south are made of this soft material. Thus, scenes that most likely show soft blocks (even limestone can be as soft as a sugar cube) being shaped with either bronze or copper chisels do not explain how more ancient Egyptians with copper tools shaped over 12 million medium-hard to hard pyramid blocks. The overwhelming majority of pyramid blocks do not exhibit tool marks. Some of the tool marks found on the minority of blocks are known to date to later attempts to cut the blocks up or pry at them in search of hidden entrances to the pyramids. We recall that Dieter Arnold abandoned the idea that copper tools were used extensively because of the insufficient copper supply for carrying out such monumental construction works. Besides, Dieter Arnold is aware of the study conducted on layers of granite debris near the pyramid of Senwosret I. As mentioned, he reported that, "In these layers, no traces of greenish discoloration from copper could be detected." Copper residue can be found on artifacts after thousands of years when copper is used to cut stone, and we can expect that copper would have been preserved in these layers if it had been used. Considering the close, corresponding fit characteristic of granite pyramid blocks, we must question how these blocks were perfected without copper combined with an abrasive, Egyptology's only option for shaping granite other than pounding balls.

We see that none of the documents or methods Egyptologists have considered explains the construction of the Great Pyramid. We next analyze the archaeological evidence from Giza used by Egyptologists to explain the construction of the Great Pyramid.

# Chapter 17

# Proof From Giza?

Egyptologists offer archaeological evidence from Giza to explain how workers built the Great Pyramid. For example, a block still sits on a small ramp connected to a small queens' pyramid in the Third Pyramid complex at Giza. The complex was built at the end of the 4th Dynasty for Pharaoh Menkaura (c. 2490–2472 B.C.). In the 1992 Nova film *This Old Pyramid*, Mark Lehner asserted that this block proved that builders had raised all pyramid blocks on ramps. He referred to this block as a "frozen moment in pyramid construction."[1] In other words, he uses this block to make the sweeping generalization that the Great Pyramid was built by means of an enormous construction ramp.

But all pyramids of the 3rd Dynasty, all 4th Dynasty queens' pyramids, and all pyramids built after the 4th Dynasty exhibit core and casing blocks small enough to be carried up ramps. One or two men are required to lift a block of the size found in these pyramids. For these and later pyramids, only features such as enormous monolithic crypts, beams, plug-blocks, and portcullises present weights that pose engineering problems. As I have explained above, the Great Pyramids, especially Khufu's pyramid, categorically defy the use of ramps.

The block Lehner had in mind may just as well represent a "frozen moment" in pyramid demolition or restoration, as carried out in ancient or modern times. Like numerous others, the Third Pyramid complex at Giza (the one Lehner referred to) was likely partly either demolished or repaired in the 19th Dynasty reign of Ramses II.[2] This pharaoh's administration partially dismantled some pyramids and restored several others. The ambitious restoration project was undertaken by his son Prince Kha-em-waset, the High Priest of Memphis, who exercised jurisdiction over the entire pyramid necropolis.

From the Old Kingdom's 5th Dynasty (c. 2465–2323 B.C.) forward, blocks were expropriated from older pyramids, until Kha-em-waset's major reconstruction program marked the end of a millennium of pilfering and neglect. Stonemasons' inscriptions suggest that his restoration work started on the 3rd Dynasty pyramid complex of Zoser on the tenth day of the third month of summer, in the 36th year of Ramses II's reign (c. 1243 B.C.). Also known to have benefited were the 4th Dynasty rectangular

56. Signs of block quarrying at Giza are unmistakable and found in the quarry next to Khafra's Great Pyramid. The volume of the quarry equals only about three percent of Khafra's masonry. This quarry bears the inscriptions of Pharaoh Ramses II, and so the quarrying may date to his restoration operation at Giza. Photograph by Jon Bodsworth

cenotaph of Pharaoh Shepseskaf, the 5$^{th}$ Dynasty pyramids of both Sahure and Unas, and a Sun temple of Neuserre.

Egyptologists suggest that Kha-em-waset's operation may have also contributed to the restoration of Khufu's Great Pyramid. During Herodotus' 5$^{th}$ century B.C. trip to Egypt, he reported seeing inscriptions on the Great Pyramid.[3] His report cannot be verified, because almost all casing blocks are now gone. However, Kha-em-waset prominently inscribed large, conspicuous hieroglyphic characters on the outer casing blocks of one face of each pyramid he restored; therefore, the inscriptions Herodotus saw may have been those of Kha-em-waset. Kha-em-waset's writings still appear on several pyramids. The inscriptions of Ramses II and those of Kha-em-waset's architect Mey are still visible in a quarry at the foot of Khafra's Great Pyramid, the quarry at Giza with conspicuous signs of block quarrying.

These demolition and restoration works carried out under Ramses II's administration, and later phases of reconstruction, may explain the block Lehner deemed a "frozen moment" in the original construction work.

An account by Abd el-Latif (A.D. 1161–1231) pertains to the very pyramid complex that Lehner had in mind.[4] El-Latif described an ill-fated government-ordered operation that set out to demolish Menkaura's pyramid. El-Latif described the tremendous toil and expense involved when stripping off a great many pyramid blocks and dumping them nearby. But the project proved so demanding that it had to be abandoned, and, after all the work, only a small part of the pyramid had been defaced. Perhaps the queen's pyramid in Menkaura's complex—the monument Lehner takes issue with—was affected.

Pyramids were also routinely robbed of ready-made blocks by 5$^{th}$ and 6$^{th}$ Dynasty pharaohs and by modern operations, as well. In the hope of finding an intact burial site, a crew of Napoleon's men attempted to demolish the westernmost queen's pyramid in this complex. After tearing down its upper north quarter, they abandoned the project.[5] Treasure hunters over many centuries have pried and moved blocks. Giza has experienced post-19$^{th}$ Dynasty Egyptian, Greek, Roman and modern reconstruction activity.[6] In their quests for artifacts, early Egyptologists dismantled parts of pyramids, frequently using boring rods, gunpowder, and dynamite. Tradition holds that Egyptian Arabs removed many blocks from the Giza monuments for constructions in Cairo, and Petrie witnessed the removal of blocks from a number of structures during his seasons of work in Egypt. We see that the "frozen moment" Lehner perceived as original construction work can easily date to a subsequent period. In other words, rather than an abandoned block left during construction, the block remaining on the ramp could have been abandoned after being torn off of the pyramid. In any case, we have already considered why a giant ramp of the size needed to raise blocks for the Great Pyramid is unworkable. For reasons we have already considered, it is not logical to assume that small blocks carried up earthen ramps translate into a scenario in which enormous blocks for the Great Pyramid were transported up a giant earthen ramp.

To explain how the pyramid builders quarried blocks, Lehner pointed out a hole in a quarry at Giza made by the removal of a block. He insisted that this hole proves that all core blocks for the Great Pyramid were quarried at Giza. His sweeping generalization protested claims by Petrie, and more recently by geologists from Waseda University, that pyramid builders hauled core blocks from a distant quarry. For Lehner, this quarry hole represented another "frozen moment" in pyramid construction.

His assertion ignores simple established facts: First, anyone can see the one area where trenches were made and rectangular stumps remain (See Figure 56 on page 181), i.e., clear evidence of block removal. Anyone can compare this area, located next to Khafra's pyramid, with the huge "quarries" (excavated pits) associated with the Great Pyramid. The comparison shows how very small the quarry with the trenches and stumps (clear evidence of block quarrying) is relative to the large excavation pits (showing no comparable areas of quarried blocks) associated with the Giza pyramids. As mentioned, Mark Lehner estimated the volume of the "quarry" associated with the Great Pyramid as equal to the monument itself. Petrie was the first to point out that the area showing quarried blocks (Figure 56) at Giza is too small to account for the Great Pyramid.

In 2002 Systems Engineer Mike Carrell studied surveys and maps of Giza to provide an estimate for publication here. Based on his estimate of the height of the walls and other dimensions of this quarry near Khafra's pyramid (the one with clear evidence of block quarrying), he calculated its volume at only 2 percent of the volume of Khufu's pyramid.

Second, Dieter Arnold and Dietrich Klemm recognized that 4th Dynasty quarrying was not characterized by holes, like the one Lehner pointed out during the Nova film. Klemm established that Old and Middle Kingdom quarry walls are instead covered with the marks of pointed picks. Lehner's assertion ignores the long history of quarrying at Giza. Indeed, geochemist Klemm, of the University of Munich, in Germany, and his wife Egyptologist Rosemarie Klemm carefully studied quarrying techniques by historical period.[7] These researchers identified and classified the quarrying techniques used from the Pyramid Age to the Roman occupation of Egypt in A.D. 30. By comparing tool marks and considering inscriptions, and by dating pottery shards, the Klemms produced a chronology of the quarrying techniques used in the sandstone quarries at Silsila and in the limestone quarries. In other words, they used the type of tool marks found in the quarries to date these quarries to specific historical periods.

The Klemms observed evidence of the crudest quarrying method, which involved inserting wooden poles into holes made in the bedrock. Ancient workers then saturated these large dowel rods with water. The water-swollen poles afforded enough pressure to cause the limestone bedrock to split along a single plane. Quarrymen repeated the operation at 90-degree angles until they isolated a rough block. Workers then undercut the block to extract it. Until the study by the Klemms, Egyptologists thought that this method was the oldest, because it is the crudest. But the Klemms showed that this was the Roman method, and that this method was used in Egypt 2,500 years after the Great Pyramid was built. There is little evidence of this method at Giza, assuring that it was not used to obtain millions of blocks for the Great Pyramid. Thus, in the Nova film, Mark Lehner incorrectly used holes at Giza to draw a conclusion about Pyramid Age quarrying.

Another method was to bash out long, straight trenches in the bedrock at right angles until a block was isolated on four sides. Quarrymen crouched in these trenches and bashed out more rock from below to separate the blocks from the quarry floor. The Klemms showed that this technique does not match Pyramid Age quarrying, either. This technique shows up in the quarry field near Khafra, which is very small (equaling about 3 percent of Khafra's pyramid) compared with the huge "quarries" (excavation pits) near the Giza Pyramids, as already mentioned.

Egyptology has no true picture of the quarrying process used for building the Great Pyramid. Acknowledging the study by the Klemms, Arnold admitted:

> The question as to what kind of tools were used to cut the separation trenches and to lift the blocks from their beds has not been answered satisfactorily because of the contradiction between the tool marks left on the quarry walls and the tools actually found in ancient Egypt.[8]

The tool marks on quarry walls to which Arnold alluded are crude, the marks of primitive pickaxes. Like copper tools, stone pickaxes are unsuitable for block quarrying. We see that Egyptologists cannot reconcile these crude tool marks, which characterize Old and Middle Kingdom quarrying, with making trenches to produce blocks. This is an important point, because Arnold's admission shows that Egyptology really has not determined how workers made blocks for the Great Pyramid.

Egyptology's inability to show how the Egyptians could have quarried blocks to build the Great Pyramid establishes yet another serious weakness in the accepted construction theory. In these pages, I have shown three fundamental, fatal flaws in the accepted theory of how the Great Pyramid was constructed.

First, the Egyptological literature itself shows that Egyptology has not determined how the Great Pyramid's blocks could have been raised. Studies show that huge ramps are unworkable.

Second, Egyptology has not determined how millions of limestone and harder stone blocks could have been shaped, because the Pyramid Age Egyptians did not have adequate supplies of appropriate metal tools for creating giant pyramid shapes with beautifully sloped surfaces and tight-fitting, conforming blocks made of medium-hard to hard rock. Pounding balls, Egyptology's last option for shaping pyramid blocks, cannot produce the special features existing on the scale of the giant pyramids, a fact admitted by Dieter Arnold (quoted earlier in these pages).

Third, Egyptology has not determined how even crudely shaped limestone blocks could have been quarried at Giza during the Pyramid Age on such a massive scale. Clearly, there is a dire need for an entirely new and different pyramid-construction theory that can solve these germane problems.

A third problem with Lehner's assertion is that there are major geological differences between the Giza limestone bedrock and the pyramid blocks, differences observed by a number of geologists. As mentioned, fossiliferous pyramid and temple blocks exhibit jumbled seashells. In contrast, the quarry walls contain the same types of shells, but the quarry walls are characterized by normal sedimentary layering in which the fossils mostly lie flat.

The evidence above shows how important it is to sort out the different periods of quarry work at Giza and at other quarries so that we can get a true picture of ancient construction methods. Most books and articles on pyramid construction show the stumps north of Khafra's pyramid and assert that they explain the method of obtaining blocks for pyramid construction. The quarried area consists of rows of what appear to be stumps left over from the removal of blocks. However, this grid is associated with Khafra's pyramid; therefore, it did not exist when the Great Pyramid was built. It could not have been the source of rock for the Great Pyramid, and, for that reason, it is not involved in Mark Lehner's reconstruction (The Giza Mapping Project) of the source of stone for Khufu's Great Pyramid.

Before the study by the Klemms, Egyptologists assumed that these so-called stumps proved how blocks were quarried for the Great Pyramid, thereby ignoring Petrie's observation that the quarried area is too small to account for the Great Pyramids (an observation that can easily be confirmed now that Giza has been carefully mapped).

Comments appear in the most popular book of all on the pyramids *The Pyramids of Egypt* (1985 edition), by former keeper of Egyptian antiquities at the British Museum I.E.S. Edwards:

> Limestone . . . presented the pyramid builders with no serious difficulties of its quarrying. A discovery by W.B. Emery in the early dynastic cemetery of Saqqara has shown that even in the 1st Dynasty the Egyptians possessed excellent copper tools, including saws and chisels, which were capable of cutting any kind of limestone. . . . Chisels and wedges were, however, the tools most favoured for quarrying limestone, the former for cutting the blocks away from the rock on every side except the bottom and the latter

for detaching the blocks at the base.[9]

Although the body of the Sphinx and some blocks in the Giza complexes are soft enough to be cut with copper, Edwards' remarks are out of date and erroneous, as the trials with copper tools, the relative dearth of copper supplies, and the study by the Klemms we have already explored have all shown.

Given that the most up-to-date Egyptological findings show that the flat-topped stumps near Khafra's pyramid are uncharacteristic of Pyramid Age quarrying, they should no longer be used to explain how blocks were made for the Great Pyramids. Unfortunately, however, Dieter Arnold's *Building in Egypt*, which will long remain the new standard on ancient Egyptian masonry, fails specifically to mention that this grid is characteristic of post-Pyramid Age quarrying. Arnold also failed to point out that the grid is vastly too small to have supplied blocks for the Great Pyramids. As mentioned, this grid of stumps is associated with Khafra's pyramid, and did not exist when the Great Pyramid was built. The grid of stumps may represent the restorations of Ramses II's reign. Inscriptions of Ramses II's administration appear in this quarry next to Khafra's pyramid; however, the block quarrying could date to even later than his reign.

The long history of intermittent building activity at Giza spans thousands of years and includes several phases. After the original work was completed, maintenance cults preserved the Giza pyramid estates. These cults disintegrated over time, and Egyptians of later times eventually used the pyramids and temples as sources of ready-made blocks. Later still, Ramses' son Kha-em-waset restored the pyramids and reestablished their maintenance cults. The endowment estates were large, and priests of Snofru, Khufu, and other pharaohs were still officiating in Ptolemaic times.[10]

Building activity at Giza was also conducted during the Saite Period, in the 26$^{th}$ Dynasty (664–525 B.C.).[11] The work was so extensive that some Egyptologists suggest that the sarcophagus lid found in the Third Pyramid at Giza, built for Pharaoh Menkaura, was replaced during Saite times.[12] When clearing a chamber in this pyramid, John S. Perring found a fragment of a lid with Menkaura's name on it. But its style is identified as dating to the 26$^{th}$ Dynasty.

There was also Greek activity at Giza, as evidenced by the large number of Greek Sphinxes discovered in 1994. As mentioned, a Greco-Roman village of considerable size at Giza was first reported by Howard Vyse. Evidence of Roman restoration appears near the Sphinx, where there are inscriptions belonging to the Roman emperors Marcus Aurelius Antoninus (A.D. 161–180) and Septimus Severus (A.D. 193–211). Both restored the court of the Sphinx. The Roman Emperors Antonius Pius (A.D. 138–161) and Lucius Versus (A.D. 161–169) had the Sphinx's retaining walls restored.

Only a minority of pyramid blocks exhibit tool marks, and these blocks contrast

57. The south face of the pyramid of the 5th Dynasty Pharaoh Unas still exhibits portions of the large banner inscribed during the 19th Dynasty restoration operation of Prince Kha-em-waset, son of Ramses II. The banners were inscribed as follows:

> His Majesty decreed an announcement (thus): It is the High Priest (of Ptah), the Sem-Priest, Prince Kha-em-waset, who has perpetuated the name of King...[in this case Unas]. Now his name was not found upon the face of his pyramid. Very greatly did the Sem-Priest, Prince Kha-em-waset, desire to restore the monuments of the Kings of Upper and Lower Egypt, because of what they had done, the strength of which [monument] was falling into decay. He [Kha-em-waset] set forth a decree for its [the pyramid's] sacred offerings...its water...[endowed] with a grant of land, together with its personnel...

Photograph by John Reid

sharply to the overwhelming majority of blocks at Giza. Egyptologists assume that workers ground off the tool marks on most pyramid and temple blocks. However, Egyptologists offer no explanation for why Egyptians would grind off tool marks on the blocks, which are sometimes highly irregular in shape and not meant to look perfect, and were supposed to remain forever hidden behind giant, beautifully made casing blocks. Egyptology offers no demonstration of how workers could have ground tool marks from in between huge form fitted blocks, some demonstrating hairline joints as close as 1/500 inch or in perfect contact along their lengths, or those with undersides that conform to the bedrock below.

Some blocks bear tool marks that should not be confounded with original work. Many tool marks were made by treasure hunters who pried pyramid blocks in search of hidden entrances to the monuments. It is known that some of the marks are the result of Arab workers of the Middle Ages, who cut up some blocks and left others partially cut and/or marred. It is, therefore, logical to think that the minority of blocks, in both the quarries and monuments, that exhibit certain distinctive marks, represent either post-Pyramid Age restoration or attempts to utilize the blocks for new construction.

We see that the archaeological record vies against Lehner's assertion that all blocks original to the Great Pyramid were quarried as he supposes. As mentioned above, Arnold admitted that the evidence associated with block extraction was very puzzling. Moreover, Petrie was correct to assert that there is a dearth of evidence for the extraction of whole blocks at Giza, no matter what the quarry method employed, to account for the construction of the Great Pyramid.

In the Nova film *This Old Pyramid,* Lehner also attempted to explain how the ancient workers shaped pyramid blocks. To do so, Lehner pointed out stone debris strewn around the floor of the crudely made subterranean chamber of the Great Pyramid. He said that this debris proved that the ancient builders cut all limestone blocks for the Great Pyramid with primitive tools. His assertion is illogical.

Stone picks and pounding balls are suitable for breaking up limestone to tunnel crude shafts and bash out rough subterranean rooms, like the one in which Lehner was standing. The work mainly involved removing tons of rubble. The main challenge for the workers engaged in this task was overcoming the difficulty of preventing the bedrock from caving in when encountering softer strata of desert conglomerate and cracks in the bedrock.

It is illogical to compare a crude, bashed-out room to the masonry of the Great Pyramid itself. The special masonry features of the Great Pyramid include its giant form-fitting casing blocks that fit as closely as 1/500 an inch, the angle they produced up the sides of the pyramid, its 13-acre level foundation, its more than 200 corresponding tiers made in about 73 tier heights (covering a great many acres) accurate to within ½ centimeter, its four amazingly accurate subtly curved faces, and the near perfect planes of these vast sloping faces. All require a vastly more sophisticated technology than the ability to bash and hack rock to produce crude underground chambers, such as the one Lehner showed in the Nova film. Besides, limestone is more moist and easier to cut when it is underground.

In these pages I have shown that the accepted theories of pyramid construction are not supported by hard evidence. They are supported only by the sheer weight of very entrenched ideas that are gradually being displaced by the most up-to-date Egyptological findings.

To summarize, the small block on a small ramp at Giza cannot legitimately be used to explain the method of building the Great Pyramid. Small ramps attached to small pyramids do not demonstrate that workers used a huge ramp to elevate blocks for the Great Pyramid. Engineering studies we have already considered show that construction ramps are unworkable for building the Great Pyramid.

There is too little evidence of block quarrying at Giza to account for the construction of the Great Pyramid, and this shows that something is fundamentally wrong with the accepted construction-theory paradigm. Evidence of block quarrying at Giza is characteristic of much later building activity. Arnold admits that Old Kingdom quarrying is very puzzling to him. The crude tool marks, made with pointed picks in the huge quarries associated with the Great Pyramids, do not offer him a clue about how pyramid blocks could have been quarried.

All this evidence may seem very strange, given the existence of enormous pyramids at Giza. But it is a mistake to use the monuments themselves as proof of method. The true method of pyramid construction, which I explain in Volume 2, causes all of these seemingly overwhelming problems to vanish.

# Chapter 18

# The Resistance To New Knowledge

In response to the wild speculation of occultists and poorly researched books, the trend in Egyptology these days is to dismiss or downplay unresolved masonry and engineering enigmas.[1] Consider Dieter Arnold's remarks in Building in Egypt (1991):

> The discussion of how the pyramids could have been built seems, however, to be never-ending and continues to produce fantasies. In this respect, Egyptology shares the fate of other archaeological fields that deal with monumental architecture. But although Egyptian builders accomplished great feats in moving and lifting enormous weights, everything was achieved with the relatively simple building methods that are well attested for Pharaonic Egypt. The Egyptian builders used three basic methods to lift a weight: by pulling it up an inclined plane; by lifting it with ropes and primitive devices; and by levering.[2]

These remarks imply that Arnold assumed that the pyramid builders had overcome the impossible task of elevating millions of massive building units on a ramp much more massive than the Great Pyramid itself. While Arnold himself acknowledged unresolved problems with ramps, he nevertheless made light of unsolved engineering puzzles:

> The laying of blocks of extraordinary size seems to have presented no real problems for the Egyptian builders. Also, the lifting of core and casing blocks of the pyramids to great heights seems to have been routine work for them.[3]

Arnold was implying that because the Great Pyramid exists, raising enormous weights to great heights did not present a problem. Indeed, Egyptologists have an intellectual obligation to go beyond such perfunctory observations, which anyone untrained in the principles of valid reasoning and argumentation can make. Egyptologists have the obligation of explaining how enormous building units were elevated on such a grand scale. Egyptologists have the responsibility of explaining problems like how workers can use instruments such as stone pounding balls and sandstone rubbers to create 20 acres of tightly-fitted casing blocks with smooth surfaces all beautifully angled—according to historical reports and examples including Khafra's pointed tip—to form an enormous pyramid shape. If an Egyptologist cannot figure out these problems, then that individual should have the presence of mind to recognize and admit to fundamental problems rather than ignore and/or brush them aside.

Esteemed scholars do a serious disservice by dismissing enigmas that continue to perplex trained engineers and stone masons, as well as defy common sense. Because great weight is accorded to the opinions of learned scholars, the average reader will be greatly persuaded by dismissive comments that may not be correct or even relevant. I write this book to appeal to readers who think deeply, and I present sufficient evidence to prove that the Great Pyramid would not exist if its construction were solely dependent on the means proposed by Egyptology. Remarks by the scientific-minded Reginald Engelbach, chief inspector of antiquities of Upper Egypt early in the 20$^{th}$ century, can serve to summarize the problem.

> While the publication of a new grammatical form or historical point will evoke a perfect frenzy of contradiction in the little world of Egyptology, the most absurd statements on a mechanical problem will be left unquestioned and, what is worse, accepted.[4]

Dieter Arnold was not always so willing to dismiss problems. He recognized that building Snofru's two large pyramids had involved a total volume of about four million cubic yards of rock. Workers incorporated this huge amount of material during this pharaoh's 24-year reign. The Great Pyramids of Khafra and Khufu each have a volume of about two million cubic yards of material. Arnold calculated that in 80 years, workers had built 12 million blocks into the major pyramids.[5] The number of blocks set per day depended on how long it took to choose, plan and prepare construction sites. We must also factor in the usual delays of getting ambitious projects underway. There was also time off, since the ancient Egyptians enjoyed a number of religious holidays per year. To avoid hazards, workers had to be off the construction sites after daylight hours. Considering the various factors, Arnold deduced that the number of blocks set per day could lead to "astronomical numbers."

He saw no solution other than doubling or tripling the life spans of these pharaohs. His proposal is conservative compared with that of engineers from Japan's Waseda University. As mentioned, after building a relatively small model of the Great Pyramid, they calculated that the monument required a 1,200-year construction period.[6]

Mark Lehner, too, dismisses the construction enigmas of the Great Pyramid. After Nova's *This Old Pyramid* aired, Lehner's remarks were published in the January 1995 issue of *National Geographic*:

> To gauge the extent of that labor [for building the Great Pyramid], Mark Lehner and a team built a 30-foot-high pyramid near Giza out of the same Tura limestone used by the ancient Egyptians. The men who built Khufu's pyramid, hauling and positioning an estimated 2.3 million limestone blocks, most weighing 2.5 tons, would have had to set a block in place every two and a half minutes. Using a helical ramp winding upward around their pyramid, Lehner's team found that just ten to twelve men could slide a block up the ramp, using desert clay and water as a lubricant, and lever it into place. Herodotus declared that 100,000 men were needed to build one of the Pyramids of Giza. Lehner calculates that as few as 10,000 could have pulled off the job. As he puts it, "A pyramid turns out to be a very doable thing."[7]*

*THE NATIONAL GEOGRAPHIC REPORTER HAS MADE A NUMBER OF ERRORS. NOVA'S MINIATURE PYRAMID WAS 18 FEET HIGH, NOT 30. THE TURA LIMESTONE USED BY NOVA WAS VERY SOFT, UNLIKE THE HARDER CORE AND CASING BLOCKS OF THE GREAT PYRAMID. THE SIZES OF THE GREAT PYRAMID'S BLOCKS ARE AVERAGED AT 2.5 TONS (THE POINT IS MISSED THAT THE MUCH LARGER ONES AT GREAT HEIGHTS POSE THE GREAT CHALLENGE). NOVA'S RAMP DID NOT WIND UPWARD AROUND THE MINIATURE PYRAMID, BUT ONLY AROUND ONE CORNER—AFFORDING THE ONLY CLUE THAT THE PYRAMID WAS NOT REALLY BUILT BY HAND.

Since the above-quoted *National Geographic* article was published, Lehner has revised his 10,000-man figure. In *The Complete Pyramids* (1997), he offered revised calculations. Lehner concluded that a grand total of 25,000 men was required. He listed most as logistical workers, including copper-tool sharpeners, cooks, and brewers.[8] For the critical work of quarrying, elevating, shaping, and setting stones for the Great Pyramid, Lehner's figure is too low:

> Our calculations suggest that Khufu's pyramid could have been built by two crews of 2,000.[9]

I have already shown above that Mark Lehner came to his low estimate with erroneous calculations. Lehner substitutes the calculation of the number of men needed to haul blocks on a flat surface for the calculation needed for elevating blocks on an incline—which allows him to discard many thousands of workers.[10] Compare Petrie's estimate of 100,000 men. Sadly, the enigmas of pyramid construction cannot be appreciated as long as people in responsible positions incorrectly report them, as I show in these pages Mark Lehner has done repeatedly.

Nova's *This Old Pyramid* ignored the unanswered masonry and engineering questions. Producer Michael Barnes planned and scripted the film based on consultations with a number of well-known Egyptologists. In addition to Mark Lehner and Jean-Philippe Lauer, one of these Egyptologists was Dieter Arnold, whose *Building in Egypt*, despite its mixed messages, did point out inadequacies of Pyramid Age tools and some severe problems with ramp theories. Here are the most critical points that Nova ignored to base *This Old Pyramid* on outdated ideas that Egyptology is gradually abandoning:

- Arnold admits that Egyptology does not really know how limestone blocks could have been quarried. Arnold wrote: "The question as to what kind of tools were used to cut the separation trenches and to lift the blocks from their beds has not been answered satisfactorily because of the contradiction between the tool marks left on the quarry walls and the tools actually found in ancient Egypt. . . ."[11]

- Arnold admits that Egyptology does not know how blocks could have been shaped: "We do not know exactly how the masons achieved two corresponding and neatly fitted planes on two neighboring blocks. . . ."[12]

- Regarding helical ramps, designs that would work with the topography of the Giza site, Arnold writes: ". . . one would even doubt their feasibility. In spite of the ingeniousness of such a device, spiral ramps would have created serious problems."[14]

- Arnold's remarks can serve to sum up the ramp problems associated with constructing the Great Pyramid: ". . . the most ingenious and scrupulous system developed on the drawing board is nothing but one more example of unproven speculation. . . ."[13]

In short, Nova ignored the most fundamental problems: Egyptology does not know how the Great Pyramid's blocks could have been quarried, shaped or elevated. The film misrepresented the problems and then claimed to have reconciled them.

PBS repeated the same old mistakes in a newer film that first aired on February 20, 2001, titled *Secrets of the Pharaohs, Part 2: Lost City of the Pyramids*. The film featured a study of pyramid construction by contractor Craig Smith. Here are excerpts from an online article by Mark Rose, Managing Editor of *Archaeology* magazine (dated February 21, 2001), which summarize the project:

> In an interesting experiment, American contractor Craig Smith is called in. Familiar with managing large-scale construction projects, like airports, Smith is primed with what we know of Old Kingdom construction methods: stone and flint implements from the tombs, copper-working, and quarrying at Giza (partially cut-out blocks and ramps along which stones were hauled), an inscription depicting a colossal statue being dragged using ropes and water (to reduce friction), and results of failed stone-levering experiments inspired by Herodotus' tale of how blocks were moved. Smith gets to work, first determining how the pyramids were built. Computer modeling shows that a ramp built perpendicular to one side of the pyramid's base was most economical for positioning blocks until the structure reached one-third of its height (at which point one-half of the blocks would have been laid). Only then would the ramp be built, more narrowly since the blocks farther up would be smaller, spiraling around the upper part of the pyramid. A ramp spiraling up all the way from the base, explains Smith, would require much more fill and construction time. Having established the most economical way to build a pyramid, he looks at the numbers of people required. Surprisingly, Smith says it could be done in only ten years: two or three for preparation, five for the actual construction, and two to remove the ramp and finish the site. This schedule would require 40,000 workmen during the peak years, four through six. Lehner and Hawass believe more time was used, perhaps 20 years, which would bring the annual labor pool down toward the figure proposed by Hawass.

In other words, Smith was provided incorrect data and information, and so he incorrectly assumed that copper, flint and other stone tools are capable of quarrying and cutting millions of limestone blocks and can achieve the perfection of the Great Pyramid. Smith does not explain where vast supplies of copper could have come from, or consider that copper is softer than most blocks in the Great Pyramid. Smith does not address the absence of tool marks on the vast majority of blocks.

Smith advocates the use of a gigantic ramp, although no ramp remains have been found attached to the Great Pyramid. There are vastly insufficient ramp remains at Giza that would suggest the existence of such an enormous ramp. Smith supplies no data on the strength of the ramp he proposes. Remember that engineers such as Peter Hodges showed that a solid stone ramp would be needed, and the blocks making up such a ramp would have to be heavy enough not to slide out of place when beams up to 70 tons are raised to the level of the ceiling of the King's Chamber. The stones would have to be of good quality so that they would not crack or give way beneath the workers. As mentioned in the Nova pyramid-building experiment, Roger Hopkins confirmed the need for a solid masonry ramp. Roger Hopkins remarked in the film that their stone rubble ramp was falling apart after raising only a couple of stones weighing one ton each, and that a concrete ramp was needed. Egyptologists presume that a concrete ramp did not exist, making a stone ramp mandatory.

Smith proposes a partial ramp design, covering 2/3 of the monument, that eliminates the ability to measure from true reference points. The upper 2/3 of his ramp completely engulfs the Great Pyramid, and so we can expect a distorted pyramid shape as the work outcome because he offered no way around the problem.

He did not simulate tests of his design using actual tier height measurements. We must keep in mind that tier 201 was measured as taller than tier four at the base, and that tier 35 is taller than tier two. His calculation is also devoid of the time required to prepare, set, and cement (with paper-thin cement) huge, form-fitted casing blocks, a feat that baffled W.M.F. Petrie: "To merely place such stones in exact contact at the sides would be careful work; but to do so with cement in the joint seems almost impossible."

When critical data are ignored and computer modeling substitutes for real experiments, it is easy to minimize the construction rate and manpower required. Smith's idea that the actual construction work could be done in only five years arises from the flawed information and data he was "primed with." The very idea that millions of blocks can be converted into 73 tier heights (which heights show an error of less than half a centimeter when measured with precise modern instruments) made up largely of conforming masonry to form evenly bowed faces (which show a mean optical plane touching the most prominent points of the blocks at an average variation of only 1.0 inch), staggers the mind and must be factored into legitimate calculations.

Computer modeling is only as good as the data input, and in this instance the input is seriously flawed. Proper study shows that the Great Pyramid, with its unprecedented precision, exceeds even modern capabilities (assuming a construction rate of only about 25 years)—unless one is working with the special technology that is the subject of Volume 2 of this book.

Egyptology is abandoning unworkable theories, but the process is slow, because there has been nothing acceptable to replace them—until the discovery came about that is the subject of this book. The great resistance to change we can sense from all of this, and the reluctance to look at problems thoroughly and in new ways is not atypical. Intellectual progress often moves very slowly. A statement by the famous British author George Orwell (1903–50) appropriately describes the situation:

> Progress is not an illusion, it happens, but it is slow and invariably disappointing.[15]

# Chapter 19

# The Supertech Theories

In 1883 William M. Flinders Petrie's book *The Pyramids and Temples of Gizeh* introduced the world to the grand features of the Great Pyramid, along with perplexing puzzles associated with its construction. The enigmas he identified glare after more than a century of cumulative study, and challenging questions continue to arise. As society has become more technology-minded, a number of popular books have advanced speculative theories based in futuristic technology.

Although they existed earlier, the supertech idea was popularized about 30 years ago by author Erich von Daniken in his best-seller *Chariots of the Gods?* (1969). There has since been no shortage of variations and elaboration on his theme. Von Daniken and others advocate that space-alien technology is responsible for all ancient monuments exhibiting unexplained engineering or masonry features.

Predictably, Egyptologists react by denouncing these ideas and asserting established theories. Nevertheless, there is no denying the need for a theory that solves the enigmas and anomalies I have presented in the previous pages. In the absence of such a truly convincing explanation, alternative explanations abound. Some are outlandish and others fail to properly address problems. Some popular books propose exotic power sources for running supertech devices ranging from crystal generators to harmonic or magnetic levitation. But if we think along these lines, then we would have to entertain a tremendous wealth of supertechnology to satisfy all of the features of the Great Pyramid.

Antigravity devices are a favorite for transporting granite beams up to 27 feet long from Aswan, 500 miles south of Giza. We would need a matter scrambler to jumble up fossil shells for the nummulitic limestone building blocks of the Great Pyramid.[1] A machine that recalibrates time would allow for very rapid construction during Khufu's reign. A supercomputer would be useful for addressing the inventorying, storing, and assorting problems associated with the vast masonry patterns. Computer-driven power saws could shape the multitudes of form-fitted blocks and cut the deep hieroglyphic and decorative reliefs in items made of hard rock. A large, exotic power saw could rapidly cut the lid from Khufu's granite sarcophagus in the Great Pyramid. Because this sarcophagus is too large to fit through the long hallway leading to the King's Chamber, a matter shrinker would be useful for installation. The ultrasonic

58. THE ANCIENT MODEL HOUSE ABOVE DATES FROM THE MIDDLE KINGDOM (2040-1640 B.C.) AND HELPS TO OFFER US A SENSE OF THE TECHNOLOGICAL LEVEL OF THAT TIME. BRITISH MUSEUM NUMBER 22783; PHOTO BY MICHAEL HOLFORD, LOUGHTON, ESSEX, UK

59. NEXT PAGE. A MODEL HOUSE DATING TO THE 19TH CENTURY B.C. A WOMAN IS SHOWN KNEADING BREAD, WHILE A FARM STEWARD SITS UPSTAIRS. ALTHOUGH VERY BEAUTIFIED AND ELABORATE, EVEN ROYAL PALACES WERE BUILT WITH MUD-BRICK AND WOOD IN PHARAONIC TIMES. BRITISH MUSEUM PHOTOGRAPH

drill Christopher Dunn envisions might play a role, too. The same devices would be useful for post-Pyramid Age objects that defy conventional explanations. Such technology would have had to exist alongside mud-brick houses and the primitive technology of the times, an unlikely scenario.

Although I reject such fanciful ideas, it is important to recognize that the supertech theories exist, to a significant degree, because orthodox theories have failed. To make matters worse, orthodox books and articles tend to ignore or gloss over the most difficult enigmas, causing proponents of the supertech theories to suspect a conspiracy of censorship.

Some proponents of an Atlantean origin of the Great Pyramid propose that evidence for advanced technologies must be buried deeper than archaeologists have excavated. But this line of reasoning is invalid, because the technology that afforded extraordinary masonry works appears throughout Egyptian history.

For example, Pharaoh Amenemhet III's huge, spectacular monolithic quartzite sarcophagus, which is unrivaled by modern stonework, was constructed only 600 years before the events that came to be recorded in the Bible as the Hebrew Exodus. Many extraordinary artifacts date from much later than Amenemhet III's quartzite sarcophagus. The 63-foot-high quartzite Colossi of Memnon immediately come to mind. A yellow quartzite bust of Queen Nefertiti dates to the 18th Dynasty. Curators consider the detailed, lifelike bust a masterpiece. As mentioned, a number of quartzite sarcophagi were made for 18th Dynasty pharaohs.

Inscriptions on hard-stone vessels, statuary, sarcophagi, and obelisks serve to date these items. Among a great many examples, inscriptions etched into a diorite bowl found at Saqqara date this object to Hotep, the first king of the 2nd Dynasty. Another example is the hieroglyphic writings in the vaults above the King's Chamber

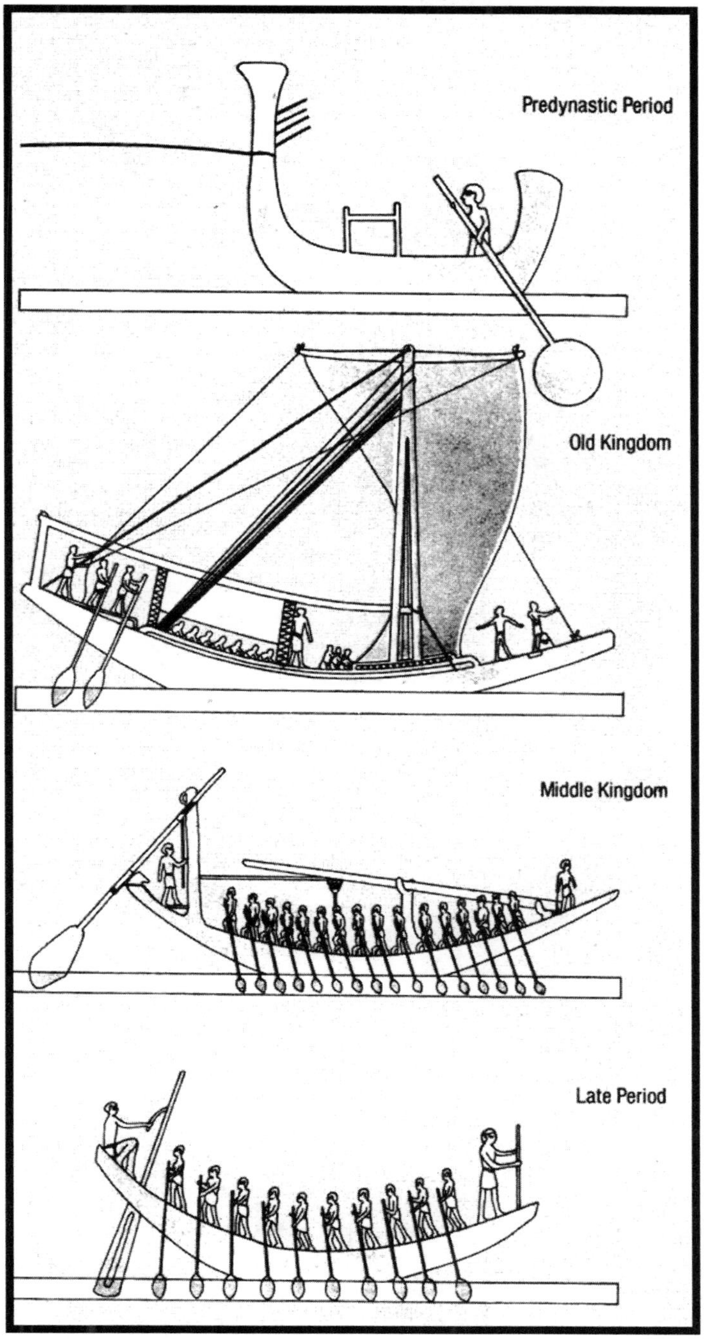


60. THE STATE-OF-THE-ART IN BOAT BUILDING DURING EGYPTIAN ANTIQUITY OFFERS US A SENSE OF THE OVERALL TECHNOLOGICAL LEVEL. THE MATERIALS USED WERE SIMPLE AND INCLUDED LEATHER, WOOD AND ROPE.

A MYSTERY OF EGYPTOLOGY IS HOW THE RUDIMENTARY CRAFT KNOWN FROM ANCIENT EGYPTIAN HISTORY COULD HAVE BEEN STRONG ENOUGH TO CARRY MONOLITHIC OBJECTS WEIGHING THOUSANDS OF TONS. HERODOTUS REPORTED A MONOLITHIC TEMPLE, MADE WITH GRANITE, IN THE DELTA CITY OF BUTO THAT JOHN G. WILKINSON ESTIMATED AT ABOUT 5,000 TONS. PLINY THE ELDER MEASURED OBELISKS THAT WOULD HAVE WEIGHED AT LEAST 2,000 TONS. THE SIMPLE LATE STONE AGE TECHNOLOGY THAT IS THE SUBJECT OF VOLUME 2 OF THIS BOOK SOLVES THE PROBLEM.

DRAWINGS BY D. BARNARD, LONDON, BASED ON G. REISNER, H. WINLOCK AND B. LANDSTROM

of the Great Pyramid, dated to the reign of Khufu.

For most of his career as an archaeo-Egyptologist, Mark Lehner promoted the idea that the Great Pyramid is an artifact of Atlantis. In his book *The Egyptian Heritage: Based on the Edgar Cayce Readings* (1974), Lehner suggests that Atlanteans painted

61. The state-of-the-art in ship building during the 4th Dynasty (c. 2590 B.C.) offers us a sense of the technological level of the Pyramid Age. The photograph to the left shows one of Khufu's funerary boats. In the 1950s it was excavated from a pit near the Great Pyramid. The ship was made of 1,200 pieces of wood, mostly cedar, all pegged or sewn together with rope. In water, papyrus rope shrinks and wood swells, making this craft water-tight without tar or caulking. It displaced about 40 tons of water and measured 120 feet long. Photograph by John Ross

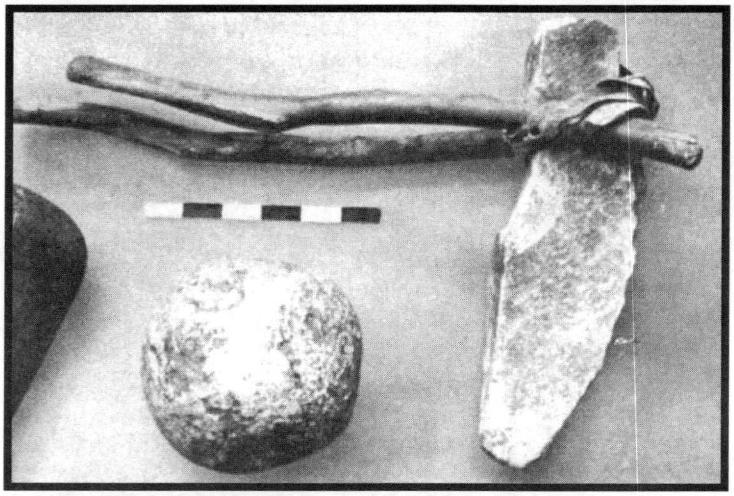

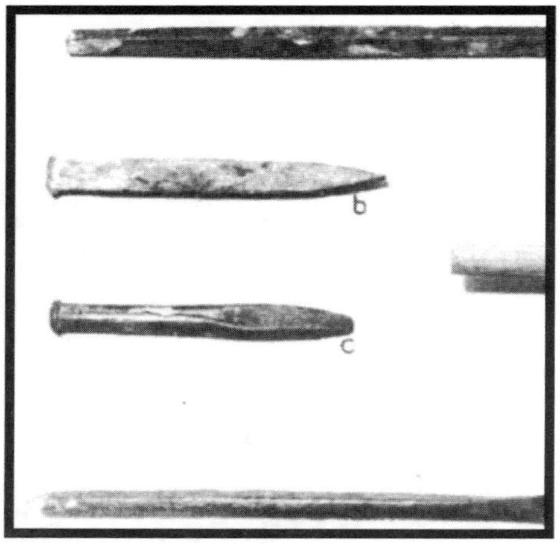


62-63. Stone tools like those shown above (Figure 62, left) were in common use as late as the 26th Dynasty in Egypt. Along with copper chisels (b and c, Figure 63, right), these tools allow us to witness the level of toolmaking in the Pyramid Age. The Late Stone Age technology that is the subject of Volume 2 was used in combination with primitive tools like these to produce artifacts that are remarkable by modern standards. The ax blade tied to sticks and the pounding ball are made of diorite (also called dolerite). Photos by Somers Clarke and Reginald Engelbach at the Cairo Museum

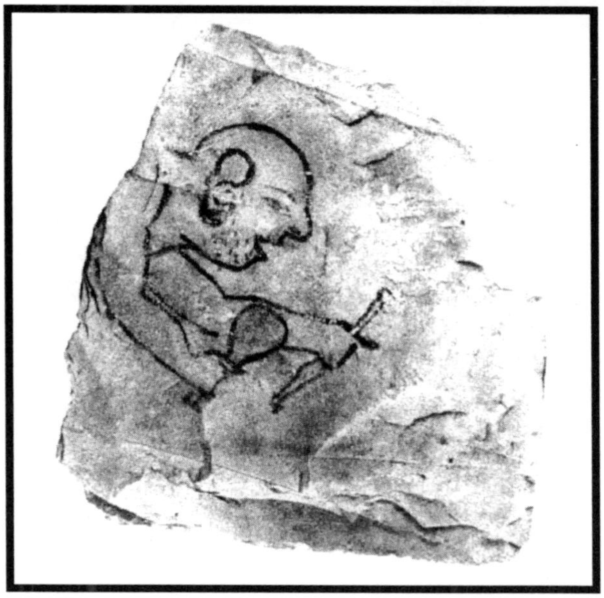

**64-65.** THE SKETCH OF THE STONE CUTTER DATES TO THE NEW KINGDOM, AT ABOUT THE SAME TIME SARCOPHAGI WITH EXTREMELY FLAT SURFACES WERE BEING MADE AND THE COLOSSI OF MEMNON WERE CONSTRUCTED. ALL OF THE DRAWINGS AND OTHER DIRECT EVIDENCE FROM ANCIENT EGYPT DEFIES THE IDEA OF THE EXISTENCE OF SUPER ADVANCED TECHNOLOGY. THE DRAWING IS IN RED AND BLACK INK ON A CHUNK OF LIMESTONE AND IS HELD BY THE FITZWILLIAM MUSEUM, IN CAMBRIDGE. THE PHOTOGRAPH ON THE RIGHT SHOWS A SQUARE, A LEVEL AND A PLUMB-RULE FROM THE 20TH DYNASTY AND AN OLD KINGDOM MASON'S MALLET. THIS GROUP OF TOOLS WAS PHOTOGRAPHED IN THE CAIRO MUSEUM BY CLARKE AND ENGELBACH.

Khufu's inscription (Khufu's cartouche dated to year 17 of his reign) in the vault above the King's Chamber. Lehner suggested that the purpose was to confound modern researchers, and so Lehner described Khufu's cartouche as a:

> ...'red herring' for modern man until the time was right for the real meaning of this Pyramid to be brought to light. This, of course, would require considerable prophetic skill.[2]

As Mark Lehner has since discovered, it is unnecessary to entertain the notion that Atlanteans—supposedly in about 10,500 B.C.—planted hieroglyphics to confound modern researchers. There is nothing un-Egyptian about the Great Pyramid.[3] As we have considered in these pages, other examples of stunning ancient Egyptian masonry bear characteristics that are remarkable by modern standards, and they date from Neolithic times to the late periods of Egyptian history. Thus, there is no reason to postulate that technology from the fabled Atlantis afforded the Great Pyramid and that further evidence of such technology is buried more deeply than the earliest known ruins.

There is a logical solution to all of the masonry and engineering enigmas. The all-encompassing solution operates upon the technical horizon of the primitive tools, materials and methods known even during the Neolithic Period (c. 7,000 B.C.). It allowed workers to build each pyramid within a pharaoh's reign. The archaeological evidence, including the features of the pyramids, quarries, and tomb artifacts, supports only the real solution. The real solution is clearly demonstrated in the pages of Volume 2 as the method used to build the Great Pyramids.

# APPENDIX

# TIER HEIGHTS OF THE GREAT PYRAMID

The following tier heights of the Great Pyramid are the measurements, in centimeters, made by Egyptologist Georges Goyon and published in 1978.[1] Goyon rounded off the tier height measurements to ½ centimeter: The margin of error of the tier heights is less than ½ centimeter. In general, the Great Pyramid incorporates blocks made with 73 different heights (rounded to less than ½ centimeter). By the time Goyon made his measurements, tier 201 was missing. Thus, he lists the measurement of the Napoleonic Expedition for that tier.

Increases in tier heights can be observed at tiers 35, 98 and several other tiers high in the Great Pyramid, including the missing tier 201. Tier 35 is taller than tier two and tier 201 was taller than tier four. Although the monument exhibits a general decrease in tier height as it rises, tall tiers high in the masonry present engineering problems because of the difficulties of lifting thousands of massive blocks to great heights.

**TABLE 1: TIER HEIGHTS OF THE GREAT PYRAMID**

| Tier Number | Height In Cm. | Tier Number | Height In Cm. | Tier Number | Height In Cm. |
|---|---|---|---|---|---|
| 1 | 150 | 13 | 76 | 25 | 80 |
| 2 | 124 | 14 | 75 | 26 | 74 |
| 3 | 120 | 15 | 75 | 27 | 78 |
| 4 | 102 | 16 | 73.5 | 28 | 69 |
| 5 | 99 | 17 | 75 | 29 | 65 |
| 6 | 90 | 18 | 83 | 30 | 64 |
| 7 | 100 | 19 | 95 | 31 | 73 |
| 8 | 97 | 20 | 62 | 32 | 72 |
| 9 | 93 | 21 | 58 | 33 | 54 |
| 10 | 91.5 | 22 | 87 | 34 | 66 |
| 11 | 86.5 | 23 | 89 | 35 | 127 |
| 12 | 76 | 24 | 83 | 36 | 100 |

| TIER NUMBER | HEIGHT IN CM. | TIER NUMBER | HEIGHT IN CM. | TIER NUMBER | HEIGHT IN CM. |
|---|---|---|---|---|---|
| 37 | 97 | 69 | 78 | 101 | 85 |
| 38 | 95 | 70 | 64 | 102 | 74 |
| 39 | 84 | 71 | 71 | 103 | 76 |
| 40 | 84 | 72 | 67.5 | 104 | 68 |
| 41 | 83 | 73 | 66 | 105 | 67.5 |
| 42 | 72 | 74 | 80 | 106 | 64 |
| 43 | 83 | 75 | 76 | 107 | 63.5 |
| 44 | 106 | 76 | 62 | 108 | 75.5 |
| 45 | 97 | 77 | 64 | 109 | 68 |
| 46 | 73 | 78 | 60 | 110 | 59 |
| 47 | 90 | 79 | 59.5 | 111 | 60.5 |
| 48 | 90.5 | 80 | 62.5 | 112 | 59.5 |
| 49 | 86 | 81 | 60 | 113 | 60 |
| 50 | 70 | 82 | 60 | 114 | 58 |
| 51 | 72.5 | 83 | 60 | 115 | 57.5 |
| 52 | 61 | 84 | 67 | 116 | 67.5 |
| 53 | 68 | 85 | 57.5 | 117 | 58 |
| 54 | 63 | 86 | 67 | 118 | 90.5 |
| 55 | 69 | 87 | 66 | 119 | 83 |
| 56 | 55 | 88 | 58 | 120 | 75 |
| 57 | 62 | 89 | 61 | 121 | 74.5 |
| 58 | 68.5 | 90 | 97 | 122 | 67 |
| 59 | 75 | 91 | 90.5 | 123 | 66 |
| 60 | 70 | 92 | 83.5 | 124 | 63 |
| 61 | 67.5 | 93 | 77.5 | 125 | 58 |
| 62 | 63.5 | 94 | 68 | 126 | 60.5 |
| 63 | 65.5 | 95 | 63 | 127 | 59.5 |
| 64 | 67.5 | 96 | 60.5 | 128 | 59 |
| 65 | 66 | 97 | 61 | 129 | 70 |
| 66 | 60.5 | 98 | 100 | 130 | 65 |
| 67 | 86 | 99 | 99.5 | 131 | 60.5 |
| 68 | 83.5 | 100 | 90.5 | 132 | 56.5 |

| Tier Number | Height In Cm. | Tier Number | Height In Cm. | Tier Number | Height In Cm. |
|---|---|---|---|---|---|
| 133 | 55.5 | 159 | 54.5 | 185 | 53 |
| 134 | 54.5 | 160 | 54.5 | 186 | 52 |
| 135 | 61 | 161 | 60 | 187 | 52.5 |
| 136 | 58 | 162 | 59 | 188 | 52 |
| 137 | 68 | 163 | 64.5 | 189 | 52.5 |
| 138 | 65 | 164 | 54 | 190 | 54 |
| 139 | 57 | 165 | 54.5 | 191 | 51.5 |
| 140 | 56 | 166 | 54 | 192 | 52 |
| 141 | 56 | 167 | 54.5 | 193 | 52 |
| 142 | 56.5 | 168 | 52.5 | 194 | 52 |
| 143 | 74 | 169 | 53.5 | 195 | 58.5 |
| 144 | 68.5 | 170 | 54 | 196 | 60.5 |
| 145 | 60 | 171 | 53 | 197 | 56.5 |
| 146 | 59 | 172 | 52 | 198 | 55 |
| 147 | 56 | 173 | 49.5 | 199 | 57.5 |
| 148 | 56 | 174 | 53 | 200 | 56.5 |
| 149 | 70 | 175 | 53 | 201* | 112 |
| 150 | 63.5 | 176 | 52.5 | | |
| 151 | 59.5 | 177 | 53 | | |
| 152 | 59 | 178 | 53 | | |
| 153 | 55 | 179 | 67.5 | | |
| 154 | 55 | 180 | 63.5 | | |
| 155 | 54 | 181 | 60 | | |
| 156 | 54.5 | 182 | 58 | | |
| 157 | 54.5 | 183 | 56 | | |
| 158 | 54.5 | 184 | 54.5 | | |

* Missing tier number documented by the Napoleonic measurements.

# NOTES

## Chapter 1: A Secret Of The Ages Revealed

1. For the theory that stone pounding balls were used to build the pyramids, refer to Arnold, D., *Building in Egypt: pharaonic stone masonry,* New York, N.Y., Oxford University Press (1991), 48. On the Mohs' hardness scale, copper and bronze have a hardness of from 3.5 to 4. Good-quality limestone generally ranges between 4 to 5. Up-to-date Egyptological writings, e.g., Dieter *Arnold's Building in Egypt,* recognize that the demand for copper would be too great to produce about 12 million pyramid blocks in about 79 years for the 4th Dynasty pyramids. In general, the pyramid complexes are made of about 5 percent granite, which ranges from 6 to 8 on the Mohs' scale, according to Dieter Arnold. No iron tools have ever been found in a sealed tomb of the Old Kingdom, and rare examples of iron tools found around tomb sites of this era are thought to have been left by later operations to either restore the tombs or to remove ready-made blocks. Arnold lists Mohs' hardness for Egyptian stones in particular: dense limestone 4?; quartzite 6–8; granite 6–8; basalt 6–8; diorite 5–6. Refer to Arnold, D., *Building in Egypt: pharaonic stone masonry,* New York, N.Y., Oxford University Press (1991), 28. These factors lead Egyptologists who are up to date on such issues to believe that stone tools were used. Most of the Egyptological literature (including Mark Lehner's 1997 book titled *The Complete Pyramids*), however, is out of date and states that copper tools were used to build the Great Pyramids.
2. Petrie, W.M.F., *Pyramids and Temples of Gizeh*, Field, London (1883), 260 pages.
3. For the supertech theories and the problems with them, see Chapter 19 of this book.

## Chapter 2: The Great Masonry Wonder

1. Petrie, W.M.F., *Pyramids and Temples of Gizeh*, Field, London, (1883), 210. The latest figures agree with Petrie's count. Mark Lehner, who has mapped Giza, gives the same figure. Refer to Lehner, M., *The Complete Pyramids: Solving the Ancient Mysteries,* New York, Thames and Hudson (1997), 109. On page 109, the following statement appears: "The Great Pyramid contains about 2,300,000 blocks of stone, often said to weigh an average of 2.5 tons. This might be somewhat

exaggerated; the stones certainly get smaller towards the top of the pyramid, and we do not know if the masonry of the inner core is as well-cut and uniform as the stone courses that are now exposed. . . . On the other hand some of the casing stones at the base may weigh as much as 15 tons, and the large granite beams roofing the King's Chamber and the stress-relieving chambers above it have been estimated to weigh from 50 to 80 tons. Such statistics, while repeated frequently, never cease to astound." In the 5th century B.C., when the Great Pyramid was still in perfect condition, Herodotus wrote that he saw many casing blocks 30 feet long, and Abd el-Latif gave the same figure in the 12th century. The tier heights have been measured, and these measurements show massive blocks at levels high in the Great Pyramid (see my Appendix). Some blocks in the outer masonry of the Great Pyramid, situated at about the level of the King's Chamber, occupy the height of two tiers.

2. Arnold, D., *Building in Egypt: pharaonic stone masonry,* New York, N.Y., Oxford University Press (1991), 165.
3. Arnold, D., *Building in Egypt: pharaonic stone masonry,* New York, N.Y., Oxford University Press (1991), 167–8.
4. For the study by Goyon, refer to Goyon, G., "Les Rangs d'assises de la Grande Pyramide," *Bulletin de l'Institut Francais d'Archeologie Orientale,* Cairo (1978), Vol. 78, No. 2, 405–413.
5. Arnold, D., *Building in Egypt: pharaonic stone masonry,* New York, N.Y., Oxford University Press (1991), 165–167.
6. For the study by Goyon, refer to Goyon, G., "Les Rangs d'assises de la Grande Pyramide, Bulletin de l'Institut Francais d'Archeologie Orientale, Cairo (1978), Vol. 78, No. 2, 405–413. Refer also to Vyse, Richard William Howard (1784–1853), *Operations carried on at the pyramids of Gizeh in 1837: with an account of a voyage into Upper Egypt, and an appendix*, London, Pub. J. Fraser (1840-1842).
7. Davidovits, J., Morris, M., *The Pyramids: An Enigma Solved,* Hippocrene, NY (1988), 109–112.
8. Davidovits, J., Morris, M., *The Pyramids: An Enigma Solved,* Hippocrene, NY (1988), 109–112.
9. The feature was photographed in about 1940 by a British Air Force pilot named P. Groves who took aerial photographs. According to J.P. Lepre, "One very unusual feature of the Great Pyramid is a concavity of the core that makes the monument an eight-sided figure, rather than four-sided...That is to say, that its four sides are hollowed in or indented along their central lines, from base to peak. This concavity divides each of the apparent four sides in half, creating a very special and unusual eight-sided pyramid; and it is executed to such an extraordinary degree of precision as to enter the realm of the uncanny." See Lepre, J.P., *The Egyptian Pyramids: A Comprehensive, Illustrated Reference,* McFarland, Jefferson, N.C. (1990), 65.

10. Petrie, W.M.F., *Pyramids and Temples of Gizeh*, Field, London (1883 reprint 1990), 37.
11. Arnold, D., *Building in Egypt: pharaonic stone masonry*, New York, N.Y., Oxford University Press (1991), 122–123, note 56 on page 203; ibid., 123, Arnold adds, "In pyramid casing, oblique joints are therefore more frequent in granite than in limestone."
12. Owing to their smooth surfaces, casing blocks still intact at the tip of Khafra's Pyramid reflect moonlight. John Greaves (1602–1652), a professor of mathematics and an astronomer at Oxford University, mistook Khufu's granite sarcophagus for marble; refer to his book *Pyramidographia* (1646). Petrie referred to unusually colored limestones as marble.
13. Petrie, W.M.F., *Pyramids and Temples of Gizeh*, Field, London, Histories and Mysteries of Man, Ltd., London (1883 reprint 1990), 13.
14. Petrie, W.M.F., *Pyramids and Temples of Gizeh*, Field, London, Histories and Mysteries of Man, Ltd., London (1883 reprint 1990), 13.
15. Abd al-Latif, *The Eastern key: Kitab al-ifadah wa'l-i'tibar of 'Abd al-Latif al-Baghdadi, Translated in English by Kamal Hafuth Zand, John A. and Ivy E. Videan*, Allen and Unwin London (1964), 117.
16. Herodotus, *The History of Herodotus*, New York, L. MacVeagh, The Dial press, Toronto, Longmans, Green & company (1928), 124–126; Herodotus, Histories 2.124.5 reads, "The pyramid itself was twenty years in the making. Its base is square, each side eight hundred feet long, and its height is the same [Herodotus could not have measured the height, whereas he could have measured some individual blocks and some sides]; the whole is of stone polished and most exactly fitted; there is no block of less than thirty feet in length." To say that all of the blocks were that long, Herodotus must have been generalizing or he examined the Great Pyramid when the smaller casing blocks remaining now at the lower level were covered with sand.
17. The official Egyptian government survey found that the foundation of the Great Pyramid does not exceed 7/8 inch from dead level, and that this variation may be due to subsidence. Refer to Cole, J. H., "Determination of the exact size and orientation of the great pyramid of Giza," *Government Press*, Cairo (1925), Series: Egypt. Finance, Ministry of, Survey dept. Survey of Egypt, paper; no. 39. The paper can be found in 1 ERMM European Register of Microform Masters (Master microform), 2 NYBA The Brooklyn Museum, 3 NYMA Metropolitan Museum of Art Library, 4 UKBX British Library (Master microform).
18. Arnold, D., *Building in Egypt: pharaonic stone masonry*, New York, N.Y., Oxford University Press (1991), 147.
19. For explanations of making the foundation, refer to Lepre, J.P., *The Egyptian Pyramids: A Comprehensive, Illustrated Reference*, McFarland, Jefferson, N.C.

(1990), 235 and Edwards, I.E.S. (Iorwerth Eiddon Stephen), *The pyramids of Egypt*, Rev. and updated, repr. with minor revisions, Harmondsworth, Middlesex, England; New York, N.Y., Penguin Books (1988), 310 pp.

20. Diodorus witnessed the Great Pyramid when it was intact, see Diodorus, *Library of History*, Book I, 63 (Oldfather translation).

## CHAPTER 3: INCREDIBLE CONSTRUCTION SPEED

1. Arnold, D., "Ueberlegungen zum Problem des Pyramidenbaus," *Mitteilungen des Deutschen Archäologischen Instituts Kairo* (1981), 37, 15–28.
2. Ashley, M., *Seven Wonders of the World*, Ashley Pub., London (1980), 288 pp. *New York Times*, March 12, 1978, Section IV, p. 7, col. 5. The project was led by Sakuji Yoshimura, formerly of Waseda University, and sponsored and filmed by Nippon TV.
3. Kitchen, K.A., *Pharaoh Triumphant: the life and times of Ramesses II, King of Egypt* (edition: third corr. impression), Warminster, Wiltshire, England: Aris & Phillips; Mississauga, Ont., Canada: Benben (1985, c. 1982), 107.
4. *Kitchen, K.A. Pharaoh Triumphant: the life and times of Ramesses II, King of Egypt* (edition: third corr. impression), Warminster, Wiltshire, England: Aris & Phillips; Mississauga, Ont., Canada: Benben (1985, c. 1982), 107. For Giza's cults dedicated to guarding and maintaining the sepulchres of dead pharaohs, refer to Zivie, C.M., *Giza au deuxieme millenaire*, Cairo (1976), 185 ff; for Teti's cult, refer to Yoyotte, J., "A Propos De La Parente Feminine Du Roi Teti (VI Dynastie)," *Bulletin de l'institut d'archeologie orientale* 57 (1958), 96, n. 4; for Sahure, Martin, G.T., "The tomb of Hetepka and other reliefs and inscriptions from the Sacred Animal Necropolis, North Saqqâra 1964–73," *Egypt Exploration Society*, London (1979), p1. 55.
5. Stadelmann, R., "Snofru und die Pyramiden von Meidum und Dahschur," *Mitteilungen des Deutschen Archäologischen Instituts Kairo*, 36 (1980), 438–439; Arnold, D., *Building in Egypt: pharaonic stone masonry*, New York, N.Y., Oxford University Press (1991), 61, which reads: ". . . the pyramids of the Fourth Dynasty would have consumed at least 9 million cubic meters of limestone, mortar, and sand, which had to be delivered quickly in small quantities." More precisely, to convert cubic meters to cubic feet multiply by 35.31 and this equals 317,790,000 cubic feet or 9,000,000 cubic meters. Add to this amount hundreds of thousands of tons of granite and basalt.
6. Lehner, M., *The Egyptian Heritage: Based on the Edgar Cayce Readings*, Virginia Beach, Va., A.R.E. Press (1974), 135 pp.
7. For the mortar dating tests, refer to Haas, H., et al., "Radiocarbon Chronology and the Historical Calendar in Egypt," *British Archaeological Report, International*

*Series*, Archaeological Series, No. 3, Chronologies in the Near East, pp. 585–606; Lehner M., "Radiocarbon Dating the Pyramids," *Venture Inward* (1985), 40–45. An analysis of mortar in two boat pits on the south side of the Great Pyramid was made. Refer to Noür, M.Z., Iskander, Z., Osman, M.S., and Moustafa, A.Y., *The Cheops Boats*, Cairo (1960), 31: "The mortar . . . is coarse and pinkish white. Chemical analysis showed that it is mostly composed of calcium sulfate and contains some silica, iron and aluminum oxides, calcium carbonate, sodium chloride and magnesium carbonate." Although the charcoal and reeds in the mortar underwent acid leaching to remove carbon contamination before the dating process, there is no pretreatment that can remove contamination due to a concentrated alkaline solution of sodium or potassium carbonate. The scientific literature provides examples of errors dating aquatic plants that grew in hard-water lakes similar to the Egyptian lakes where natron was gathered. Refer to Aitken, M.J., *Physics and Archaeology*, Clarendon Press, Oxford (1974), 42; Shotton, F.W., "An example of hard-water error in radiocarbon dating of vegetable matter," *Nature* (1972), 460–61; Deevey, E.S., Gross, M.S., Hutchinson, G.E., and Kraybill, H.L., "The natural C14 contents of materials from hard-water lakes," *Proceedings of the National Academy of Science*, Washington, 40 (1954), 285–88. Trees and reeds taken from natron lakes and burned will typically date older. Cellulose fibers chemically react with sodium carbonate. Because of its high porosity, charcoal absorbs a great deal of natron solution and also carbon dioxide, which results from the decomposition of natron. There is also speculation that burning of old wood produced the date discrepancies; see Volume 2 of this book.

8. For the issue of carbon pollution, refer to Davidovits, J., Morris, M., *The Pyramids: An Enigma Solved*, Hippocrene, NY (1988), 232. In addition, consider that carbon-14 dating of a mortar sample removed by Lehner from between two blocks in the Sphinx Temple resulted in two different dates from two different laboratories. One laboratory produced a date of 2086 B.C. and the other of 2746 B.C.
9. For a description of how the ancient Egyptians made gypsum (lime-gypsum) mortar, refer to Davidovits, J., Morris, M., *The Pyramids: An Enigma Solved*, Hippocrene, NY (1988), 107–108. The geopolymeric (silicoaluminate) mortar corresponds to chemical analysis. Refer to Nour, M.Z., Iskander, Z., Osman, M.S., and Moustafa, A.Y., *The Cheops Boats*, Cairo (1960), 31, which reads, "The mortar . . . is coarse and pinkish white. Chemical analysis showed that it is mostly composed of calcium sulfate [gypsum] and contains some silica, iron and aluminum oxides, calcium carbonate, sodium chloride and magnesium carbonate."
10. For the odd results of the mortar-dating study, refer to the Nov./Dec. 1985 *Venture Inward* and a follow-up article in 1986 titled "The Great Pyramid Reveals Her Age," published by the Association for Research and Enlightenment (A.R.E.). The A.R.E. is the international headquarters of the work of Edgar Cayce.

11. For the mortar-dating tests, refer to Haas, H., Devine, J., Wenke, R., Lehner, M., Wolfli, W., Bonani, G., "Radiocarbon Chronology and the Historical Calendar in Egypt, Chronologies in the Near East," Aurenche O., Evin J. and Hours P. eds., *British Archaeological Report, International Series* No. 379, Part II (1987), 585–606. Page 592 illustrates this point, ". . . Table 4 illustrates the range and average of dates for the Khufu Pyramid. An attempt has been made to determine the spread of age dates from samples from the lower levels of the monuments, as compared with samples from the apex. The spread is nearly 100 years, but the trend is reversed, the youngest dates are from the bottom samples. . . ." Also refer to Lehner M., "Radiocarbon Dating the Pyramids," *Venture Inward* (1985), 40–45.
12. Lehner, M., *The Egyptian Heritage: Based on the Edgar Cayce Readings*, Virginia Beach, Va., A.R.E. Press (1974), 136 pp.
13. Arnold, D., *Building in Egypt: pharaonic stone masonry*, New York, N.Y., Oxford University Press (1991), 186.
14. *Newsweek*, Feb. 13, 1978, p. 55; Ashley, M., *Seven Wonders of the World, Ashley Pub.*, London (1980), 288 pp.; *New York Times*, March 12, 1978, Section IV, p. 7, col. 5.
15. Joseph Davidovits, founder of the Geopolymer Institute, in France, was invited to Egypt by Nova producer Michael Barnes. Dr. Joseph Davidovits witnessed the entire pyramid building operation. Joseph Davidovits was able to compare the limestone used.
16. For Tura limestone, refer to Klemm, R., Klemm, D., *Steine und Stein-Burche im Alten Agypten*, Springer-Verlag, Berlin (1993), 60–71; Harrell, J. A., "An Inventory of Ancient Egyptian Quarries," *Newsletter of the American Research Center in Egypt,* 146 (1989), pp. 1-7.
17. Arnold, D., *Building in Egypt: pharaonic stone masonry*, New York, N.Y., Oxford University Press (1991), 72.

## CHAPTER 4: ENIGMATIC INTERIOR FEATURES

1. For a theory about the plug blocks, refer to Lepre, J. P., *The Egyptian Pyramids: A Comprehensive, Illustrated Reference*, Jefferson, N.C.: McFarland (1990 reprint), 235, and Edwards, I.E.S., *The pyramids of Egypt*, Rev. and updated, repr. with minor revisions, Harmondsworth, Middlesex, England; New York, N.Y., Penguin Books (1988), 75–86. An entire chapter is devoted to the theories of the plug blocks in Tompkins, P., *Secrets of the Great Pyramid. With an appendix by Livio Catullo Stecchini* (1st ed.) New York, Harper & Row (1971), Ch. XIX titled "Why were the Pyramid Passages Plugged? When? and How?" pp. 236–255 (diagrams included).
2. For the measurements of the plug blocks in the Ascending Passageway, refer

to Kingsland, W., *The Great Pyramid in Fact and Theory*, Mokelumne Hill, Calif., Health Research (1923–72), Part I, 50, 64–66, 74. Edwards, I.E.S., *The pyramids of Egypt*, Rev. and updated, repr. with minor revisions Harmondsworth, Middlesex, England; New York, N.Y., Penguin Books (1988), 102, 106–110, 264; Petrie, W.M.F., *Pyramids and Temples of Gizeh*, Field, London (1883), 102, 106–110, 264.

3. Kingsland, W., *The Great Pyramid in Fact and Theory*, Mokelumne Hill, Calif., Health Research (1923–72), Part I, 65.
4. Kingsland, W., *The Great Pyramid in Fact and Theory*, Mokelumne Hill, Calif., Health Research (1923–72), Part I, 50, 64–66, 74, or Edwards, I.E.S., *The pyramids of Egypt*, Rev. and updated, repr. with minor revisions Harmondsworth, Middlesex, England; New York, N.Y., Penguin Books (1985), 109–110; Lehner, M., *The Complete Pyramids: Solving the Ancient Mysteries*, New York, Thames and Hudson (1997), 40, which presents a drawing showing how close the correspondence is between the ceiling and the plug blocks.
5. Kingsland, W., *The Great Pyramid in Fact and Theory*, Mokelumne Hill, Calif., Health Research (1923–72), Part I, 65; Petrie, W.M.F., *Pyramids and Temples of Gizeh*, Field, London (1883), 65.
6. Arnold, D., *Building in Egypt: pharaonic stone masonry*, New York, N.Y., Oxford University Press (1991), 79.
7. For the Ascending Passageway running through the girdle stones, which range from 12 to 15 feet long, Edwards indicated, "Borchardt considered the presence of the 'girdle-stones' in the Ascending Corridor as proof that the Great Pyramid followed the standard pattern, each 'girdle-stone' being part of an internal casing, but two equally eminent authors, Somers Clarke and R. Engelbach, refused to accept Borchardt's arguments." Edwards, I.E.S., *The pyramids of Egypt*, 275–276, 111; Edwards gives no specific pages for the Borchardt reference, but the reference itself is Borchardt, L., "Einiges zur dritten Bauperiode der grossen Pyramide bei Gise, mit einer Bemerkung zur zweiten Bauperiode det dritten Pyramide," von Herbert Ricke, Berlin, Verlag von Julius Springer (1932). Series: *Beitrage zur agyptischen Bauforschung und Altertumskunde*, Hft. 1. Refer also to Clarke, S., Engelbach, R., *Ancient Egyptian Masonry: The Building Craft*, London, Oxford University Press, Milford (1930), 242 p. Edwards' footnote to Clarke and Engelbach refers to pages 123–4. Refer also to Kingsland, W., *The Great Pyramid in Fact and Theory*, Mokelumne Hill, Calif., Health Research (1923–72), Part I, 66–68, 70. Petrie also discussed the girdle stones, "Several of the roof-blocks are girdle-blocks, being all in one piece with the walls, either wholly round the passage, or partially so. These vertical girdle-blocks are a most curious feature of this passage (first observed and measured by Mr. Waynman Dixon, C.E.), and occur at intervals of 10 cubits (206.3 to 208.9 inches) in the passage, measuring along the slope. All the stones

that can be examined round the plugs are partial girdle-blocks, evidently to prevent the plugs forcing the masonry apart, by being wedged into the contracted passage." Refer to Petrie, W.M.F., *Pyramids and Temples of Gizeh*, Histories and Mysteries of Man, Ltd., London (1990 reprint), 21 (Note that this quote differs from the original version of *The Pyramids and Temples of Giza*, as the 1990 new and revised edition has been abbreviated).

8. The Grand Gallery is discussed by Edwards. Refer to I.E.S., *The pyramids of Egypt*, Rev. and updated, repr. with minor revisions Harmondsworth, Middlesex, England; New York, N.Y., Penguin Books (1985), 103, 107–9.
9. For a description of the King's Chamber and the compartments above, refer to Edwards, I.E.S., *The pyramids of Egypt*, Rev. and updated, repr. with minor revisions Harmondsworth, Middlesex, England; New York, N.Y., Penguin Books (1985), 103, 105–6, 264.
10. The problems of cutting granite with simple tools are raised in Edwards, I.E.S., *The pyramids of Egypt* (1985), 240; Lucas, A., *Ancient Egyptian Materials and Industries*, 82–83. While granite can be cut with long, hard work with abrasives and simple tools, features found in ancient Egyptian artifacts have not been replicated. These include subtle and complex curves, such as those found in portrait statues, examples of rapid cutting (the latter of which Petrie determined for the sarcophagus in Khufu's Great Pyramid and other artifacts made with sharp points), surfaces as flat as .0002 inch (according to machinist Christopher Dunn, who measured large areas of three sarcophagi). Compare that with .01 flatness Denys Stocks can account for when working with replicas of ancient Egyptian tools.
11. Kingsland, W., *The Great Pyramid in Fact and Theory*, Mokelumne Hill, Calif., Health Research (1923–72), 95.
12. Stocks, D.A., "Stone Sarcophagus Manufacture in Ancient Egypt," *Antiquity* 73, 918–922. Stocks cut granite with a bow drill and sand. He believes that all of the work was done slowly but surely. However, it is impossible to believe that the ancient workers used the slow cutting method employed by Stocks only to achieve the mistakes Petrie described for their effort. Surely, these stray cuts are signs of rapid cutting. Machinist Christopher Dunn discusses some instances of rapid cutting in his *The Giza Power Plant, The Technologies of Ancient* Egypt, Bear & Company, Sante Fe (1998), NM, 70–93. Although Dunn's ideas about advanced machining in ancient Egypt and the notion that the Great Pyramid functioned as a power plant are untenable, Dunn is an expert machinist with long experience. His observations about cutting rates are compelling and should be given full consideration. Refer to a review by Systems Engineer Mike Carrell in *Infinite Energy* magazine, Issue 32 (July/August 2000). Mike Carrell's review does not go into detail about the many problems with Dunn's power plant system, but Mike Carrell corresponded with Dunn and sent me his list of extensive explanations

describing why the King's Chamber of the Great Pyramid will not support maser activity. Dunn still contends that the Great Pyramid is a power plant and has not presented arguments contesting the problems Mike Carrell raised, although years have passed.

13. Lepre, J.P., *The Egyptian Pyramids: A Comprehensive Illustrated Reference*, McFarland & Co., Inc., Jefferson, NC and London (1990), 110.
14. For a study asserting that only solid masonry could provide the necessary strength needed for ramps, refer to Peter Hodges, *How the Great Pyramids Were Built*, Element Books, Wilshire (1989); The PBS Nova film confirmed Hodges' assertions. Stonemason Roger Hopkins observed that the Nova miniature ramp was unsuitable after raising only a few one-ton stones.
15. Kingsland, W., *The Great Pyramid in Fact and Theory*, Mokelumne Hill, Calif., Health Research (1923–72), Part I, 89, 97.
16. Kingsland, W., *The Great Pyramid in Fact and Theory*, Mokelumne Hill, Calif., Health Research (1923–72), Part I, 89. Kingsland wrote, "The roof of the Chamber consists of nine granite beams, varying in width from 44.8 to 62.7 inches (refer to Plates XXXVI and XXXVII). They extend about 5 feet beyond the side walls, and are therefore about 27 feet long. The 62.7 inch stone has a depth of about 7 feet, and therefore a cubic capacity of approximately 987 cubic feet. Reckoning 165 pounds per cubic foot, it will weigh about 73 tons, or about the weight of a modern locomotive. How did the builders raise this enormous weight to a height of 160 feet, and up the steep angle of the Pyramid?" Arnold reckoned these beams to weigh 50–60 tons. Refer to Arnold, D., *Building in Egypt: pharaonic stone masonry*, New York, N.Y., Oxford University Press (1991), 60. Lehner alludes to estimates up to 80 tons, see Lehner, M., *The Complete Pyramids: Solving the Ancient Mysteries,* New York, Thames and Hudson (1997), 109.
17. Arnold, D., *Building in Egypt: pharaonic stone masonry*, New York, N.Y., Oxford University Press (1991), 61.
18. Lepre, J.P., *The Egyptian Pyramids: A Comprehensive, Illustrated Reference*, McFarland, Jefferson, N.C. (1990), 95–97.

## CHAPTER 5: EGYPTOLOGY HAS NO EXPLANATION

1. Lehner, M., "Development of the Giza Necropolis: The Khufu Project," *Mitteilungen des Deutschen Archäologischen Instituts Kairo* (1985), 109–143.
2. Davidovits, J., Morris, M., *The Pyramids: An Enigma Solved*, Hippocrene, NY (1988), 106 (for Petrie's observations); pages 108–12 cover a masonry feature that complicates the issue raised by Petrie, as does the lack of broken blocks that must be present in all block quarrying operations, 78–79.
3. Lehner, M., *The Complete Pyramids: Solving the Ancient Mysteries*, New York,

Thames and Hudson (1997), 206.

4. For pyramid blocks as hard as the head of the Sphinx, refer to Klemm, R, and Klemm, D.D., *Steine und Steinbrüche im Alten Ägypten*, Springer-Verlag, Berlin (1993), 193–194, Figures 213 and 214.
5. Arnold, D., *Building in Egypt: pharaonic stone masonry*, New York, N.Y., Oxford University Press (1991), 31. On page 31, Arnold exhibits Figure 2.4 showing the field of open quarrying at Giza, near Khafra's pyramid, with the stumps of squared blocks. This form of block quarrying is not typical for Giza and resembles later-style quarrying. For the marks of Old Kingdom quarrying, refer to ibid. page 34, Fig. 2.7 and then consider the difficulties of extracting millions of pyramid blocks with pointed stone picks. Clearly, the quarrying technique Arnold describes for the later work of cutting the unfinished Aswan quarry does not apply to the method used at Giza for extracting stone for the Great Pyramid. Refer to ibid. pages 27 to 40 for Arnold's discussion of quarrying hard and softer stones.
6. Arnold, D., *Building in Egypt: pharaonic stone masonry*, New York, N.Y., Oxford University Press (1991), 261, Fig. 6.14.
7. Petrie, W.M.F., *Pyramids and Temples of Gizeh*, Field, London (1883), 209. Yoshimira, S., *Studies in Egyptian Culture, No. 6, non-destructive pyramid investigation (1) by Electromagnetic Wave Method*, Waseda University Press, Tokyo, 2 Vols; Davidovits, J., Gaber, H., in Davidovits, J., Morris, M., *The Pyramids: An Enigma Solved*, Hippocrene, NY (1988), 97–108, 89. A drawing of the jumbled shells that characterize Giza pyramid and temple blocks appears in Jomard, E.F. (ed.), *Description de l'Egypte, ou, Recueil des observations et des recherches qui ont été faites en Egypte pendant l'expédition de l'armee française*, Paris, Pub. Imprimerie Imperiale (1809-1828) and is reproduced in Davidovits, J., Morris, M., *The Pyramids: An Enigma Solved*, Hippocrene, NY (1988), Fig. 14; Kingsland, W., *The Great Pyramid in Fact and Theory*, Mokelumne Hill, Calif., Health Research (1923–72), Part I, 25. Aigner, *T.*, "Facies and Origin of Nummulitic Buildups: An Example from the Giza Pyramids Plateau (Middle Eocene, Egypt)," *Neues Jahrbuch für Geologie und Paläontologie, Abhandlung, V. 166 (1983), 347–368. Mark Lehner commented on Aigner's study as follows: "* . . . According to Aigner's model, the Pyramids Plateau began as a bank of nummulites seen to exceed 30 m in thickness in the northern escarpment. A shoal and reefal facies was laid over the southern slope of the nummulites bank. A "back bank" facies was, in turn, laid over the shoal reef, forming a series of limestone/marl beds which 'lens out' over the shoal reef to the N. In practical terms, this left the very hard and brittle limestone of the nummulites bank to the NNW part of the Pyramids Plateau, and the softer thickly bedded layers to the lower SSE area of the plateau. . . ." Refer to Lehner, M., "The Development of the Giza Necropolis: The Khufu Project," *Mitteilungen des Deutschen Archäologischen Instituts Kairo,* 41 (1985), 113–114. Also on page

118, Lehner wrote: ". . . According to Aigner's depositional model of the plateau, the pyramid was based on the harder, more massive nummulites bank which swells up along the N–NW part of the formation. . . ." Joseph Davidovits showed in the 1992 Nova film *This Old Pyramid* that limestone from the Sphinx quarry is so high in kaolin clay content that it comes apart within 24 hours of soaking in water. In short, the limestone from the Giza quarries does not match the better-quality blocks that characterize the Giza pyramids and temples.

8. Jomard, E.F. (ed.), *Description de l'Egypte, ou, Recueil des observations et des recherches qui ont été faites en Egypte pendant l'expédition de l'armee française*, Paris, Pub. Imprimerie Imperiale (1809-1828), 23 v.
9. Petrie, W.M.F., *Pyramids and Temples of Gizeh*, Field, London (1883), 209.
10. Kingsland, W., *The Great Pyramid in Fact and Theory*, Mokelumne Hill, Calif., Health Research (1923–72), 25.
11. Yoshimira, S., *Studies in Egyptian Culture, no. 6, non-destructive pyramid investigation (1) by Electromagnetic Wave Method*, Waseda University Press, Tokyo, 2 vols., 4–5.
12. Davidovits, J., Morris, M., *The Pyramids: An Enigma Solved*, Hippocrene, NY (1988), 97–104.
13. For the quote by Diodorus Siculus, refer to Diodorus of Sicily, *Library of History*, Book I, Ch. 63, lines 6–7. The translation is by Oldfather, the Loeb Classical Library edition, William Heinemann Ltd., London, and G.P. Putnam's Sons, New York (1933), Vol. I, 217.
14. Strabo, *The Geography of Strabo* 17.1.34, which reads, "One of the marvelous things I saw at the pyramids should not be omitted: there are heaps of stone-chips lying in front of the pyramid; and among these are found chips that are like lentils both in form and size; and under some of the heaps lie winnowings, as it were, as of half-peeled grains. They say that what was left of the food of the workmen has petrified; and this is not improbable." For this translation, refer to *The geography of Strabo with an English translation by Horace Leonard Jones; Based in part upon the unfinished version of John Robert Sitlington Sterrett*, W. Heinemann, G. P. Putnam's sons, London; New York (1917–33). Contributors, Jones, Horace Leonard, Vol. 8, 95.

## CHAPTER 6: EGYPTIAN MASONRY MARVELS

1. Emery, W.B., *Archaic Egypt: Culture and Civilizations in Egypt Five Thousand Years Ago*, Penguin Books, Baltimore (1961 edition), 214–215. Also refer to Hoffman for the primitive level of technology used to produce hard diorite and basalt vases at the Nagada II ritual complex at Hierakonpolis, Hoffman, M.A., "The Predynastic of Hierakonpolis: An Interim Report," *Egyptian Studies Association*, Publication No.

1, Cairo, 130. This primitive technological level mystifies geologists who recognize the difficulties of drilling tough diorite. Diorite is almost as difficult to drill as quartzite, the drilling of which is difficult with the best modern tools equipped with tungsten carbide drill bits and thousands of pounds of pressure applied to the bits. Also refer to el-Khouli, A., *Egyptian Stone Vessels: Predynastic Period to Dynasty III typology and analysis*, von Zabern, Mainz/Rhein (1978). In Vol. II titled *Manufacture of Stone Vessels - Ancient and Modern*, page 797, el-Khouli summarizes, and his summary shows that the method for making hard-stone vessels is not really known. Thus, it is not described in detail by Egyptologists. He wrote, "Hundreds of thousands of stone vessels have been discovered in the pyramids and tombs of Egypt. The making of stone vessels must have been, therefore, a very common industry. . .Many Egyptologists (e.g. von Bissing, Petrie, Quibell, Bonnet, Emery, Reisner, Balcz, Lucas, Baumagartel, Hartenberg and Schmidt) have discussed the method of production of stone vessels, using the evidence of the Old Kingdom tomb-scenes and materials excavated in the field (especially partially worked stone vessels). Much of the discussion was somewhat brief."

2. Emery, W.B., *Archaic Egypt: Culture and Civilizations in Egypt Five Thousand Years Ago,* Penguin Books, Baltimore (1961 rev.), 11.
3. Lange, K., *Des Pyramides, des Sphinx, des Pharaons, Ed. Plon*, Paris, 169–174.
4. Refer also to remarks by A. el-Khouli, *Egyptian Stone Vessels: Predynastic Period to Dynasty III typology and analysis*, von Zabern, Mainz/Rhein (1978). In Vol. II, titled *Manufacture of Stone Vessels - Ancient and Modern*, page 789, Rl-Khouli wrote, "No other country, before or since, has achieved such perfection in this skilled industry in its efforts to produce not only objects of utility but also of beauty. A high level of achievement in this respect was reached in the Predynastic Period and during the first three Dynasties." On page 801 el-Khouli wrote, "Stone vessel craftsman soon showed his mastery over the material by producing vessels of floral and leaf shapes, and in the shapes of fish, animal, birds, etc." On page 789, "No stone was too hard or intractable for the ancient craftsman."
5. Petrie referred to diorite bowl fragments he believed were made by turning, *see* Petrie, W.M.F., *The Pyramids and Temples of Gizeh*, Field, London (1883), *176 and pl. XIV, 14, 15.*
6. Maspero, G., *Manual of Egyptian archaeology and guide to the study of antiquities in Egypt*. For the use of students and travellers, 6th ed., rev. and enl. London, H. Grevel and co. (1914): Article on stone vessels, pp. 281–282.
7. For the quote by l'Hote, refer to Perrot G, Chipiez, C., *Histoire de l'Art dans l'Antiquité*, Vol. 1, Paris (1882), 676.
8. Arnold, D., *Building in Egypt: pharaonic stone masonry,* New York, N.Y., Oxford University Press (1991), 174. Refer also to Emery, W.B., *Archaic Egypt: Culture and Civilizations in Egypt Five Thousand Years Ago*, Penguin Books, Baltimore (1961),

182. Large granite blocks first appeared in the 2nd Dynasty. Refer to Petrie, W.M.F., The Royal Tombs of the Earliest Dynasties (1900–1901), II, pl. 31 (The stelae of Peribsen); Fischer, H.G., "An Egyptian Royal Stela of the Second Dynasty," *Artibus Asiae*, 24 (1961), 45 ff.

9. Arnold, D., *Building in Egypt: pharaonic stone masonry*, New York, N.Y., Oxford University Press (1991), 174.
10. Garstang, J., *Mahâsna and Bêt Khallâf (With a chapter by Kurt Sethe)*, B. Quaritch, London (1903), 9, 11, pls. 7, 17, 18.
11. For the splendid Valley Temple, refer to Hoelscher, U., *Das Grabdenkmal des Konigs Chephren*, Veroflentlichungen der Ernst von Sieglin Expedition in Agypten, Vol. 1, Leipzig (1912).
12. Only two industrial cranes exist with the necessary capacity. The K-10000 tower crane by Kroll Giant Towercranes, in Denmark, is the world's largest tower crane as of this writing. The capacity of the standard 269-foot crane is 132 tons. A diagram showing the hook radius and crane capacity appears at this company's Web site: http://www.towercrane.com.
13. Perrot G, Chipiez, C., *Histoire de l'Art dans l'Antiquité*, Vol. I, Hachette et Cie, Paris (1882), 775.
14. Arnold, D., *Building in Egypt: pharaonic stone masonry*, New York, N.Y., Oxford University Press (1991), 184–189.
15. Petrie, W.M.F., *Pyramids and Temples of Gizeh*, Field, London (1883), 168. Strabo, *Geography* 17. 1. 33. Strabo visited Egypt in 24 B.C. and wrote an extensive history that has not survived. His surviving geographical appendix indicates that the swivel door in the Great Pyramid allowed access to a square passage descending 374 feet to a pit. Greek and Roman initials made with torches appear on the ceiling of the pit, showing that the Descending Passageway and pit were explored during this era.
16. Petrie, W.M.F., *Pyramids and Temples of Gizeh*, Field, London (1883), 168. Any remains of such a door would have disappeared when the casing blocks were stripped away. Refer to Edwards, I.E.S., *The Pyramids of Egypt*, 130 ff; Tompkins, P., *Secrets of the Great Pyramid*, Harper & Row, New York (1971), 3, which mentions an attempt to reconstruct a pivoting door.
17. Arnold, D., *Building in Egypt: pharaonic stone masonry*, New York, N.Y., Oxford University Press (1991), 192, Fig. 4.130. ibid. 61, "Blocks of huge dimensions, weighing up to 90 tons, were also found in the gable-roof constructions of the pyramids of the Fifth and Sixth Dynasties."
18. Arnold, D., *Building in Egypt: pharaonic stone masonry*, New York, N.Y., Oxford University Press (1991), 120, Fig. 4.129.
19. Arnold, D., *Building in Egypt: pharaonic stone masonry*, New York, N.Y., Oxford University Press (1991), 40.

20. For Lucas' general remarks, see Lucas, A., *Ancient Egyptian Materials and Industries*, Dover Publications, Mineola, N.Y. (1999 1962), 70–4. For quarrying quartzite, Arnold remarked that the methods were not clear. He wrote, "The extent to which dolerite balls were used for pounding quartzite is not clear. . . . There seems to be no clear indication for the pounding method, and we must assume that chiseling was employed. This work could have been achieved only by experienced laborers, who probably were not numerous enough to produce huge quantities of quartzite. Still, the sepulchral chamber of Amenemhat III at Hawara and the statues of Memnon were made of that stone, and their production certainly required a sizable number of such people." Arnold, D., *Building in Egypt: pharaonic stone masonry*, New York, N.Y., Oxford University Press, (1991), 40. In other words, Egyptologists have no idea whatsoever how large quartzite items could have been quarried. The Colossi of Memnon were originally monolithic and stand, including the statues mounted on separate pedestals, 63 feet high. No one has found an extraction site showing dug-out trenches of this great size in the quartzite quarries. Arnold cannot and does not try to explain what kind of chisels could possibly have been used to quarry the huge monoliths of quartzite. In short, there is no evidence of pounding balls at the quartzite ranges and no ancient chisel would be adequate for quarrying quartzite blocks. The best that could be done is to strike off aggregates by hitting tools with mallets. We can detect a fundamental flaw in the accepted paradigm.
21. The first undoubted reference to diamond appears in the writings of the Roman poet Manilius (A.D. 16): "The diamond [Latin: *adamas, meaning* unconquerable or invincible] a stone no bigger than a dot, is the most precious of substances in the world." Pliny (A.D. 100) also described six types of diamonds. Refer to Pliny, *Natural History*, Book 37, page 15, line 55 (Wormington 1972).
22. Petrie, W.M.F., *Kahun, Gurob, and Hawara* (London, 1890); Petrie, W.M.F., *Hawara, Biahmu and Arsinoe*, London (1889). Arnold reported the weight of the sepulcher at 110 tons (he assumed that it was made from a block of this size) and he indicated that it had come from the quarries at Gebel el-Ahmar, 61.
23. For the Labyrinth, see Lloyd, A.B., "The Egyptian Labyrinth," *Journal of Egyptian Archaeology,* 56 (1970), 81–100; Arnold, D., "Das Labyrinth und Seine Vorbilder," *Mitteilungen des Deutschen Archäologischen Instituts Kairo* , 35 (1979), 1–9; Uphill, E.P., *Pharaoh's Gateway to Eternity, The Hawara Labyrinth of King Amenemhat III*, Keagan and Paul, London (2000). Wainwright, G.A., and Mackay, E., *The Labyrinth, Gerzeh and Mazghuneh, British School of Archaeology in Egypt and Egyptian Research Account, 18th Year,* Bernard Quaritch, London (1912). Arnold, D., "Labyrinth," *Lexikon der Ägyptologie, Band* III (1980), 905–908.
24. Herodotus, 2.148.1; Strabo, *The geography of Strabo with an English translation by Horace Leonard Jones; based in part upon the unfinished version of John Robert*

*Sitlington Sterrett*. W. Heinemann; G. P. Putnam's sons, London; New York (1917–33), Contributors: Jones, Horace Leonard, Vol. 8, 103–105.

25. A well-known example is the French Gothic Chartres Cathedral, built around 1230, which incorporated a labyrinth design into its floor plan. The labyrinth is forty feet across, set with blue and white stones into the floor of the nave of the church. Other French Gothic cathedrals with labyrinths are Amiens, Rheims, Sens, Arras, and Auxerre.
26. The heights of the figures are about 51 feet and the pedestals (on which the feet rest) are about 13 feet high. The original heights of the total structures may have reached 69 feet with their crowns, which are now destroyed. The legs (from the soles of the feet to the knees) each measure 19½ feet. Pliny mentioned the hardness of the stone, which he called basalt (to denote a stone harder than iron). Pliny, *Natural History*, Volume 36, Chapter XI reads: ". . . The Egyptians have found a stone in Ethiopia that has the color and hardness of iron, and consequently, it was called basalt. It is said that there exists at Thebes, in the Temple of Serapis, a statue which was made with this same stone. It represents Memnon, and makes a sound all during the day when touched by sunbeams. . . ." Jollois and Devilliers of the Napoleonic Egyptian Expedition also described the hardness of the stone. Jollois and Devilliers, *Description de l'Egypte*, Edition Panckoucke, Paris (1809-828), Vol. II, Chap. IX, Section II, page 153 reads, ". . .The Colossi are facing the southeast, and are standing parallel to the Nile. They are known in this country by the names of Tama and Chama. Chama is the southern Colossus, and Tama is the northern Colossus. Both are alike in many ways. They show differences in their dimensions that we will indicate step by step: both are made from a variety of conglomerate consisting of a mass of agatized flint, bound together by a cement of exceptional hardness. This material is very dense, and has a highly heterogeneous structure which is much more difficult to sculpt than granite. What we have witnessed shows that the Egyptian sculptors have mastered their task with the greatest success." For more on the colossi, refer to R.F. Heizer, F. Stross, T.R. Hester, A. Albee, I. Perlman, F., Asaro, H. Bowman. 1973. "The Colossi of Memnon revisited" *Science*, 182, 1219–25. Bowman, H., et al., "The Northern Colossus of Memnon: New Slants," *Archaeometry* (1984), Vol. 26, 218–229.
27. Petrie, W.M.F., *A History of Egypt During the XVIIth and XVIIIth Dynasties*, London, Metheun & co. ltd. (1904), 192; Breasted, J.H., *Ancient Records of Egypt; historical documents from the earliest times to the Persian conquest, collected, edited, and translated with commentary*, New York, Russell & Russell (1962), Vol. II, 355–356.
28. The statue was found in 1820 and the Egyptian ruler Mohammed Ali donated it to the British Museum.
29. The Egyptian *Hikuptah* ("The Palace of Ptah") was corrupted into *Aigyptos* in Homeric Greek, coming to our time as "Egypt." The word Coptic is a later cor-

ruption, as well. Refer to Baines, J., Malek, J., *Atlas of Ancient Egypt*, Facts on File Publications, NY (1985), 134.

30. The remarks of Stuart M. Edelson are quoted from West, J., *The Traveler's Key to Ancient Egypt: A Guide to the Sacred Places of Ancient Egypt*, Knopf, New York (1985), 193–194.
31. For the stele of Djehutihotep, refer to Baines, J., Malek, J., *Atlas of Ancient Egypt*, Facts on File Publications, NY (1980), 126–127. Arnold, D., *Building in Egypt: pharaonic stone masonry*, New York, N.Y., Oxford University Press (1991), 61.
32. For theories on lowering stones, refer to Arnold, D., *Building in Egypt: pharaonic stone masonry*, New York, N.Y., Oxford University Press (1991), 73–79.
33. Jomard, E.F. (ed.), *Description de l'Egypte*, Volume III, Section XI, Panckoucke Ed., Paris (1809-1828), 181.
34. Jomard, E.F. (ed.), *Description de l'Egypte*, Vol. III, Section XI, Panckoucke Ed., Paris (1809–1828), 181.

## CHAPTER 7: IT STAGGERS THE IMAGINATION

1. Stocks, D., "Tools of the ancient craftsman," *Popular Archaeology, 7* (1986), 24–29. Arnold, D., *Building in Egypt: pharaonic stone masonry*, New York, N.Y., Oxford University Press (1991), 41.
2. Arnold, D., *Building in Egypt: pharaonic stone masonry*, New York, N.Y., Oxford University Press (1991), 48.
3. Yoshimira, S., *Studies in Egyptian Culture, No. 6, non-destructive pyramid investigation (1) by Electromagnetic Wave Method*, Waseda University Press, Tokyo, 2 vols. 4–5.
4. Zuber, A., "Techniques Der Travail Des Pierres Dures Daus L'Ancienne Egypt," *Techniques et Civilizations 30*, Vol. 5, No. 5 (1956), 161–178.
5. Baines, J., Malek, J., *Atlas of Ancient Egypt*, Facts on File Publications, N.Y. (1980), 19.
6. Arnold, D., *Building in Egypt: pharaonic stone masonry*, New York, N.Y., Oxford University Press (1991), 33–34, 50.
7. Arnold, D., *Building in Egypt: pharaonic stone masonry*, New York, N.Y., Oxford University Press (1991), 48.
8. Refer to Roder, J., "Zur steinbruchgeschichte des rosengranits von Assuan," *Archalogischer Anzeiger* 3, Jahrbuch des Deutschen Archaeologischen Instituts (1965), 523.
9. Lehner, M., *The Complete Pyramids: Solving the Ancient Mysteries*, New York, Thames and Hudson (1997), 211.
10. Arnold, D., *Building in Egypt: pharaonic stone masonry*, New York, N.Y., Oxford University Press (1991), 43.

11. Petrie, W.M.F., *Pyramids and Temples of Gizeh*, Field, London (1883 reprint 1990), 37.
12. Arnold, D., *Building in Egypt: pharaonic stone masonry*, New York, N.Y., Oxford University Press (1991), 48.
13. Arnold, D., *Building in Egypt: pharaonic stone masonry*, New York, N.Y., Oxford University Press (1991), 122. On page 42, Arnold wrote, ". . . toolmarks left on numerous unfinished or unsmoothed limestone blocks from the Old and Middle Kingdoms show such a distinctive rectangular shape with very sharp inner corners that it is difficult to believe that they were produced by stone tools (fig. 2.21)." With regard to shaping rock, Arnold wrote, "But again for reasons of metal consumption, the sawing of stone was restricted to rare and special cases." Ibid. 50.
14. For the rockers and an illustration, refer to Clarke, S., Engelbach, R., *Ancient Egyptian Construction and Architecture*, Dover pub., N.Y. (1990) (a reprint of *Ancient Egyptian Masonry*), 102–4, Figs. 89, 109.
15. Arnold, D., *Building in Egypt: pharaonic stone masonry*, New York, N.Y., Oxford University Press (1991), 72.
16. Moores, R., "Evidence for Use of a Stone-Cutting Drag Saw for the Fourth Dynasty Egyptians," *Journal of the American Research Center in Egypt* XVIII (1991), 141 Fig. 3, 4. Also refer to Petrie, W.M.F., *Pyramids and Temples of Gizeh*, Field, London (1885), 14 and 75; Clarke, S., Engelbach, R., *Ancient Egyptian Masonry*, London (1930), 204; Lucas, A., *Ancient Egyptian Materials and Industries*, 4th Edition, Mineola, N.Y., Dover Publications (1962), 69–72.
17. Moores, R., "Evidence for Use of a Stone-Cutting Drag Saw for the Fourth Dynasty Egyptians," *Journal of the American Research Center in Egypt*, XVIII (1991), 142–3, Fig. 5. Moores also suggested that the basalt slabs were hammer-dressed on top. Hammering tends to break basalt along its internal fractures. It makes no sense to use this crude method in conjunction with the method that allowed workers to produce plunge cuts in basalt! It seems more likely that the signs Moores interpreted as hammer dressing resulted from later activity on the basalt slabs, such as the dismantling operation W.M.F. Petrie witnessed.
18. Arnold, D., *Building in Egypt: pharaonic stone masonry*, New York, N.Y., Oxford University Press (1991), 251–268. For more information, refer to Petrie, W.M.F., *Tools and Weapons: illustrated by the Egyptian Collection in University college, London and 2,000 outlines from other sources*, British School of Archaeology in Egypt and Egyptian Research Account, London (1917), 71 p.
19. De Garis Davies, N., *The Tomb of Rekh-mi-Re' at Thebes*. Publications of the Metropolitan Museum of Art Expedition 11, New York (1943), pls. 52–55. Arnold, D., *Building in Egypt: pharaonic stone masonry*, New York, N.Y., Oxford University Press (1991), 258.
20. The blocks above the King's Chamber are among the examples of large, form-fit-

ted masonry units. Such blocks hug one another very closely along their whole joints, although the joints deviate from being purely straight up and down. Much of the core masonry fits this way, while many core blocks have gaps between them where mortar or tafla cushioning has disappeared.

21. Mendelssohn, K., *The Riddle of the Pyramids*, Praeger (1974), New York, Illustration 18. The caption reads, "The slabs forming the corbelled roof of the tomb chamber in the Meidum pyramid are perfectly fitted but remain undressed." More precisely, they are highly irregular and snugly fit with form-fitting irregularities.
22. Arnold, D., *Building in Egypt: pharaonic stone masonry*, New York, N.Y., Oxford University Press (1991), 168–169. Arnold also commented with regard to granite (which was used to partially case some of the pyramids). Arnold wrote as follows on ibid. pages 47–48, "The dressing of hard stones, which were used abundantly in the Egyptian building industry, was certainly a problem for the ancient masons, and the work in granite quarries was used as a punishment for criminals. Because of this difficulty, Egyptian masons avoided working in hard stones as much as possible and restricted the dressing of such material to an absolute minimum and to visible parts of the blocks only. The underside and the rear of blocks, which came into contact with bedrock, were often left rough, and the bedrock was cut accordingly to take into account the protuberances of the granite." Contrasting Arnold's remarks, Joseph Roder estimated that during the 450-year-long Old Kingdom a little less than 1.6 million cubic feet of granite was removed from the Aswan quarries to incorporate into monuments! Joseph Roder, "Zur steinbruchgeschichte des rosengranits von Assuan," *Archalogischer Anzeiger* 3, Jahrbuch des Deutschen Archaeologischen Instituts (1965), 461–551. Granite casing blocks covered the first course of Khafra's pyramid, the first sixteen courses of Menkaura, the first course of Menkaura IIIa, the first course of Shepseskaf, the first course or more of Neferirkara, and possibly covered the whole of the pyramid of Djedefra. Refer to ibid., 169. Moreover, Arnold's statement does not take into consideration the difficulties of cutting granite blocks so that they would conform to one another. An example is the King's Chamber of the Great Pyramid, where all of the blocks made with granite fit together with conforming hairline joints. Conforming basalt slabs characterize Old Kingdom temple flooring.
23. Arnold, D., *Building in Egypt: pharaonic stone masonry*, New York, N.Y., Oxford University Press (1991), 168–169.
24. Arnold, D., *Building in Egypt: pharaonic stone masonry*, New York, N.Y., Oxford University Press (1991), 147.
25. Arnold, D., *Building in Egypt: pharaonic stone masonry*, New York, N.Y., Oxford University Press (1991), 47.
26. Arnold, D., *Building in Egypt: pharaonic stone masonry*, New York, N.Y., Oxford University Press (1991), 46–47.

## CHAPTER 8: IRON IS NOT THE SOLUTION


1. Fakhry, A., *The Pyramids*, University of Chicago Press, Chicago; London (1969 ed.), 9.
2. British Museum # 2433.
3. Caliph Al-Ma'moun (A.D. 813–833). Tourists enter the Great Pyramid today through the rough passage cut by Al-Ma'moun.
4. Abd al-Latif, *The Eastern key: Kitab al-ifadah wa'l-i'tibar of 'Abd al-Latif al-Baghdadi. Translated in English by Kamal Hafuth Zand, John A. and Ivy E. Videan.* London, Allen and Unwin (1965), 286.
5. *The Egyptian History of Murtada ibn al-Khafif.* Also see *Land of Enchanters: Egyptian Short Stories from the Earliest Times to the Present Day*, edited by Bernard Lewis, Stanley M. Burstein, and Stanley Burstein. Markus Wiener, Princeton, NJ, 183 pp. The book includes the "Miraculous Stories of the Pyramids Of Queen Charoba of Egypt and Gebirus the Metapheguian."
6. *Arnold, D., Building in Egypt: pharaonic stone masonry*, New York, N.Y., Oxford University Press (1991), 257.
7. For Vyse's discovery of the iron plate, refer to Vyse, R.W.H., *Operations Carried On at the Pyramids of Gizeh in 1837: with an account of a voyage into Upper Egypt, and an appendix*, Pub. J. Fraser, London (1840 1842), vol. I, 275–276.
8. Theophrastus, *De lapidibus*, edited, with introduction, translation and commentary, by D. E. Eichholz, Oxford, Clarendon Press (1965), 73. Engelbach indicated, "I have spent hours trying to cut granite with iron, copper, and even dolerite chisels, and though granite can be cut—in a manner of speaking—with all of them I am convinced that the Egyptians used a much harder tool." Engelbach, R., *The Problem of the Obelisks, From a Study of the Unfinished Obelisk at Aswan*, T.F. Unwin, limited, London (1923), 40. The problem is that the Egyptians did not have harder tools. Refer also to el-Khouli, A., *Egyptian Stone Vessels: Predynastic Period to Dynasty III typology and analysis*, von Zabern, Mainz/Rhein (1978). In Vol. II titled *Manufacture of Stone Vessels - Ancient and Modern*, page 789, Alexander el-Khouli wrote, "To my knowledge, until a few years ago villagers in some parts of Middle and Upper Egypt were still manufacturing mortars of limestone in a rather simple fashion, boring out the interiors of the vessels . . . or manufacturing spindles from such horns using a very small chisel of iron. They spent a long time even on one stone vessel, and the finished product, it must be admitted, was hardly commensurate with the labour and trouble expended."
9. Wilkinson, J.G., *The Manners and Customs of the Ancient Egyptians*, New ed. rev. and corrected by Samuel Birch, London, J. Murray (1879). 252–253.
10. Lehner, M., *The Complete Pyramids: Solving the Ancient Mysteries*, New York, Thames and Hudson (1997), 206.

## CHAPTER 9: HOW WAS IT POSSIBLE?

1. Zuber, A., "Techniques Der Travail Des Pierres Dures Daus L'Ancienne Egypt," *Techniques et Civilizations* 29, Vol. 5, no. 5 (1956), 170.
2. Wilkinson, J.G., *The Manners and Customs of the Ancient Egyptians*, New ed. rev. and corrected by Samuel Birch, London, J. Murray (1879), 255.
3. Stocks, D., "Tools of the ancient craftsman," *Popular Archaeology, 7* (1986), 24–29.
4. Arnold, D., *Building in Egypt: pharaonic stone masonry*, New York, N.Y., Oxford University Press (1991), 261, Fig. 6.14.
5. Arnold, D., *Building in Egypt: pharaonic stone masonry*, New York, N.Y., Oxford University Press (1991), 261, Fig. 6.13.
6. Arnold, D., *Building in Egypt: pharaonic stone masonry*, New York, N.Y., Oxford University Press (1991), 261, Fig. 6.14.
7. Arnold, D., *Building in Egypt: pharaonic stone masonry*, New York, N.Y., Oxford University Press (1991), 261, Fig. 6.14.
8. Zuber, A., "Techniques Der Travail Des Pierres Dures Daus L'Ancienne Egypt," *Techniques et Civilizations 29*, Vol. 5, no. 5 (1956), 201–202.
9. Antoine Zuber, "Techniques Der Travail Des Pierres Dures Daus L'Ancienne Egypt," *Techniques et Civilizations 29*, Vol. 5, no. 5 (1956), 161–178.
10. Edwards, I.E.S., *The pyramids of Egypt*, Rev. and updated, repr. with minor revisions Harmondsworth, Middlesex, England; New York, N.Y., Penguin Books (1988), 249. The topic was long debated, and Edwards, referring to Lucas, indicated, "The methods employed in the Pyramid Age for quarrying granite and other hard stones are still a subject of controversy. One authority even expressed the opinion that hard-stone quarrying was not attempted until the Middle Kingdom; before that time, the amount needed could have been obtained from large boulders lying loose on the surface of the ground." Lucas, A., *Ancient Egyptian Materials and Industries* (1948), 82–83. Arnold, D., *Building in Egypt: pharaonic stone masonry*, New York, N.Y., Oxford University Press (1991), 39, wrote, "For a long time, Egyptologists believed that granite was quarried with the help of wooden wedges inserted into wedge holes (made with copper chisels), since long chains of wedge holes could still be seen in the quarries of Aswan. This theory was abandoned for two reasons. First, Roder showed that no such wedge holes could be dated before 500 B.C. Second, most specialists seem to agree that wooden wedges, after being watered, would not be able to break granite. This new finding contradicts the remarks of Petrie, who described what he interpreted as wedge marks on the floor of the fourth construction chamber of the Cheops Pyramid." Besides, copper chisels are too soft to wedge slots in granite.
11. Zuber, A. "Techniques Der Travail Des Pierres Dures Daus L'Ancienne Egypt,"

*Techniques et Civilizations 29*, Vol. 5, no. 5 (1956), 161–178.

12. Roder, J., "Zur steinbruchgeschichte des rosengranits von Assuan," *Archalogischer Anzeiger* 3, Jahrbuch des Deutschen Archaeologischen Instituts (1965), 461–551.
13. For Roder's study showing that wedge holes date to after 500 B.C., refer to Roder, J., "Zur steinbruchgeschichte des rosengranits von Assuan," *Archalogischer Anzeiger* 3, Jahrbuch des Deutschen Archaeologischen Instituts (1965), 523.
14. The method was used during the New Kingdom and later at Aswan. Refer to Engelbach, R., *The Problem of the Obelisks, From a Study of the Unfinished Obelisk at Aswan*, T.F. Unwin, limited, London (1923), 42–43.
15. For Lehner's test, refer to Lehner, M., *The Complete Pyramids: Solving the Ancient Mysteries*, New York, Thames and Hudson (1997), 207. In addition, Lehner recalled (at the Nova Web site) that after pounding the surface at a granite quarry for several hours he could hardly type on his computer. He said that after 20 minutes of pounding all he had to show for his effort was a baby's palmful of granite dust, and that the granite bedrock looked no different from when he started. For Engelbach's study of Aswan, refer to *The Aswan Obelisk, with Some Remarks on the Ancient Engineering*, Cairo (1922). Refer also to Engelbach, R., *The Problem of the Obelisks, From a Study of the Unfinished Obelisk at Aswan*, T.F. Unwin, limited, London (1923), 40. Refer also to Labib Habachi, *The Obelisks of Egypt: Skyscrapers of the Past*, The American University in Cairo Press, Cairo (1994).
16. See Chapter 5 above. The large number of blocks that should have broken and be strewn around must be considered relative to the size of the Great Pyramid. For the size, refer to Cole, J.H., "The Determination of the Exact Size and Orientation of the Great Pyramid of Giza," Survey of Egypt, Paper No. 39, Cairo (1925).
17. Pyramids with granite casing are Khafra's first course; the first sixteen courses of Menkaura; the first course of Menkaura IIIa; the first course of Shepseskaf; at least the first course of Neferirkara, and possibly the entire casing of the pyramid of Djedefra.
18. For the pyramid of Djedefra at abu Roash, refer to Lehner, M., *The Complete Pyramids: Solving the Ancient Mysteries*, New York, Thames and Hudson (1997), 120. For this and other pyramids, refer to Arnold, D., *Building in Egypt: pharaonic stone masonry*, New York, N.Y., Oxford University Press (1991), 168.
19. For the Valley Temple, refer to Hoelscher, U., *Das Grabdenkmal des Konigs Chephren*, Veroflentlichungen der Ernst von Sieglin Expedition in Agypten, Vol. 1, Leipzig (1912).
20. For more on the Mastabat el-Fara'un, refer to Jequier, G., *Le Mastabet Faraoun*, Cairo (1928); Fakhry, A., *The Pyramids*, University of Chicago Press, Chicago and London (1969 ed.), 151–53.
21. Arnold, D., *Building in Egypt: pharaonic stone masonry*, New York, N.Y., Oxford

University Press (1991), 197.
22. Arnold, D., *Building in Egypt: pharaonic stone masonry*, New York, N.Y., Oxford University Press (1991), 199.
23. Arnold, D., *Building in Egypt: pharaonic stone masonry*, New York, N.Y., Oxford University Press (1991), 66. Here is a translation (by Joseph Davidovits) of Jean Paul Adams, *L'Archeologie devant l'mposture*, Ed. Robert Laffont, Paris (1975), 135. "Nowadays, it is difficult to imagine workers attacking a rocky cliff with stone axes. It is, however, in this way that numerous megaliths were detached and squared." Edwards, I.E.S., *The pyramids of Egypt, Rev. and updated, repr. with minor revisions*, Harmondsworth, Middlesex, England; New York, N.Y., Penguin Books (1988), 249.

## CHAPTER 10: STANDARD MASONRY THEORY DISPROVED

1. Petrie, W.M.F., *Journal Royal Anthropology Institute*, 13 (1884), 90–1.
2. Petrie, W.M.F., *Pyramids and Temples of Gizeh*, Field, London, Histories and Mysteries of Man, Ltd., London (1883 reprint 1990), 29. Petrie wrote, "On the outer sides the lines of sawing may be plainly seen: horizontal on the N., a small patch horizontal on the E., vertical on the S., and nearly horizontal on the W.; showing that the masons did not hesitate at cutting a slice of granite 90 inches long, and that the jeweled bronze [copper] saw must have been probably about 9 feet long. On the N. end is a place, near the W. side, where the saw was run too deep into the granite, and was backed out again by the masons; but this fresh start they made was still too deep, and two inches lower they backed out a second time, having altogether cut out more than 1/10 inch deeper than they intended. On the E. inside is a portion of a tube drill hole remaining, where they tilted the drill over into the side by not working it vertically. They tried hard to polish away all that part, and took off about 1/10 inch thickness all round it; but still they had to leave the side of the hole 1/10 deep, 3 long, and 1.3 wide; the bottom of it is 8 or 9 below the original top of the coffer. They made a similar error on the N. inside, but of a much less extent."
3. Stocks, D.A., *Testing Ancient Egyptian Granite-Working Methods in Aswan. Upper Egypt*, Antiquity, (2001) 75, 89-94.
4. Stocks, D.A., "Stone sarcophagus manufacture in ancient Egypt," *Antiquity* (1999) 73, 918-22. For more on tools and crystal cutting, see Long, F.W., *The Creative Lapidary: Materials, Tools, Techniques, Design,* Van Nostrand Reinhold, New York (1976), 136 p.; Petrie, W.M.F., *Tools and Weapons:* illustrated by the Egyptian Collection in University College London and 2,000 outlines from other sources, British School of Archaeology in Egypt and Egyptian Research Account, London (1917), 71 p; Sinkankas, J., *Gem Cutting: A Lapidary's Manual,* Van Nostrand

Reinhold, New York (1984), 365 p.; Stocks, D.A., *Industrial technology at Kahun and Gurob: experimental manufacture and test of replica and reconstructed tools with indicated uses and effects upon artifact production*. Unpublished Masters thesis (1988), University of Manchester; Wainwright J., *Discovery of Lapidary Work*, Mills & Boon, London (1971), 216 p.

5. Antoine Zuber, "Techniques Der Travail Des Pierres Dures Daus L'Ancienne Egypt," *Techniques et Civilizations* 29, Vol. 5, no. 5 (1956), 161–178.
6. Naum, G., *Of Divers Arts*, Pantheon Books, New York (1962), 170.
7. Petrie, W.M.F., *Pyramids and Temples of Gizeh*, Field, London, Histories and Mysteries of Man, Ltd., London (1883 reprint 1990), 78.
8. Dunn, C., *The Giza Power Plant, The Technologies of Ancient Egypt*, Bear & Company (1998), Sante Fe, N.M., 67–106.
9. Petrie, W.M.F., *Pyramids and Temples of Gizeh*, Field, London (1883), 173–4. Lucas argued that the cutting was done with quartz sand. Refer to Lucas, A., *Ancient Egyptian Materials and Industries*, Mineola, N.Y., Dover Publications (1999 1962), 71.
10. Petrie, W.M.F., *Pyramids and Temples of Gizeh*, Field, London, Histories and Mysteries of Man, Ltd., London (1883 reprint 1990), 75.
11. Clarke, S., Engelbach, R., *Ancient Egyptian Construction and Architecture*, Dover pub., N.Y. (1990) (a reprint of *Ancient Egyptian Masonry*), 202. Petrie's lecture is titled "On the Mechanical Methods of the Ancient Egyptians," *Journal of the Anthropological Institute of Great Britain and Ireland* (August 1883).
12. Clarke, S., Engelbach, R., *Ancient Egyptian Construction and Architecture*, Dover pub., N.Y. (1990) (a reprint of *Ancient Egyptian Masonry*), 202.
13. Gorelick, L., Gwinnett, J., "Ancient Egyptian Stone Drilling: An Experimental Perspective on a Scholarly Disagreement," *Expedition* (Spring 1983) 40–46.
14. For Lucas' general discussion of emery, refer to Lucas, A., *Ancient Egyptian Materials and Industries*, Dover Publications, Mineola, N.Y. (1999 1962), 70–4.

## CHAPTER 11: ARTIFACTS DEFY MODERN REPRODUCTION

1. Stocks, D., "Tools of the ancient craftsman," *Popular Archaeology*, 7 (1986), 24–29.
2. Dunn, C., *The Giza Power Plant, The Technologies of Ancient Egypt*, Bear & Company (1998), Sante Fe, NM, 281 pp.
3. For Mariette's discovery of the Serapeum, refer to Mariette, A., *Le Sérapeum de Memphis*, F. Vieweg, Paris (1882).
4. For all of these objects, refer to Emery, W.B., *Archaic Egypt: Culture and Civilizations in Egypt Five Thousand Years Ago*, Penguin Books, Baltimore (1961), 38–39.
5. For the tiny beads, refer to Lucas, A., *Ancient Egyptian Materials and Industries*, Dover Publications, Mineola, N.Y. (1999 1962), 44.

## CHAPTER 12: A TECHNOLOGICAL RIDDLE

1. Lange, K., *Des Pyramides, des Sphinx, des Pharaons, Ed. Plon*, Paris, 169–174. Lucas, A., "Egyptian Prehistoric Stone Vessels," *Journal of Egyptian Archaeology*, XVI (1930), 210, n.9. Alexander el-Khouli, author of *Egyptian Stone Vessels: Predynastic Period to Dynasty III typology and analysis*, von Zabern, Mainz/Rhein (1978). In Vol. II titled *Manufacture of Stone Vessels - Ancient and Modern*, 796.
2. Arnold, D., *Building in Egypt: pharaonic stone masonry*, New York, N.Y., Oxford University Press (1991), 141.
3. Arnold, D., *Building in Egypt: pharaonic stone masonry,* New York, N.Y., Oxford University Press (1991), 147.
4. Aldred, C., *The Egyptians*, Thames and Hudson, London; New York (1984), 120–122.
5. Most 5th and 6th Dynasty pyramids are little more than mounds of rubble. They were built of loose stone rubble and sand sandwiched between stone walls. Once the casing blocks were removed, the structures degraded.
6. Wildung, D., *Egyptian Saints: Deification in Pharaonic Egypt*, New York University Press, New York (1977), 8–28, Fig. 6, 7.
7. Wildung, D., *Egyptian Saints: Deification in Pharaonic Egypt*, New York University Press, New York (1977), 8, Fig. 4.
8. Arnold, D., *Building in Egypt: pharaonic stone masonry*, New York, N.Y., Oxford University Press (1991), 61, which reads: ". . . the pyramids of the Fourth Dynasty would have consumed at least 9 million cubic meters of limestone, mortar, and sand, which had to be delivered quickly in small quantities." Arnold cites Stadelmann, R., *Mitteilungen des Deutschen Archäologischen Instituts Kairo,* 36 (1980), 438–439.
9. Jomard, E.F. (ed.), *Description de l'Egypte*, Panckoucke Ed., Paris (1809–1828), Vol. I, 245.
10. Badawy, A., A *History of Egyptian Architecture*, Giza, Studio Misr (1954). Refer to his Vol. 1 for the Old Kingdom and Vol. 3 for New Kingdom architecture.
11. *Temples and Tombs of Ancient Nubia: The International Rescue Campaign at Abu Simbel, Philae, and Other Sites*, general editor, Torgny Säve-Söderbergh, New York, N.Y. Thames and Hudson; Paris, France: UNESCO (1987). Between 1964 and 1966, the United Nations Educational, Scientific and Cultural Organization (UNESCO) and the Egyptian government reinforced with resin, cut up, and moved two temples, one dedicated to Hathor and the other to Ra-Harakhte, and reconstructed them on a cliff 200 feet above the site.
12. Arnold, D., *Building in Egypt: pharaonic stone masonry*, New York, N.Y., Oxford University Press (1991), 174–175.
13. Arnold, D., *Building in Egypt: pharaonic stone masonry*, New York, N.Y., Oxford

University Press (1991), 175.
14. Arnold, D., *Building in Egypt: pharaonic stone masonry*, New York, N.Y., Oxford University Press (1991), 175; Arnold wrote, "In general, either the limestone core walls were completely cased with granite or at least the lower parts received a casing of orthostats made of granite or, as in the case of Niuserra, of basalt." For granite, examples include the mortuary temples of Khafra and Menkaura at Giza. For the granite orthostats, refer to Borchardt, L., *Das Grabdenkmal des Konigs Sahu-Re*, Vol. 1, Der Bau. Ausgrabungen der Deutschen Orient-Gesellschaft in Abusir (1902–08), No. 6. Leipzig, (1910), 12, 16, 22, 33, and 40. For basalt, ibid. 24, Fig. 20, and Borchardt, L., Das Grabdenkmal des Konigs Ne-user-Re. Ausgrabungen der Deutschen Orient-Gesellschaft in Abusir (1902–04), No. 1. Leipzig, (1907), 56.
15. Arnold, D., *Building in Egypt: pharaonic stone masonry*, New York, N.Y., Oxford University Press (1991), 124.
16. Kitchen, K.A. (ed. and trans.), *Ramesside Inscriptions.* Translated and Annotated, Blackwell, Oxford, UK; Cambridge, MA (1993–2000).

## Chapter 13: The Trouble With Ramps

1. Clarke, S., Engelbach, R., *Ancient Egyptian Construction and Architecture*, Dover pub., N.Y. (1990) (a reprint of *Ancient Egyptian Masonry*); Wilkinson observed, "Diodorus tells us (Diodorus i., 63), that machines were not invented at that early period [for raising pyramid blocks] and that the stone was raised by mounds of inclined planes; but we may be excused for doubting his assertion, and thus be relieved from the effort of imagining an inclined plane five hundred feet in perpendicular height, with a proportionate base." Wilkinson, J.G., *The Manners and Customs of the Ancient Egyptians*, New ed. rev. and corrected by Samuel Birch, London, J. Murray (1879). 309. Besides, Diodorus indicated that the mounds were made of salt, which would not be suitable for hauling blocks. Diodorus may have been extrapolating based on inclined ramps situated at some of the small pyramids, which exhibit blocks small enough to be carried by one or two men. A mud-brick ramp associated with the Great Pyramid is situated in the quarry. It was useful for climbing in and out of the quarry, but is not strong enough for raising the pyramid blocks out of the quarry. Dieter Arnold remarks, Arnold, D., *Building in Egypt: pharaonic stone masonry*, New York, N.Y., Oxford University Press (1991), 83, "It was probably used for the delivery of stones to the plateau, probably not for the pyramids but for one of the mastabas of later Fourth Dynasty." In other words, it was not strong enough for raising a great many massive stone pyramid blocks. This begs the question of how large blocks could be raised from the quarries, which show no evidence of strong stone ramps.

2. Arnold, D., *Building in Egypt: pharaonic stone masonry*, New York, N.Y., Oxford University Press (1991), 67.
3. Arnold, D., *Building in Egypt: pharaonic stone masonry*, New York, N.Y., Oxford University Press (1991), 98–99.
4. Hodges, P., *How the Great Pyramids Were Built*, Element Books, Wilshire (1989), 11.
5. Hodges, P., *How the Great Pyramids Were Built*, Element Books, Wilshire (1989), 11.
6. For ramp studies, Hodges, P., *How the Great Pyramids Were Built*, Element Books, Wilshire (1989); Isler, M., "Ancient Egyptian Methods of Raising Weights," *Journal of the American Research Center In Egypt*, 13 (1976), 31–41; Isler, M., "On Pyramid Building," *Journal of the American Research Center In Egypt* 24 (1987), 95–112; Dunham, D., "Building An Egyptian Pyramid," *Archaeology* 9, no. 3 (1956), 159–165; Fitchen, J., "Building Cheops' Pyramid," *Journal of the Society of Architectural Historians*, 37 (1968), 3–12. A report by Georges Legrain shows that 52 tons can be pulled on a ramp. Refer to Legrain, G., *Les Temples de Karnak*, Brussels (1929), 166–171, Figs. 102–7. However, hauling one block is feasible, whereas hauling many will cause a ramp to quickly degrade. Legrain's report is sometimes misused to justify the theory that the ramp system can be used to place millions of huge pyramid blocks in about twenty-three years. Also refer to Arnold, D., *Building in Egypt: pharaonic stone masonry*, New York, N.Y., Oxford University Press (1991), 79–101.
7. Arnold, D., *Building in Egypt: pharaonic stone masonry*, New York, N.Y., Oxford University Press (1991), 84.
8. Garde-Hansen, P., *On the Building of the Cheops Pyramid*, Dansk ingeniørforening, Copenhagen, (1974), 36 p. Garde-Hansen's study is commented on by Egyptian engineer Moustafa Gadalla, *Pyramid Illusions: A Journey to the Truth*, Bastet Publishing, Erie, PA (1997), 98–99. "There are many problems with the existence of such a ramp. If such a ramp existed, how could so much material disappear?" Because the figures are so staggering, Garde-Hansen theorized that some kind of additional lifting device would have been involved. Garde-Hansen's theories amount to a building rate of 6.67 blocks per minute.
9. Gadalla, M., *Pyramid Illusions: A Journey to the Truth*, Bastet Publishing, Erie, PA (1997), 98–99.
10. Hamblin, D.J., "A Unique Approach to Unraveling the Secrets of the Great Pyramid," *Smithsonian*, April (1986), 88–89.
11. Arnold, D., *Building in Egypt: pharaonic stone masonry*, New York, N.Y., Oxford University Press (1991), 100. Also, Arnold notes that "The oldest true pulley in Egypt possibly dates to the late Twelfth Dynasty and was probably not used to gain mechanical advantage. . . ." ibid., 71.

12. For Arnold's criticism of the helical ramp design, refer to Arnold, D., *Building in Egypt: pharaonic stone masonry*, New York, N.Y., Oxford University Press (1991), 100. For the Nova film, refer to *This Old Pyramid,* South Burlington, VT: Pub. WGBH Video (1992), Audiovisual, 1 videocassette (VHS) (57 min.): sd., col.; ½ in.
13. The viewer was my Mother, who kindly wrote a letter because Barnes does not respond to my letters that explain fundamental problems with the film and show the need for a disclaimer.
14. The congressional staff people included Alison Pascal from Michigan Senator Carl Levin's Washington office. She called me 9/15/94 in response to my letter of August 1994 regarding Michael Barnes' disclaimer. Tom Hestor of Michigan Senator Donald Riegle's office called Nova producer Michael Barnes in August of 1994, during which conversation Barnes promised that the revised film would include a disclaimer.
15. I sent David Suzuki copies of all of my correspondence attempting to correct the problem, until he wrote to me indicating that he refused to consider any more information or attempts to correct the problem.
16. Lehner, M., *The Complete Pyramids: Solving the Ancient Mysteries*, New York, Thames and Hudson (1997), 209.
17. Joseph Davidovits was invited by Nova to participate in the film. Here is a description of Joseph Davidovits' career profile: Dr. Joseph Davidovits is an internationally recognized, award-winning materials scientist who holds numerous patents for his products and processes. He is involved in major international technology development programs, for which he coordinates research and development projects that are carried out at major institutions and/or universities in Europe, the U.S.A., Brazil, Japan, and Australia. These research programs include, 1) the development of fire-resistant composites for the Fire Research Section of the U.S. Federal Aviation Administration, 2) the rehabilitation of uranium-mining sites for the German Government's WISMUT program, and 3) the mitigation of global warming for the European Commission in Brussels, Belgium. Dr. Joseph Davidovits has published many scientific papers over his long career. He has participated in scientific committees and held university posts in the U.S.A, including the position of Visiting Professor of Solid State Science at Pennsylvania State University (a primary hub of materials science in the U.S.). He is the founder and president of the Geopolymer Institute, a nonprofit organization based in Saint-Quentin, France. In 1994 he received a Gold Ribbon award from the National Association for Science, Technology, and Society (NASTS), in Washington, D.C., U.S.A. The NASTS issued Gold Ribbon awards for "the most significant real advances in materials research of the last decade." He is the founder of the chemistry of geopolymerization.
18. The viewer was my Mother, who wrote to Barnes on my behalf, because he does

not respond to my letters.

## CHAPTER 14: BLOCK-RAISING ENIGMAS

1. For the stele of Djehutihotep, refer to Baines, J., Malek, J., *Atlas of Ancient Egypt*, Facts on File Publications, N.Y. (1980), 126–127. Arnold, D., *Building in Egypt: pharaonic stone masonry*, New York, N.Y., Oxford University Press (1991), 61.
2. For the 1,000-ton statue at the Ramesseum, refer to Leblanc, Ch., "Les sources grecques et les colosses de Ramsès Rê-en-hekaou et de Touy, au Ramesseum," *Memnonia,* IV-V, Cairo (1994), 71–101 and Pls. XVI–XX, and Leblanc, Ch., "Diodore, le tombeau d'Osymandyas et la statuaire du Ramesseum," *Mélanges Gamal Eddin Mokhtar*, B d'E XCVII/2, Cairo (1985), 69–82 and Pls. I–VI.
3. For Ramses II's 1,000-ton statues in Tanis, refer to Uphill, E.P., *The Temples of Per Ramesses*, Aris & Phillips, Warminister, England (1984), 129–132. Arnold, D., *Building in Egypt: pharaonic stone masonry,* New York, N.Y., Oxford University Press (1991), 62, which reads, "At Tanis, fragments of up to four granite colossi were found that could even have surpassed the size of that in the Ramesseum and certainly weighed about 1,000 tons."
4. For Arnold's estimate of oxen and men, refer to Arnold, D., *Building in Egypt: pharaonic stone masonry*, New York, N.Y., Oxford University Press (1991), 64. Arnold's estimate also requires a slick, flat surface all of the way from Aswan to Tanis, a distance of hundreds of miles. No evidence that such a long, flat surface existed has been found and such a surface is not realistic. The idea of barges strong enough to float this kind of weight along the Nile is highly speculative and does not correlate with the strength of the known ship building capabilities. We would also expect to find the remains of a suitable, gigantic loading dock at Aswan if the weight was floated, but no such feature is known.
5. Arnold, D., *Building in Egypt: pharaonic stone masonry*, New York, N.Y., Oxford University Press (1991), 64.
6. Engelbach, R., *The Problem of the Obelisks, From a Study of the Unfinished Obelisk at Aswan*, T.F. Unwin, limited, London (1923), 53.
7. For Ramses II's 1,000-ton statues in Tanis, refer to Uphill, E.P., *The Temples of Per Ramesses*, Aris & Phillips, Warminister, England (1984), 129–132. For the 1,000-ton statue at the Ramesseum, refer to Leblanc, Ch., "Les sources grecques et les colosses de Ramsès Rê-en-hekaou et de Touy, au Ramesseum," *Memnonia*, IV–V, Cairo (1994), 71–101 and Pls. XVI–XX and Leblanc, Ch., "Diodore, le tombeau d'Osymandyas et la statuaire du Ramesseum," *Mélanges Gamal Eddin Mokhtar*, Cairo (1985), 69–82 and Pls. I–VI. Engelbach, R., refer to *The Aswan Obelisk, with Some Remarks on the Ancient Engineering*, Cairo (1922), 36–43; Engelbach, R., *The Problem of the Obelisks, From a Study of the Unfinished Obelisk at Aswan*, T.F. Unwin,

limited, London (1923), 66–84.
8. Engelbach, R., *The Problem of the Obelisks, From a Study of the Unfinished Obelisk at Aswan*, T.F. Unwin, limited, London (1923), 67.
9. Chevrier, H., *Revue d Egyptologie*, 22, Paris (1970), 20–21. Chevrier, H., *Le temple reposoir de Ramsès III à Karnak*, Impr. de l'Institut français d'archéologie orientale, Cairo (1933), 21 p.
10. The account of Herodotus stating that 2,000 men were needed to haul the "green naos" of Nectanebos II, weighing 580 tons, corresponds with Chevrier's findings of each man being able to pull about 1/3 ton. Refer to Herodotus, *History*, II, 175. Refer also to Chevrier, H., *Revue d Egyptologie* 22, Paris (1970), 20–21. Lauer, J.-P., "Comment furent construites les pyramids," *Historia*, 86 (1954), 57–66.
11. Lehner, M., *The Complete Pyramids: Solving the Ancient Mysteries*, New York, Thames and Hudson (1997), 224–225.
12. Lehner, M., *The Complete Pyramids: Solving the Ancient Mysteries*, New York, Thames and Hudson (1997), 224.
13. Petrie, W.M.F., *Pyramids and Temples of Gizeh*, Field, London (1885), 210. Edwards repeats Petrie's gross oversimplification of the problem, but notes that "In the face of so many unknown or unconfirmed factors, speculations regarding the number of men required for building one of the larger pyramids and the time needed for the work may perhaps appear vain." Refer to Edwards, I.E.S., *The pyramids of Egypt*, Rev. and updated, repr. with minor revisions, Harmondsworth, Middlesex, England; New York, Penguin Books (1988), 270.
14. Parry, R.H.G., "On the Construction of the Great Pyramid at Giza," *Cambridge University Engineering Department Report* No. DUED - Struct/TRI53 (1995). For the rockers that inspired Dick Parry, refer to Clarke, S., Engelbach, R., *Ancient Egyptian Construction and Architecture*, Dover pub., N.Y. (1990) (a reprint of *Ancient Egyptian Masonry*), 102–4, Figs. 89, 109. Arnold, D., *Building in Egypt: pharaonic stone masonry*, New York, N.Y., Oxford University Press (1991), 271–2, Figs. 6.29, 6.30.
15. Hodges, P., *How the Great Pyramids Were Built*, Element Books, Wilshire (1989), 8.
16. For the quote, refer to Engelbach, R., *The Problem of the Obelisks, From a Study of the Unfinished Obelisk at Aswan*, T.F. Unwin, limited, London (1923), 56.

## CHAPTER 15: THE MYSTERY OF OBELISKS

1. Engelbach, R., *The Problem of the Obelisks, From a Study of the Unfinished Obelisk at Aswan*, T.F. Unwin, limited, London (1923), 67. Also refer to Noakes, A., *Cleopatra's Needles*, H.F. & G. Witherby, London (1962), 128 pp.
2. Engelbach, R., *The Problem of the Obelisks, From a Study of the Unfinished Obelisk*

*at Aswan*, T.F. Unwin, limited, London (1923), 67.
3. Engelbach, R., *The Problem of the Obelisks, From a Study of the Unfinished Obelisk at Aswan*, T.F. Unwin, limited, London (1923), 67.
4. Engelbach, R., *The Problem of the Obelisks, From a Study of the Unfinished Obelisk at Aswan*, T.F. Unwin, limited, London (1923), 56.
5. Engelbach, R., *The Problem of the Obelisks, From a Study of the Unfinished Obelisk at Aswan*, T.F. Unwin, limited, London (1923), 67, 118.
6. Engelbach, R., *The Problem of the Obelisks, From a Study of the Unfinished Obelisk at Aswan*, T.F. Unwin, limited, London (1923).
7. Pliny the Elder, *Natural History*, Book 36, Ch. 14.
8. Engelbach, R., *The Problem of the Obelisks, From a Study of the Unfinished Obelisk at Aswan*, T.F. Unwin, limited, London (1923), 88–89. Excerpts from a Nova online article titled "Gifts of the River," by Peter Tyson, dated March 19, 1999, read: "Herodotus, the father of history, said famously that Egypt was the 'Gift of the River.' The same could be said of obelisks, that they are a gift of the Nile, for without the river, the task of shuttling these massive pillars of stone hundreds of miles from quarry to temple would have been orders of magnitude more challenging." As mentioned, however, Engelbach found no evidence of a canal at Aswan when he cleared the quarries and the ship designs known from ancient Egypt will not tolerate hauling the heaviest surviving colossi and the obelisks reported in ancient literature. Herodotus measured a much heavier monolithic temple in the Delta that would have weighed about 5,000 tons! Studies that calculate the strength requirements and speculate on a suitable craft, made of known ancient building materials, for the Memnon Colossi do not correlate with actual ancient Egyptians ships. The archaeological information on ship and barge building from ancient Egypt is abundant and allows for a good understanding of the technological level and strength of the river and sea crafts. For a more detailed analysis of the problems, see Volume 2 of this book.
9. Engelbach, R., *The Problem of the Obelisks, From a Study of the Unfinished Obelisk at Aswan*, T.F. Unwin, limited, London (1923), 80.

## CHAPTER 16: PROOF FROM ANCIENT TEXTS?

1. For Unas' causeway, refer to Raslan, M.A.M., "The Causeway of Ounas Pyramid," in *Annals du Service des Antiquites de l'Egyp*t, LXI (1973), 151–60.
2. Arnold, D., *Building in Egypt: pharaonic stone masonry*, New York, N.Y., Oxford University Press (1991), 52; ibid. 2. Arnold wrote, "The transport scenes from the causeway of Unas and the temple of Hatshepsut indicate that columns, architraves, and obelisks were dressed to their final shape in the quarry . . ." ibid. 39. Engelbach showed that the transport scene at Hatshepsut's temple is

impressionistic. Engelbach, R., *The Problem of the Obelisks, From a Study of the Unfinished Obelisk at Aswan*, T.F. Unwin, limited, London (1923), 57.

3. Joseph Davidovits investigated the site and inspected the temple column units. Davidovits, J., Morris, M., *The Pyramids: An Enigma Solved*, Hippocrene, N.Y. (1988), 62–63.
4. Davidovits, J., Morris, M., *The Pyramids: An Enigma Solved*, Hippocrene, N.Y. (1988), 60.
5. Fakhry, A., *The Pyramids*, University of Chicago Press, Chicago and London (1969 ed.), 12.
6. Junker, H., *Gîza. Bericht über die von der Akademie der Wissenschaften in Wien auf gemeinsame Kosten mit Dr. Wilhelm Pelizaeus unternommenen Grabungen auf dem Friedhof des Alten Reiches bei den Pyramiden von Gîza*, Wien, Leipzig Hölder-Pichler-Tempsky A.G., (1929–55), Vol. x, 16; Arnold, D., *Building in Egypt: pharaonic stone masonry*, New York, N.Y., Oxford University Press (1991), 262.
7. For Engelbach's quote concerning the wheel, refer to Clarke, S., Engelbach R., *Ancient Egyptian Construction and Architecture*, Dover pub., N.Y. (1990) (a reprint of *Ancient Egyptian Masonry*), 87–88. Refer to ibid. Fig 83 for a small ladder mounted on wheels from the 5th Dynasty. The invention does not appear to have flourished, however, perhaps because wheels do not function well in the sand. The tomb scene is unique, and all known further development of the wheel dates to much later times.
8. Newberry, P.E., *The Life of Rekhmara*, Constable, London (1900).

## Chapter 17: Proof From Giza?

1. Lehner made this statement in the 1992 WGBH Nova film titled *This Old Pyramid*, South Burlington, VT: Pub. WGBH Video (1992), Audiovisual, 1 videocassette (VHS) (57 min.): sd., col.; ½ in.
2. Kitchen, K.A., *Pharaoh Triumphant: the life and times of Ramesses II, King of Egypt* (edition: third corr. impression), Aris & Phillips, Warminster, Wiltshire, England; Mississauga, Ont., Canada: Benben (1985, c. 1982), 107.
3. Refer to Herodotus, *The History of Herodotus*. New York, L. MacVeagh, The Dial press; Toronto, Longmans, Green & company (1928), 124–6.
4. Abd al-Latif, *The Eastern key: Kitab al-ifadah wa'l-i'tibar of 'Abd al-Latif al-Baghdadi, Translated in English by Kamal Hafuth Zand, John A., and Ivy E. Videa*, Allen and Unwin, London (1964), 119–123.
5. Lehner, M., *The Complete Pyramids: Solving the Ancient Mysteries*, Thames and Hudson, New York, (1997), 47, which reads: "In 1801 Coutelle and Lepere began to dismantle Pyramid GIII-c, the westernmost queen's pyramid of Menkaure, in the hope of finding an undisturbed burial. They abandoned their efforts after

removing the upper north quarter of the pyramid."

6. For the extensive 19th Dynasty repairs, refer to Kitchen, K.A., *Pharaoh Triumphant: the life and times of Ramesses II, King of The Egypt* (edition: third corr. impression), Warminster, Wiltshire, England: Aris & Phillips; Mississauga, Ont., Canada: Benben (1985, c. 1982), 107. In 1853 Auguste Mariette found the Inventory Stela (also called the Stela of Khufu's Daughter) dated to the 26th Dynasty (c. 500 B.C.) Saite Period. The stela indicates that the Sphinx was repaired in the Saite Period. Zahi Hawass found a number of Greek Sphinxes at Giza in 1994. Roman restorations incorporated a protective layer of small brick-sized stones to the paws and two sides of the Sphinx. The floor of the Sphinx sanctuary was also paved in the Roman period. Modern activity at Giza is apparent from Portland-cement-based concrete blocks on the pyramids, placed to keep some blocks from falling. In a letter from the Egyptian Antiquities Organization, I was told that natural stone blocks were also used whenever possible.
7. A study by Klemm, D., and Klemm, R., show that quarrying methods that have been associated with pyramid building at Giza match Roman-style quarrying techniques. This evidence is, therefore, to be associated with Roman activity at Giza. The Klemms presented their study at the Second International Congress of Egyptologists in 1979. Here is the abstract of their paper describing Roman-style quarrying, as the quarrying appears at the sandstone quarries of Gebel el-Silsila: "Most quarries were dated to well-defined historical periods with the aid of chisel marks, block technique, inscriptions, and pottery shards. The most anciently quarried areas are at the northern edges of Gebel el-Silsila. These were quarried prior to the New Kingdom, perhaps in the Middle Kingdom. The chisel marks of this period are irregularly oriented (Fig. 7). The northern part of Gebel el-Silsila was exploited during the New Kingdom, in about the Eighteenth Dynasty, and chisel marks form a herringbone pattern. In the Nineteenth Dynasty, Ramses II introduced a fine parallel pattern that still prevailed when the Ptolemies exploited large quarries at the site. At the southern end of Gebel el-Silsila are the Roman quarry sites. No chisel marks of the previous types are found, but only wedge marks made by wooden dowels." The Klemms subsequently studied the limestone quarries, including those at Giza. Fourth Dynasty rock excavation was carried out with pointed stone tools. Refer to Klemm, R. and Klemm, D. D., *Steine und steinbrüche im alten Ägypten: Spring-Verlag*, Berlin (1993); Arnold, D., *Building in Egypt: pharaonic stone masonry*, New York, N.Y., Oxford University Press (1991), 33.
8. Arnold, D., *Building in Egypt: pharaonic stone masonry*, New York, N.Y., Oxford University Press (1991), 33.
9. Edwards, I.E.S., *The pyramids of Egypt, Rev. and updated, repr. with minor revisions*, Penguin Books, Harmondsworth, Middlesex, England; New York, N.Y. (1988),

248.

10. For Giza's cults dedicated to guarding and maintaining the sepulchres of dead pharaohs, refer to Zivie, C., "Giza au deuxième millénaire," Bibliothèque d'étude, *Fouilles de l'Institut francais, d'Archaeologie oriental,* Cairo (1976), 185 ff; for Teti's cult, refer to Yoyotte, J., "A Propos De La Parente Feminine Du Roi Teti (VI Dynastie)," *Bulletin de l'institut d'archeologie orientale,* 57 (1958), 96, n. 4; for Sahure, refer to Martin, G.T., *The tomb of Hetepka and Other Reliefs and Inscriptions from the Sacred Animal Necropolis, North Saqqâra, 1964–73* (with chapters by Alan B. Lloyd and J.J. Wilkes, and a contribution by R.V. Nicholls), Egypt Exploration Society, London (1979), p1. 55. Fakhry, A., *The Pyramids,* University of Chicago Press, Chicago and London (1969 ed.), 18–19. Fakhry cites Junker, H., Giza, VI (*Gîza. Bericht über die von der Akademie der Wissenschaften in Wien auf gemeinsame Kosten mit Dr. Wilhelm Pelizaeus unternommenen Grabungen auf dem Friedhof des Alten Reiches bei den Pyramiden von Gîza,* Wien, Leipzig Hölder-Pichler-Tempsky A.G., [1929–55]), 6–25 for a study of priests and officials of the pyramid cult.
11. Fakhry, A., *The Pyramids,* University of Chicago Press, Chicago and London (1969 ed.), 164. Arnold, D., *Building in Egypt: pharaonic stone masonry,* New York, N.Y., Oxford University Press (1991), 173. In Arnold's caption for Fig. 4.104, he says, "Granite casing blocks of the Chephren Pyramid, with medieval wedge holes for splitting." In other words, his photo shows an abandoned attempt to cut apart an existing granite casing block. In 1853 Auguste Mariette found the Inventory Stela (Stela of Khufu's Daughter) dated to the 26th Dynasty (c. 500 B.C.) Saite Period. The stela indicates that the Sphinx was repaired in the Saite Period.
12. Edwards, I.E.S., *The pyramids of Egypt,* Rev. and updated, repr. with minor revisions, Penguin Books, Harmondsworth, Middlesex, England; New York, N.Y. (1988), 141.

## CHAPTER 18: THE RESISTANCE TO NEW KNOWLEDGE

1. Arnold, D., *Building in Egypt: pharaonic stone masonry,* New York, N.Y., Oxford University Press (1991), 66. Here is a translation (by Joseph Davidovits) of Jean Paul Adams, *L'Archeologie devant l'mposture,* Ed. Robert Laffont, Paris (1975), 135. "Nowadays, it is difficult to imagine workers attacking a rocky cliff with stone axes. It is, however, in this way that numerous megaliths were detached and squared." Refer also to Edwards, I.E.S., *The pyramids of Egypt,* Rev. and updated, repr. with minor revisions, Penguin Books, Harmondsworth, Middlesex, England; New York, N.Y. (1988), 249; Arnold, D., *Building in Egypt: pharaonic stone masonry,* New York, N.Y., Oxford University Press (1991), 62, 66.
2. Arnold, D., *Building in Egypt: pharaonic stone masonry,* New York, N.Y., Oxford University Press (1991), 66. One of the purposes of Arnold's book is to protest

alternative theories. He wrote, "This book also tries to combat speculative literature on how the ancient Egyptians solved certain technical problems. Such studies, often filled with unproven theories, obscure our outlook." Ibid., 5. With regard to levering, Arnold had in mind an experiment that raised a 32-ton block up steps almost 20 inches high using three large levering beams. He cites Mohen, J.-P., *Les Dessiers d'Archeologie*, 46 (1980), 66. It is the rapid construction speed, enormous scale of the Great Pyramid, and the potential for damaging masonry when blocks go crashing down that prohibit this method for building the Great Pyramid.

3. Arnold, D., *Building in Egypt: pharaonic stone masonry*, New York, N.Y., Oxford University Press (1991), 120.
4. Engelbach, R., *The Problem of the Obelisks, From a Study of the Unfinished Obelisk at Aswan*, T.F. Unwin, limited, London (1923), 22.
5. Arnold, D., "Ueberlegungen zum Problem des Pyramidenbaus," *Mitteilungen des Deutschen Archäologischen Instituts Kairo* (1981), 37, 15–28.
6. Ashley, M., *Seven Wonders of the World*, Ashley Pub., London (1980), 288 pp. New York Times, March 12, 1978, Section IV, p. 7, col. 5. The project was led by Sakuji Yoshimura, formerly of Waseda University and sponsored and filmed by Nippon TV.
7. Roberts, D., "Age of Pyramids: Egypt's Old Kingdom," *National Geographic Magazine*, National Geographic Society (January 1995), Vol. 187, 31, 31 ff.
8. Lehner, M., *The Complete Pyramids: Solving the Ancient Mysteries*, New York, Thames and Hudson (1997), 225.
9. Lehner, M., *The Complete Pyramids: Solving the Ancient Mysteries*, New York, Thames and Hudson (1997), 225.
10. See Chapter 14 above.
11. Arnold, D., *Building in Egypt: pharaonic stone masonry*, New York, N.Y., Oxford University Press (1991), 33.
12. Arnold, D., *Building in Egypt: pharaonic stone masonry*, New York, N.Y., Oxford University Press (1991), 122.
13. Arnold, D., *Building in Egypt: pharaonic stone masonry*, New York, N.Y., Oxford University Press (1991), 72.
14. Arnold, D., *Building in Egypt: pharaonic stone masonry*, New York, N.Y., Oxford University Press (1991), 100.
15. Orwell, G., *Dickens, Dali & Others*, Reynal & Hitchock, N.Y. (1946).

### CHAPTER 19: THE SUPERTECH THEORIES

1. Dr. Volodymyr Krasnoholovets of the Institute of Physics, in Kyiv, in the Ukraine, proposed the use of a matter scrambler. Krasnoholovets, a physicist, actually

proposed that Dunn's GizaPower plant caused the large nummulitic fossil shells (which are coin-shaped and about as big around as a quarter) to twist around in the rock matrix! Krasnoholovets has not demonstrated the process by which this amazing feat could actually happen, and Dunn has not demonstrated his GizaPower in action. Krasnoholovets does not explain how large nummulitic shells can scramble in a solid matrix without causing the pyramid blocks to become misshapen (affecting the level tiers and the contact points between backing and casing stones, etc.). He does not explain how the large nummulitic shells could twist around without causing the blocks to degrade. Even normal stresses, like salt repeatedly dissolving and recrystallizing in the pores of limestone, will cause the rock to degrade. Krasnoholovets' proposal amounts to sheer science fantasy. His surprising proposal has not been published to my knowledge, and only appears in private e-mail correspondence.

2 Lehner. M., *The Egyptian Heritage: Based on the Edgar Cayce Readings*, Virginia Beach, Va., A.R.E. Press (1974), 132.

3. Lehner has retracted certain notions, explaining that he no longer believes in the Cayce idea the same way as he did back in the 1970s. Speaking of his more recent talks before the Cayce group he wrote, "In these talks I began to suggest to the Cayce community that they look at the Egypt/Atlantis story as a myth in the sense that Joseph Campbell popularized, or that Carl Jung drew upon in his psychology of archetypes. Although the myth is not literally true, it may in some way be literally true. The Cayce 'readings' themselves say, in their own way, that the inner world of symbols and archetypes is more 'real' than the particulars of the physical world." Refer to these and other comments by Lehner renouncing his old beliefs in Hancock, G., Bauval, R., *The Message of the Sphinx: a Quest for the Hidden Legacy of Mankind*, Crown Publishing, Inc., New York (c.1996), 290–95.

## APPENDIX: TIER HEIGHTS OF THE GREAT PYRAMID

1. Goyon, G., "Les Rangs d'assises de la Grande Pyramide," *Bulletin de l'Institut Francais d'Archeologie Orientale*, Cairo, 1978, Vol. 78, No. 2, 405-413.

# INDEX

## A



## B

## C

M

## N



## O



## P

## U



## V



## W



## Y



## Z

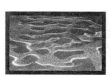